Signs of Dissent

D0700835

NEW WORLD STUDIES

A. James Arnold, *Editor*

J. Michael Dash, David T. Haberly,
and Roberto Márquez,
Associate Editors

Joan Dayan, Dell H. Hymes,
Vera M. Kutzinski, Candace Slater,
and Iris M. Zavala,
Advisory Editors

Signs of Dissent

MARYSE CONDÉ AND POSTCOLONIAL CRITICISM

Dawn Fulton

New World Studies
A. James Arnold, editor

University of Virginia Press
Charlottesville and London

University of Virginia Press

© 2008 by the Rector and Visitors of the University of Virginia

All rights reserved

Printed in the United States of America on acid-free paper

First published 2008

9 8 7 6 5 4 3 2 1

Library of Congress Cataloging-in-Publication Data

Fulton, Dawn, 1969–

   Signs of dissent : Maryse Condé and postcolonial criticism / Dawn Fulton.

     p. cm. — (New world studies)

   Includes bibliographical references and index.

   ISBN 978-0-8139-2714-5 (cloth : alk. paper) — ISBN 978-0-8139-2715-2 (pbk. : alk. paper) — ISBN 978-0-8139-2724-4 (e-book)

   1. Condé, Maryse—Criticism and interpretation. I. Title.

   PQ3949.2.C65Z66 2008

   843'.914—dc22

                                    2007044761

Contents

Acknowledgments

I AM FORTUNATE to have had the help of numerous people in the preparation of this book. Michael Thurston, Joe Keith, Françoise Lionnet, Michael Gorra, Janie Vanpée, Kevin Quashie, Nicole Ball, Jeff Rider, and Suzanne Gottschang generously provided comments and suggestions on parts of the manuscript in its various stages. I am grateful to Linda Orr, Brent Edwards, and Dan Horowitz for their support and timely professional advice, and to Lucretia Knapp, Liane Hartman, and Dan Bridgman for valuable technological insights. I also wish to thank Cathie Brettschneider at the University of Virginia Press for her steady guidance, the anonymous readers of the manuscript for their suggestions, Colleen Clark for her careful editing of the manuscript, and Nicole Calandra for her sharp proofreading eye. Finally, I thank Maryse Condé and Richard Philcox, for their generosity, for their humor, and for their work.

WORK ON this project was supported in part by a sabbatical leave from Smith College and by a Jean Picker Fellowship. Portions of chapter 3 were previously published as "Reading Death: Allegory in Maryse Condé's *Crossing the Mangrove*" in *Callaloo* 24.1 (Winter 2001): 301–9; portions of chapter 4 appeared as "'A Clear-Sighted Witness': Trauma and Memory in Maryse Condé's *Desirada*" in *Studies in Twentieth and Twenty-First Century Literature* 29.1 (2005): 47–63; and portions of chapter 7 appeared as "A Question of Cannibalism: Unspeakable Crimes in *Histoire de la femme cannibale*" in *Feasting on Words: Maryse Condé, Cannibalism, and the Caribbean Text*, ed. Vera Broichhagen, Kathryn Lachman, and Nicole Simek (Princeton, NJ: PLAS, 2006), 85–104. Early versions of chapter 5 were published as "Monstrous Readings: Transgression and the Fantastic in *Célanire cou-coupé*" in *Emerging Perspectives on Maryse Condé: A Writer of Her Own*, ed. Sarah Barbour and Gerise Herndon

(Trenton, NJ: Africa World Press, 2006), 201–15, and as "Frankenstein's Other: The Monstrous Feminine in Maryse Condé's *Célanire cou-coupé*" in *Horrifying Sex: Essays on Sexual Difference in Gothic Literature,* ed. Ruth Bienstock Anolik (Jefferson, NC: McFarland, 2007), 67–79. Permission to reprint is gratefully acknowledged.

UNLESS OTHERWISE noted, all translations are my own.

Signs of Dissent

Introduction

Critical Incorporations

IN HER 1989 novel *Traversée de la mangrove* (*Crossing the Mangrove*), Maryse Condé offers a brief glimpse of the contemporary politics of writing in a global market. Set in a small Guadeloupean village in the late twentieth century, the novel presents an array of characters absorbed in their own private hopes and desires. Among them is an aspiring novelist who, imagining the success of his yet-to-be-written masterpiece, anticipates also the questions he will confront upon its publication:

> He saw his book published by a leading publisher on the Left Bank in Paris, acclaimed by the press, but coming up against local critics.
> "Is this novel really Guadeloupean, Lucien Evariste?"
> "It's written in French. What kind of French? Did you ever think of writing in Creole, your mother tongue?"
> "Have you deconstructed the French-French language like the gifted Martinican writer Patrick Chamoiseau?" (189)

In this scarcely veiled self-referential portrait, Condé both reflects and predicts the critical reception to which her own fictional work continues to be subject. The persistent questions imagined by Lucien Evariste incisively mimic the framework that informs critical evaluations of Condé's fiction: questions concerning its authenticity, its representation of the cultural particularism of her native island, its conformity to the established models of French Caribbean literature. In citing Martinican novelist Patrick Chamoiseau in this passage, Condé also signals a fierce debate that would later take form in her widely read essay "Order, Disorder, Freedom, and the West Indian Writer," published in *Yale French Studies* in 1993, where she protests the prescriptive impetus of the *Créolité* manifesto and its authors, Jean Bernabé, Raphaël Confiant, and Chamoiseau. Pitting her own right to "disorder" against the "order" imposed by the

Créolistes, she condemns the "commands decreed about West Indian literature" ("Order," 12) in the 1989 *Eloge de la créolité (In Praise of Creoleness)* that in the name of political solidarity restrict the thematic, idiomatic, and aesthetic freedom of the Caribbean writer.[1]

The derisive tone of Condé's evocation of this polemic in *Traversée de la mangrove,* along with its bald critique of a fellow writer, signals a propensity for provocation for which Condé is now well known. But what is also worth noting about this narrative moment is the formal strategy it underwrites: in no uncertain terms, Condé inscribes a reflection on the critical reception of her fictional oeuvre into her own novel, marking her literary text with a keen awareness of the political and theoretical discussions surrounding the artistic production of Francophone Caribbean writers. Indeed, in her dual roles as novelist and critic, Condé is eminently well positioned to assess the insights and the vagaries of contemporary literary and cultural criticism, to both appreciate and resent the ideologically invested scrutiny her artistic choices will inevitably encounter.[2] As the division between metropolitan and local readers in Lucien Evariste's projection indicates, the ever-expanding geographical scope of Condé's novels and her own nomadic biography multiply the criteria for judgment: just as there may not be enough Creole in her French, the image of Africa projected in her works may be deemed too negative or divisive, while her affiliations with various U.S. academic institutions leave her open to accusations of intellectual elitism or co-opted Western feminism. While Condé has addressed these critiques at length in her essays and especially in interviews, I am interested here in the ways in which her fictional oeuvre embodies a sustained dialogue with the critical discussion surrounding her work, in the ways in which what Leah Hewitt has termed Condé's "critical self-consciousness" displays itself within her novels as an intertextual reflection on the activity of reading Condé.[3]

Strategies of intertextuality mark a signature aspect of Condé's work. The allusive range that led Vèvè Clark to characterize Condé's first novel *Heremakhonon* as an exercise in "diaspora literacy," with its intermingled references to figures and texts from French, Caribbean, African, and African American cultural traditions, has continued to proliferate along with new chronological and geographical settings. Conscriptions of music, art, literature, film, popular culture, and politics into the everyday lives of her characters signal a densely woven cosmopolitan sensibility that affirms the difficulty of categorizing Condé's cultural tradition. In a more sustained mode, Condé's works have enacted a strategy she describes as "literary cannibalism": an appropriation and revision of canonical works of Western literature.⁴ Most ostensible and heavily studied in her 1995 novel *La migration des cœurs* (*Windward Heights*), a Caribbean transposition of Brontë's *Wuthering Heights,* this "ingestion" of the classics also occurs in later works such as her 2000 *Célanire cou-coupé* (*Who Slashed Célanire's Throat?*), whose protagonist recalls Mary Shelley's monster, or her 2001 *La belle créole,* which more indirectly engages D. H. Lawrence's *Lady Chatterley's Lover.* The transnationalism of Condé's oeuvre is thus in part underwritten by this persistent interaction with multiple cultural lexicons.

While such exchanges will form an important concern in *Signs of Dissent,* the intertextual strategy I would like to examine in depth is one that specifically engages the critical discourse surrounding Condé's fiction. In particular, I am interested in the dialogue Condé stages, implicitly or explicitly, with the major theoretical preoccupations of postcolonial studies: questions of racial and cultural difference, gender, representation, and exoticism that significantly shape the critical interpretations of her work. By interpellating these metafictional discussions in her novels, I argue, Condé presents a sustained reflection on the productive and critical limits of postcolonial theory, foregrounding the ways in which the conceptual double binds and constitutive aporia endemic to the field can constrict the interpretive scope of her work. *Signs of Dissent* examines the ways in which Condé's texts challenge the various lenses through which they are read as "Caribbean," as "Third World," as "feminist," as narratives of cultural identity, or as reversals of colonial power through a particular strategy of incorporating and embodying those interpretive investments in order to test their logic. Presenting studies in cultural indeterminacy, temporal incoherence, and epistemological differentiation, Maryse Condé's "critical incorporations" expose the bounds of categorical reasoning and the burdens of representativity imposed by theories of postcolonialism, thus mounting a dialogical critique of postcolonial reading practice.

The Intransigent Writer

Born in 1937 in Pointe-à-Pitre, Guadeloupe, Maryse Condé left home at sixteen to study at the Lycée Fénelon in Paris and later at the Sorbonne. She lived and taught for twelve years in West Africa before returning to Europe and completing her doctoral work on Caribbean literature at the Sorbonne in 1975. After teaching in France for several years, she took positions at a variety of institutions in the United States, including Berkeley, the University of Virginia, Harvard, and most recently Columbia, where she is now Professor Emerita in the Department of French and Romance Philology. Although she began writing plays in the 1970s and published her first novel, *Heremakhonon*, in 1976, it was with the appearance of her third novel, the two-part African saga *Ségou* (*Segu*), in 1984 that Condé first captured widespread critical and commercial attention and gained an initial foothold as one of the most important emerging Caribbean writers. Since then, she has added over a dozen novels and numerous essays, short stories, and interviews to her oeuvre, and has achieved irrefutable standing as a writer and critic of international importance. Translations of her work into English, German, Italian, Japanese, Spanish, and Dutch have assured her a broad readership and a corresponding set of accolades, honors, and prizes from numerous institutions across the globe.[5]

The cross-linguistic and cross-cultural composition of Condé's novels has helped to generate a range of international dialogues in the critical world that few Francophone writers have accomplished. Before "cannibalizing" Brontë and Shelley, Condé was the first writer from the French Caribbean to bring together a U.S. setting and characters from the Anglophone Caribbean in her highly successful 1986 novel, *Moi, Tituba sorcière . . . noire de Salem* (*I, Tituba, Black Witch of Salem*).[6] As we have seen, the intertextuality of Condé's literary works goes insistently beyond the local, elaborating an ever more diverse lexicon as her settings and characters continue to crisscross the globe. Given this contextual agility, it is hardly surprising that Condé's work has been brought into a wide variety of critical discussions, generating studies that juxtapose her writing with that of writers from Toni Morrison to Ahmadou Kourouma, Nathaniel Hawthorne, and Simone de Beauvoir. This critical breadth is particularly evident in the collections of essays on Condé that have emerged in the past decade from the United States, France, and the Caribbean. Special issues from *World Literature Today* (1993), *Callaloo* (1995), and *Romanic Review* (2003), along with L'Harmattan's *L'Œuvre de Maryse Condé: Questions et réponses à propos d'une écrivaine politiquement incorrecte* (1996; The work of Maryse Condé: Questions and answers about a politically incorrect woman writer), Ibis Rouge's *Maryse Condé: Une nomade inconvenante* (2002; Maryse Condé: An improper nomad), Africa World Press's *Emerging Perspectives on Maryse Condé* (2006), and Princeton Latin American Studies' *Feasting on Words* (2006) bring together writers and critics from both sides of the Atlantic and display an exceptionally international collaboration that typifies the critical reception of Condé's work as a whole.[7] In many ways this element of collaboration is a testament to Condé's own role as a literary and cultural critic, whose work as an important member of a thriving intellectual community has forged connections across institutions, disciplines, and languages in edited anthologies, conferences, and colloquia in the United States and abroad.

As some of the above titles indicate ("a politically incorrect woman writer," "an improper nomad"), Condé's talent for dismantling myths, averting expectations, and provoking discomfort has become her hallmark, receiving more consistent critical attention than any other aspect of her work or career. In a 1986 article on Condé's early novels, Jonathan Ngate famously dubbed the author a "recalcitrant daughter" of Africa, while her French Caribbean readers, not least the *Créolistes,* have lashed out at her negative portrayals of her native island or her disloyal associations with elite U.S. institutions. As Condé has claimed on numerous occasions, her aim is not to please her readers but to displease them, to shock them with unflattering portraits and what Ronnie Scharfman terms "unsympathetic heroines."[8] Along with this desire to displease, the extent to which Condé's oeuvre represents a series of reinventions, dodging with each new and unexpected turn the latest reading or classification, makes critical complacency impossible.[9]

While Condé has certainly made enemies and generated open hostility thanks to her pointed remarks, she has received an equal if not greater share of admiration and praise for her persistent willingness to say what might otherwise be disguised behind curtains of idealism or political correctness.[10] In the very celebration of this intransigence, however, lies the risk of constructing a one-dimensional approach to a complex and thoughtful oeuvre. Although the discomfort and uncertainty generated by her work are undoubtedly fundamental to Condé's project, it seems inadequate to read her as purely confrontational; the urge to provoke her readers or to disagree with contemporary critics drives Condé's work but is not, I would argue, a goal in and of itself. Rather, Condé uses this skeptical stance in order to elaborate a prolonged engagement with questions of identity and difference, power and exclusion, politics and aesthetics, while the lucidity she gains from abandoning the well-beaten paths of contemporary identity politics has allowed her to offer interventions of an originality and perspicacity that go beyond shock value. Her work seems impelled above all by a conviction that the "ugly truths" from which her peers might shy away are productive not simply because they provoke fear or anxiety but because they uncover important points of friction and contradiction in the aesthetic and political conversations in which she writes. In particular, her apparent "political incorrectness" forms a caveat to ideological investments in literature that inhibit artistic freedom even as they champion a new literary voice and that suppress ambiguity in the blind celebration of difference.

Reducible Differences

The tendency to construct generalized categories of oppression has presented one of the principal stumbling blocks in postcolonial studies and more recently in theories of globalization and transnationalism. In the effort to gain new ground and forge new spaces for the articulation of previously suppressed or overlooked voices, such reconsiderations of historical inequities have often fallen into the trap of repeating the same constructions or creating new categories of identification that prove equally lacking in nuance. Fueled by the simultaneous promulgation of comparative studies, theories of particularism have expanded their scope to a vast range of political and geographical circumstances, drawing ever wider circles of consideration. To the extent that they take as a point of departure the critique of the gaps and silences of the West's master narratives, these projects are fundamentally driven by an ethics of inclusivity, and thus veer easily toward the collapsing of difference, leaving themselves open to accusations of ahistoricism and essentialism.

The problem of terminology reveals the anxiety concerning this loss of differentiation as a critical undercurrent in recent scholarship. Among the critiques of the much-maligned term *postcolonial* is that it exhibits, as Anne McClintock puts it, a "panoptic" tendency to group all non-Western subjectivities into one general package (86). As a result the term is guilty both of compressing differences, as such critics as Cooppan and Shohat have contended, and of leaving out certain subjectivities that diverge from the postcolonial template, including, as feminist scholars have argued, an entire gender.[11] Postcolonial theory also erects a critical stance that forms a source of its homogenizing effect: with the critique of the Occident as its impetus, it necessarily posits a *collective* project of dismantling this central power. Similarly, the term *globalization* has come under reproach not only for its unappealingly corporate echoes but also because of its generalizing or "globalizing" effect on discussions of difference, positing a politics of location through which the local becomes a stand-in for the global.[12]

Given that the term *Third World* writes even more stark lines of demarcation through the globe, the rejection of the term in favor of more recent terms proposed by postcolonialism, globalization, and transnationalism is not surprising. Yet perhaps because the term does less well at hiding its reductionism, critiques of "Third World" arguments offer particularly helpful reminders of the ways in which liberal-minded thinking leaves particularity behind in its effort to embrace everyone. Gayatri Spivak has explicated the myriad ways in which the "Third World" has been folded up into a generalized margin, repeating the reductive gestures of colonial discourse by presenting the Third World as a cohesive entity ready for examination by a Western intellectual eye. This vision of the Third World as a unified object of study, Spivak argues, has resulted in the creation of a "new orientalism," a new way of silencing difference through methodology ("Poststructuralism," 222). As the authors of *Third World Women and the Politics of Feminism* suggest, women from Third World countries are especially afflicted with the perception of transparency—Rigoberta Menchú is a by now classic example of an unequivocally embraced stand-in for the oppressed—and the native woman intellectual in the Western institutions that cast this reductive gaze gains an uneasy status as an informant, offering "unmediated glimpses" of this now transparent Other.[13]

One unwelcome consequence of the drive toward inclusivity is thus the glamorization of the oppressed subject that accompanies his or her transparent apparition in theoretical discourse: on the stage of cultural relativism, the marginal condition attains a state of moral immunity and unnuanced goodness. In "Woman Skin Deep: Feminism and the Postcolonial Condition," Sara Suleri points to the circularity into which the discourse of postcolonial feminism so easily slides: "While current feminist discourse remains vexed by questions of identity formation and the concomitant debates between essentialism and constructivism, or distinctions between situated and universal knowledge, it is still prepared to grant an uneasy selfhood to a voice that is best described as the property of 'postcolonial Woman.' . . . The coupling of *postcolonial* with *woman* . . . almost inevitably leads to the simplicities that underlie unthinking celebrations of oppression, elevating the racially female voice into a metaphor for 'the good'" (758–59). Suleri thus identifies the seductive pull of this unifying flag that can make an undifferentiated vision of identity as palatable for those it means to represent as for the institutions that created it. The commodification of experience generates a self-commodification, and the construction of the morally untouchable pigeonhole becomes a bipartisan effort.[14]

Theories that address the interpenetrations of "first" and "third" worlds, the hierarchies internal to nationally framed communities, and the inflection of difference in colonial Western discourse, aim to forge the way toward a more nuanced vision of identity politics. Homi Bhabha's call to reorient thinking toward a "third space" of hybrid identities suggests a means of refusing the exoticization of the multiculturalist condition and advocates an emphasis on the international inflection of heterogeneity, while the Francophone contribution of *métissage* and recent studies in transnationalism also offer ways of thinking outside or through the boundaries of colonialism, nationhood, and race.[15] The inscription of movement in such considerations brought by a greater attention to migrant and diasporic communities has encouraged a theoretical open-endedness that imagines an evolving rather than accumulative notion of multiple identities.

Yet despite this open-endedness, or perhaps because of the lack of precision necessitated by the refusal of strict delimitations, theories of syncretism have incited criticisms similar to those leveled at Third World studies and postcolonialism. Ella Shohat, for example, points out that recent usage (or overuse) of the term *hybridity* in a wide variety of contexts has succeeded in dissolving the notion itself into an ahistorical catch-all term for cultural diversity, while Arif Dirlik contends that "in its vagueness it is available for appropriation for diverse causes, including highly reactionary and exploitative ones" ("Bringing History," 104).[16] Meanwhile, the focus on migrating figures in theories of globalization and transnationalism can generate a unilateral reading of vastly distant experiences, a notion of, as Spivak puts it, "the world as immigrant" ("Poststructuralism," 228). Terminology thus betrays the Achilles heel of theories whose reach becomes overly global and whose reductive capacities are only intensified by this desire for comprehensiveness.

Critical Incorporations

Postcolonial studies and its critics, then, continue to grapple with the conceptual double binds of particularism, with the apparent incompatibilities of asserting cultural difference without fetishizing it, of deconstructing racial categories without endorsing them in the process, of questioning universalisms without creating new ones. In her novels Condé presents an ongoing engagement with these theoretical predicaments. Her work acknowledges the seductive power of undifferentiated group identities, of the authority, the "untouchability," and the collective agency offered by fixed notions of marginalized subjectivity. But, echoing the critiques of essentialism mounted in her essays, Condé's novels also work to pull apart the process of that seduction, to uncover the mechanisms through which the marginal subject becomes consumed by generalized notions of identity. Her characters live circumstances of migration, historical uncertainty, and cultural and racial discord that inevitably strike compelling chords with current theories of identity, and yet exist in tension with the temporal, epistemological, and constitutive exigencies that they create or confront in their individual and social trajectories. By embodying rather than resolving such tensions, Condé's novels foreground the slippages and reductions that continue to emerge in the blind spots of critical discourse on culture and identity. In particular, her work offers a discerning assessment of three interrelated conceptual burdens generated by these problematics: temporal continuity, internal coherence, and representativity. My inquiry in *Signs of Dissent* will thus be informed by an appreciation of the ways in which these three concerns undergird Condé's literary critique of postcolonialism and of the ways in which her novels work to expose and undo simultaneously these crucial threads in contemporary critical dialogues.

Racial and cultural categorizations are fundamentally tied to a notion of temporal continuity. To the extent that constructed identities are generated by the need for legibility, for *traceability*, the positing of a common identity simultaneously draws out a continuous line toward a common origin. It is in this sense, in part, that such social constructions mimic the false configurations of biological determinism. As Etienne Balibar writes, "*Culture can also function like nature,* and it can in particular function as a way of locking individuals and groups a priori into a genealogy, into a determination that is immutable and intangible in origin" (22). The imitation of genetic science thus invents tradition as destiny, fixing the individual in a legible chain of continuous *appartenance*. In Condé's native Caribbean, and in the African diaspora, the common heritage of slavery is apprehended *as* a temporal rift; the effort to repair that rift, to recover continuity with the past, thus becomes paramount, obscuring the fact that racial or cultural construction is being generated simultaneously.

Condé's novels expose this simultaneity by exploring both the construction of temporal continuity and the naturalism it presupposes. For a dejected gardener in *La belle créole,* for example, to stake a claim to justice in the name of collective victimhood is to embrace a past that means nothing to him, to assert a common ancestry with flickering figures on his television screen. Similarly, a Caribbean search for African origins in *Heremakhonon* is swiftly demythologized as a geographical and temporal miscalculation, while in *Desirada* the identity quest narrative contracts to a confrontation between mother and daughter. Here, as in *La migration des cœurs,* genealogy imposes knowledge: not only knowledge of the past but knowledge of the Other, demanding an epistemological transparency that is either unrealizable or untenable. By interrupting the transference of genealogical knowledge in her novels, Condé thus exposes temporal continuity and cultural identity as parallel constructions, pointing further to the dependence of theories of pan-Africanism, cultural trauma, and slavery reparations on such false frameworks.

The particular is also made legible through the projection of internal coherence. As Sara Suleri has shown, that coherence is often a moral one, garnered through the "uneasy selfhood" granted at the intersections of gender and cultural inequities. In seeking to reverse such inequities, postcolonialism reifies the oppressed subject it aims to redeem in its very celebration of that reversal; having been constituted by a history of de-humanization, the newly formed "uneasy self" must be unequivocally posited as good. But Suleri's critique also points to the fact that within a given minority group, there is often only one narrative model, since any inconsistencies or grounds for censure not only would threaten to upset the moral elevation that constituted it but also would prevent the individual member of such a group from being interchangeable with its other members and thus invalidate the terms of the collective definition. The impossibility of accounting for internal variation, discord, or ethical discrepancy thus exposes the dependence on a myth of purity in minority rights discourse. While dominant moral and social hierarchies may have been undermined, in other words, the logic of stereotype remains.

Condé resists this kind of reverse stereotyping through characters who are ethically or constitutively irreducible. Figures such as the eponymous protagonist of *Moi, Tituba sorcière . . . noire de Salem* or the widowed artist Rosélie in *Histoire de la femme cannibale* (*The Story of the Cannibal Woman*) flirt with categories of oppression by approximating familiar narratives of social ostracism and prejudice, but exhibit in other ways qualities that are inconsistent with visions of oppressed subjects as they are constituted through feminist postcolonial discourse. The extent to which these discrepancies attenuate the possibility of unequivocally celebrating the claim to power of these figures reveals the unacknowl-edged criteria upon which the morally untouchable oppressed subject is created. As the ethically deviant and racially indeterminate heroine of *Célanire cou-coupé* demonstrates, the Condéan subject exposes at once the monstrosity of epistemological uncertainty and the grotesque exag-gerations generated by the demand for coherence.

To the extent that these figures would be disqualified from represen-tative status in the category of the oppressed, moreover, Condé defies through these irreducible characters her own burden of representativity as a writer. By evoking characters who simultaneously exhibit traits from inside and outside their prescribed categories of oppression, who exceed the tolerance of identity politics, Condé refuses to allow her novels to dissolve into reproductions of alterity or to play the role of what Suleri terms an "otherness machine" (*Meatless Days,* 105). Mindful of her own imposed representative status as a "Francophone," "Non-Western," "Caribbean," "Woman" writer, Condé declines the expectation to "represent representation," following Spivak's distinction from the German *vertreten* and *darstellen,* or to portray stand-ins for the oppressed in her fiction.[17] If Condé's penchant for provocation aims to displease her readers, she accomplishes this goal in great part by refusing to reassure them with images they recognize, or with characters or landscapes they can easily reconcile with pre-scripted categories. In defending the ethical, racial, and epistemological indeterminacy of her characters, Condé exposes the unnuanced celebration of oppressed voices as an exercise in cultural determinism.

The dismantling of representativity in Condé's novels points to the intersection between theory and interpretation in her critique: Condé questions both the limits placed on the representations she offers in her texts and the constricted readings of those representations. *Signs of Dissent* proposes that she effects this latter critique through a repeated inscription of interpretive frameworks in her novels. When Lucien Evariste in *Traversée de la mangrove* jumps at the chance to discuss literature with a fellow writer because "the few Guadeloupean writers who did exist spent most of their time holding forth on Caribbean culture in Los Angeles or Berkeley" (182); when *Heremakhonon*'s Véronica exclaims, "Honestly! You'd think I'm going because it is the in thing to do. Africa is very much the thing to do lately. Europeans and a good many others are writing volumes on the subject" (3); or when the eponymous Tituba asks her seventeenth-century jail mate Hester Prynne, "What's a feminist?" (101), Condé signals the disruption of boundaries between text and critique, precociously absorbing the ideological assessment of her work into the fabric of her narrative. Just as these pointed references serve to raise questions of pan-Africanism, intellectual elitism, and postcolonial feminism, moreover, Condé's novels invoke through a sustained thematic engagement the tropes and figures that have currency in contemporary critical discussions of postcolonial literature. A search for paternal origins, a forgotten voice reclaiming history, a subjugated woman accused of cannibalism, function, I argue, as a series of signals calling up the structures of analysis concerned with colonial discourse, subaltern subjects, and cultural identity. Condé incorporates these discourses with singular insight in order to assess them critically, and by exposing this internal tension in her novels she asserts that the theoretical and conceptual limits of postcolonial studies are also its interpretive ones.

The encounter between literature and criticism as Condé stages it in her novels could not be characterized as a purely oppositional one, however, not least because of Condé's own intellectual contributions to postcolonial theory. While her novels, to follow Said's formulation, do read postcolonial criticism "contrapuntally," they do so not to refute the tenets of postcolonial theory out of hand, but to examine dialogically its ambitions and limitations in order to sharpen its critical acumen in the assessment of alterity and particularism.[18] For, as we have seen, such critiques are internal to the field of postcolonial studies; Condé's critical strategy thus aims to inform and refine the terms of this debate by bringing it into the realm of the literary, into dialogue with the thematic and narrative representations of her novels.[19] In foregrounding the incidence of postcolonialism in literary criticism, in other words, Condé's critical incorporations exhort the field of postcolonial studies to live up to its own best intentions. If postcolonial critics seek to break down stereotypes, her novels suggest, they must also be willing to allow for ethical ambiguity in a marginal subject; if they wish to eschew fetishized difference, they must also abandon immutable genealogies; and in their celebration of an intransigent writer, they must avoid stifling her creative independence.

IN A RECENT article on global literature, Shu-Mei Shih reassesses the debate sparked by Jameson's much-maligned claim that all Third World narratives are national allegories in the context of global capitalism.[20] She asserts that in the wake of this debate, Third World writers and artists began to produce "deliberate national allegorical narratives" (21) for consumption in the global marketplace. The critical expectation of national allegory, in other words, produced the conditions of a consensus between the Western reader and the Third World artist: "It is a contractual relation of mutual benefit and favor that works first to confirm the stereotyped knowledge of the audience and second to bring financial rewards to the makers of those cultural products. In other words, allegory works and sells because it makes the non-Western text manageable, decipherable, and thus answerable to Western sensibilities and expectations (sometimes even by way of the non-Western text's inscrutability)" (21). Here, with decipherability as the allegorical contract, the non-Western text succeeds by reflecting critical expectations and stereotyped knowledge back to the Western reader in harmonious replication. In her incisive attention to the field of reception of her work, then, Condé could be said to be dismantling not only the notion of the reified non-Western text but also the terms of legibility through which that reification is accomplished. Condé breaks the allegorical contract, in other words, by disrupting the process of reflection it means to guarantee. By inviting the allegorical reading of her work into her novels, Condé unhinges the dichotomous constructions of Third World text and Western critic and undermines the reductive impulses of postcolonial interpretation.

Condé accomplishes this breach of allegorical contract, I argue, by offering *imperfect* reflections of the critical expectations generated by postcolonial theory. Her critical incorporations interpellate postcolonially constructed narratives by approximating them and expose in that very gesture of approximation the interpretive limits of postcolonialism. Narratives of identity quests, historical revisionism, and reclaimed authority in her novels are "almost but not quite" the projected narratives of postcolonialism, positing in the gap of disparity a cogent critique of and resistance to reductive reading practice. In this distance between reflection and distortion lies the interpretive indeterminacy of Condé's fiction, embodying narratives that are at once serious and derisive, heroic and absurd, postcolonially legible and unrecognizable. As in parody or the fantastic, Condé's approximate imitations defend the irreducible by sustaining the reader's hesitation between competing interpretations. Similarly, Condé claims the right to both elevate and contest the precepts of postcolonialism, integrating them dialogically into her novels in order to explore their conceptual limits and test their theoretical reach. Through these critical incorporations, Condé asserts the possibility of articulating the moments of her texts that exceed the scope of postcolonial criticism, and of affirming her dissent in the name of artistic freedom.

WHILE THE focus of this study is on the articulation of such signs of resistance in Condé's novels, her extensive critical work offers helpful insights into her assessment of the politics of literary representation. The first chapter thus sketches the groundwork of Condé's literary practice as presented in her essays and in two of her early novels, focusing on the interplay of essentialism, representativity, and language. I look in particular at the link Condé elaborates between essentialist notions of identity and the prescribed visions of culture expected of the minority writer in her critical work, then turn to examine the recurring theme of alienation in her early fiction in light of this tension. The emphasis on language as the site of artistic freedom emerges in her arresting first novel *Heremakhonon*, for example, through the struggle of a young Guadeloupean woman to resist the clichés of identity quest narratives and constructed cultural difference. And in both *Heremakhonon* and her second novel, *Une saison à Rihata* (*A Season in Rihata*), the skepticism the author expresses in her critical essays concerning the politically transformative power of literature generates a literary reflection on the essentializing demands of political action in linguistic and epistemological terms.

Chapter 2 turns to Condé's most widely studied novel, *Moi, Tituba sorcière . . . noire de Salem,* in order to demonstrate her strategy of critical incorporation. In this novelistic interpretation of the Salem witch trials, Condé uses parody to subvert the unquestioned reading of the slave Tituba as a Third World heroine, and thereby the functionality of her novel as an "otherness machine." The resulting confusion and second-guessing on the part of critics—fueled in part by published interviews with Condé—mirror the interpretive constrictions denounced within the novel through the character of Tituba. By reading Condé's novel as a parody *of* these interpretive difficulties, as a parody of reading itself, I argue that the reluctance to understand this character outside of a *functional* status as a black female voice (whether as a heroine to be embraced by liberal politics or as a warranted critique of such discussions) exposes the extent to which transparency demands singularity and closes off the possibility of internal complexity either for the character or for the narrative.

The search for origins runs through many of Condé's texts, motivated in later novels, as it was in her first, by a reparative impulse on the part of the protagonist: the desire for temporal continuity underwrites a constructed notion of ancestry founded on interchangeable subjects. Chapter 3 looks at *Traversée de la mangrove* and *La migration des cœurs* to consider first how allegorical reading attempts to recover uncertain genealogies and, in Condé's revision of the Emily Brontë classic, how the romanticist vision of transcendent postmortal union might be rewritten in a context of incomplete genealogical knowledge. In each novel, the inscription of epistemological uncertainty exposes and deflects the conflation of allegorical interpretation and genetic repetition. The fourth chapter argues that *Desirada* presents a similar distortion of the identity quest narrative but addresses in particular the conscription of trauma studies in theories of collective identity. In this novel Condé thematically inscribes memory, genealogy, and rape into her narrative in order to invoke the discourse of trauma theory in the consideration of the cumulative and continuous effects of the Middle Passage. In tracing alternative landscapes of self-knowledge, however, *Desirada* reveals that the impulse to rewrite colonial narratives through the lens of trauma theory imposes an unrealizable demand for transparency and reliability. The protagonist's search for her father's name thus fails to successfully reproduce either the diasporic claim to African ancestry or the common narrative of cultural trauma.

In her most recent fiction Condé stages monstrosity as an evocation both of epistemological uncertainty and of the imposition of false coherence. Chapter 5 focuses on the eponymous heroine of *Célanire cou-coupé,* whose Frankensteinesque origins parallel a stubbornly hermetic racial and cultural indeterminacy. Condé's transformation of Shelley's creation engages the fantastic genre to foreground the epistemological implications of racial indeterminacy as a significantly more transgressive concept than conventional notions of hybridity might offer. In chapter 6 I examine the collusion between narrative integrity and caricature in Condé's 2001 novel *La belle créole,* where a legal defense strategy paints a distorted and ultimately racist vision of a young black man's experience that subjects him to the public demand for transparency even as it exonerates him from an insidious accusation of criminality. In considering the use of race in legal discourse, I argue that the novel points further to the problematic similarities between this narrative of exoneration and contemporary arguments for slavery reparations.

The sign of the cannibal is the inroad to the critique of postcolonialism in Condé's most recent novel, *Histoire de la femme cannibale.* Chapter 7 considers the ways in which Condé uses the trope of cannibalism to invoke etymologically and anthropologically informed assessments of colonial power. While the discourse of the cannibal can affirm a reversal of exoticism to unveil the violence of the colonial gaze, Condé's novel shows us that the reflective properties of the discourse *on* the cannibal can expose preexisting knowledge as equally incriminating. Her protagonist's personal narrative of discovery mimics ethnographic constructions of the Other, while the character's exaggerated identification with a fellow figure of ostracism distorts the conventionally drawn hierarchies of postcolonial liberation. The dismantling of the cannibalistic reflection through critiques of colonialism, then, can paradoxically expose the interpretive expectations of postcolonial criticism as nothing more than self-referential fabrications.

1 After Essentialism

Language, Representativity, Political Action

IN HER 1998 essay "Unheard Voice: Suzanne Césaire and the Construct of a Caribbean Identity," Condé reconsiders a Caribbean intellectual whose work was for the most part eclipsed by that of her more prominent male contemporaries. Suzanne Césaire, cofounder and regular contributor to the magazine *Tropiques*, was a critical player in the intellectual dialogues and collaborations that took place during the Second World War in Martinique, but has only recently begun to receive some notice for her role in this moment of intense creative production and theoretical innovation. Condé notes that her work was often critical of dominant literary and political trends, focusing in particular on Césaire's article "Le Grand camouflage" (The Great Camouflage), the final piece in *Tropiques*, where the author unexpectedly appears to present a lyrical and celebratory evocation of the Caribbean landscape. In fact, Condé argues, upon "reading between the lines" of Césaire's text, it is possible to discern the political message behind this apparent glorification of the native land: that the "smokescreen" referred to in the article's title is precisely this image of natural splendor, a veil of exoticism that conceals the reality of everyday Caribbean existence. "What Suzanne Césaire wants to illustrate is how difficult it is for an outsider to appreciate the inner reality of the island as he is overwhelmed and blinded by its beauty," Condé explains. "For the superficial visitor, the poverty and despair of the human beings are veiled behind the smokescreen of natural beauty" (66).

The impulse to dissipate such smokescreens has been fundamental to Condé's intellectual project. The gesture of demystification marked her career early on, and, thanks to the reception of her works, became something of a signature for her interventions in cultural and literary criticism. It is perhaps most immediately applicable to her so-called African phase, her first three novels whose African setting, in defiance of the idealizations proposed by pan-Africanist movements, emerged as a persistently complex and often culpable place. While *Ségou* has borne the brunt of such criticism, due in great part to the high visibility brought by its popular success, Condé's first two novels also delve deeply into the problems raised by utopian visions of African identity. The derisive voice of *Heremakhonon*'s narrator Véronica and the numb despair of characters in *Une saison à Rihata* paint a stark picture of African spaces where notions of community and solidarity seem unattainably idealistic. In each novel the possibility of political engagement is undercut by a blunt disillusionment with post-independence Africa that is compounded by the expectation of a preexisting common vision embedded in the call for political action. For Condé's hapless protagonists, this expectation makes demands in the realm of linguistic, epistemological, and temporal self-definition that they find impossible to meet.

In *Heremakhonon,* for example, Véronica's sardonic skepticism and flagrant disregard for political correctness appear at first glance to be purely provocative, but in fact her reflections offer a serious consideration of the epistemological shortcuts and cultural transparencies that must be constructed in order to achieve an effective solidarity. Ultimately for her it is language that interrupts the process of collective identification; this divide, however, is not only a collision between French and the African languages she fails to learn but more fundamentally a Bakhtinian standoff between the speaking subject and the heritage of usage that inheres in language, and concomitantly between the individual and the past. Condé's second novel, *Une saison à Rihata,* on the other hand, draws a critical parallel between translation of thought and translation of experience, showing how Véronica's resistance to transparent language manifests in the case of *Une saison à Rihata*'s Victor as a refusal to read his own experience in the collective language of political action. In both novels the author's trademark cynicism is soundly at play, but whereas in her essays Condé takes as a point of departure the pitfalls of political solidarity, her early fiction poses the realization of community as a possibility and as a desire. As a result, the recognition on the part of each character that such desires may be unsustainable mounts a more forceful—if more devastating—case for the dissolution of their respective smokescreens.

The Role of the Transnational Writer

Before the publication of her first novels, Condé had produced a significant body of critical work. Her five books, *La civilisation du bossale* (The civilization of the bossale), *La parole des femmes* (The voice of women),

Le roman antillais (The Antillean novel), *La poésie antillaise* (Antillean poetry), and *Cahier d'un retour au pays natal: Césaire* (Notebook of a return to the native land: Césaire), along with the numerous articles, essays, and lectures she published in the late 1970s have received significantly less critical consideration than her prose fiction, but provide much of the theoretical groundwork out of which her novels and plays have grown.[1] Although Condé's production shifted in intensity to fiction in the 1980s and 1990s, she has continued to publish essays whose demand for methodological and theoretical complexity creates an ongoing dialogue with the novels for which she has achieved international notoriety. Drawing from an extensive and eclectic literary and critical background, Condé repeatedly uses the nonfictional venue to address the inaccuracies and illusions she perceives in contemporary cultural criticism, from the unquestioning acceptance of canonical ideas to the facile lionization of new cultural figures to the omission of important unconventional voices.

Above all, Condé's critical works elaborate a sustained critique of essentialism. In her early essays, this critique takes shape primarily as an interrogation of the *Négritude* movement and its idealized vision of African unity. Her 1973 essay, "Pourquoi la Négritude?" (Why Negritude?), for example, notes that *Négritude* invokes the memory of slavery without accounting for the participation of Africans in the slave trade (151–52), while in "The Making of a West Indian Feminist," a lecture given at the Pan-Africanism Revisited Conference in California a decade later, Condé uncovers the ideological contradictions that make such visions of unity impossible.[2] In "Globalization and Diaspora" (1998), she extends the scope of her argument to position herself against any reductive vision of identity along lines of race, gender, or nation: "Novelists question the very nature of identity: what becomes if it, as I say, no longer rests on the solid pillars of language, color of skin, or land of origin?" (35–36), as later and more famously she reproaches the proponents of the *Créolité* movement for suggesting the existence of a universal Creole culture that was or should be at the core of any Caribbean artistic enterprise.

Indeed, it is in her 1993 essay "Order, Disorder, Freedom, and the West Indian Writer" that Condé most clearly formulates the relationship between essentialized visions of identity and the role of the writer. Here she enumerates the rules to which she believes the writer is subjected if he or she wishes to receive the stamp of authenticity as a Caribbean artist, noting that in terms of thematic and formal concerns the dominant literary voices in the West Indies have advocated a unified vision of the collective self through literature. "Although West Indian literature proclaims to be revolutionary and to be able to change the world," she writes, "on the contrary, writer and reader implicitly agree about respecting a stereotypical portrayal of themselves and their society. In reality, does the writer wish to protect the reader and himself against the ugliness of the past, the hardships of the present, and the uncertainty of the future?" (134).

Condé thus identifies fear as a key motivation in such projects, opposing creative imagination to the anxious attempt to preserve a predictable sense of West Indian identity. In this sense her caveat is one that points out the capacity of essentialist thought to mitigate ambiguity, affirming the belief, as she puts it, that Caribbean literature "exist[s] to provide the reader with a few reassuring images of himself and his land" ("Order," 134). Condé signals the comfort level furnished by fixed notions of identity as seductive and therefore dangerous, shutting down not only critical thought on the part of the West Indian subject but also the creative project of the writer, which in her eyes depends upon the discomforting effects of questioning convention. Some ten years earlier, Condé had already indicated a dissatisfaction with the correspondence between literature and reassurance in a brief article praising V. S. Naipaul, her contentiously received West Indian colleague, who, she finds, had succeeded in defining a new function for the writer: "not that of comforting, but of disheartening and irritating at all costs" ("Naipaul et les Antilles" [Naipaul and the Antilles], 7).[3] The disruption caused by such work is not purely hostile, but an attempt to reclaim an artistic project that reaches beyond the intellectually stifling confines of contemporary minority writing.

The relationship of the French word *rassurer* (to reassure) to consolidation, moreover, to the reinforcement brought by grouping or assembling, underscores the problem of representation as a second impetus behind Condé's objection.[4] Indeed, her essay casts a doubtful gaze on the representative role of both writer and character as it is conceived in the principal literary and theoretical works of the French Caribbean. At the inaugural moment of the "order" she condemns in her essay, for example, she critiques Aimé Césaire's characterization of poetic voice as one that will speak for the disenfranchised in his *Cahier d'un retour au pays natal:* "'My mouth will be the mouth of those who have no mouth, my voice the voice of those who despair'" ("Order," 122). In characterizing Édouard Glissant's "order," meanwhile, Condé contends that his model for artistic production envisions characters who "should not be individuals, but the collective expression of the West Indian soul" ("Order," 128). For Condé, the conflation of singular and plural narratives inheres in the demand to reassure a divided public, and the response to that demand locks the writer into a prescriptive debt to representative status.

Woven through this critique of the writer-as-synecdoche model is also a trenchant commentary on the possibility of political engagement. Here Condé posits the conflation of poetics and politics as fundamental to the problem of artistic freedom: to the extent that the project of political solidarity puts forward a unified vision of collective identity, its realization stands at odds with the writer's autonomous artistic voice. She draws a direct link between this project and the representational model imposed on the writer, citing Césaire's notion of speaking for the voiceless in his *Cahier* as the poet's "definition of committed literature" ("On the Apparent Carnivalization," 13), while maintaining that Glissant "shares with Césaire the confusion between political and poetic ambitions and the belief in the importance of community" ("Order," 127). In these essays, Condé identifies political engagement as fundamentally tied to the demand for reassuring images and characters that she seeks to dismantle: committed literature, she suggests, creates yet another smokescreen, and succeeds at the expense of artistic freedom.

To defend this creative independence, then, the writer needs to find an individual voice, unfettered by the distortion of a representative function. For Condé, language is critical in this search for artistic emancipation: language, instead of repeating the binaries of colonizer and colonized, as her *Créoliste* contemporaries might contend, or facilitating the reinforcement of stereotypical and exoticized cultural images, must provide the avenue toward a highly individualized form of expression. In a 1999 essay, "Le métissage du texte" (The hybridity of text), Condé evokes a hybrid notion of language that has begun to replace essentialized conflations of language and culture, and proposes that the language of the literary text should go further to transcend known cultures. Citing Proust's observation in *Contre Sainte-Beuve* (*Against Sainte-Beuve,* 1971) that the most beautiful texts are written in "a sort of foreign tongue," Condé draws on a Bakhtinian polyvalent model of intertextuality to imagine how this literary language might be one unfamiliar to existing languages: "The great literary work . . . would thus be one that would deconstruct, then reconstruct these clichés, these words that are contaminated in the way we say water that needs to be reprocessed in laboratories is contaminated. To achieve this effect, the writer should call upon all linguistic resources available to create what seems like a foreign tongue, different from any that has ever been used before" ("Métissage," 215).[5] Condé proposes a use of language that generates opacity rather than transparency, uncertainty rather than familiarity. This is not a foreignness that would inscribe a divergent linguistic community but a foreignness within language, one that instills internal moments of opacity.

For Condé, then, writing is not a collectively inflected act but a deeply solitary engagement, a project that not only grows out of but produces distantiation from the Other. A passage from Wilson Harris's *The Banks of the River Space* provides a particularly resonant portrait of the artist that Condé cites at the end of her 1995 essay, "Chercher nos vérités" (Searching our truths), and as an epigraph to her 1993 novel, *La colonie du nouveau monde* (The colony of the New World): "When one dreams, one dreams alone; when one writes a book, one writes alone."[6] With this repeated reference, incorporating the untranslated words of Harris into both her literary and her critical works, Condé posits solitude as crucial to her notion of artistic freedom, a solitude that marks not a physical isolation but a concentrated and intentional gesture of epistemological differentiation.

Writing Against the Grain: Proper Names and the Language of Cliché in *Heremakhonon*

In the preface to the second edition of her first novel, Condé discusses the change in title from *Heremakhonon* in the first edition of 1976 to *En attendant le bonheur* (Waiting for happiness) in the 1988 edition as a response to the perception of hermeticism. The Malinke word meaning "wait for happiness" is replaced by its French translation in the new edition, effecting what is presumably an expansive gesture, opening up the title to a wider audience—although, as Condé herself points out in an interview, the perception is a limited one, applying uniquely to readers of French with no knowledge of Malinke.[7] The title's translation also has consequences for the narrative itself, since the word "Heremakhonon" has an additional meaning established by that fictional world: it is the name of the family compound belonging to one of the major characters, an important spatial reference for the protagonist. Beyond the linguistic translation of the title, then, the new edition establishes also a shift in functional resonance, from a proper name to a phrase composed of common names. In a sense this change does privilege the first title's function in its original language by reinscribing the Malinke word as a common name, but in the process the link to the proper name use of the word in the novel is lost, or at least displaced to secondary status as a parenthetical addition to the revised title.[8] These parallel shifts are complicated further by Condé's paratextual discussion of the title's significance in the novel's preface and in interviews, where she notes the original title's resonance in her own personal experience, Heremakhonon being the name of a store she used to pass regularly during her years in Conakry.[9] To the translated meaning and proper name designation in the novel, Condé thus adds the dimension of yet another proper name, one that presumably has a wide audience within a specific locality, and which Condé has infused with her own symbolic meaning.

This interpretive vacillation highlights the contentious negotiation of language that occurs in the narrative as a whole. The novel stages an encounter between its narrator and an unfamiliar cultural landscape, presenting a range of misunderstandings and incongruities based on linguistic, cultural, and historical barriers. Although the first-person account suggests and explicitly attempts discursive control over the events in the narrative, this hermetic gesture in fact only underscores the incidence of unfamiliar elements in the narrator's immediate surroundings. In particular, the proliferation of literary, historical, and geographical allusions in the narrative points to the important role of the proper name in elaborating this interpretive tension, and suggests a further link between clichéd language and the reductive vision of cultural identity that plagues the protagonist. To the extent that it presents an interrogation of language as a collective activity, moreover, Condé's novel ultimately reveals a potential disjuncture between heterogeneous interpretation and political action. The temporal gap between the narrator and her setting, a gap that ostensibly prevents her from engaging in the violent political struggles taking place around her, can thus be seen as more than simply a narcissistic invocation of nostalgia to avoid social accountability. Instead, the novel's exploration of language as a battleground between individual and collective experience suggests that the protagonist's absorption in the past may in fact represent an insistent effort to forge an autonomous form of expression.

HEREMAKHONON'S HEROINE, Véronica Mercier, a young Guadeloupean woman who sets off from Paris for the African continent in a half-serious, half-mocking attempt to reestablish an ancestral connection to the mythical motherland, casts a stubbornly ironic gaze on her surroundings and on her experience that refutes both the notion of unity between Africa and its diasporic descendants and the idealized vision of the African continent that had become part of the *Négritude* mythology.[10] A quintessentially alienated subject, Véronica is repeatedly stricken during adolescence and early adulthood by the disdain and lack of comprehension with which the world seems to view her. In the African setting that frames the novel, her alienation expresses itself as a radical disjuncture: while she moves physically through the landscape, she seems mentally to be at a distance from her surroundings. Absorbed as she is in her own identity, she interacts with those she encounters on a secondary plane, her exchanges displaced by the urgent concerns of her self-interrogations. Véronica creates a wall of isolation, closing herself off in an exercise in egotism: "I live in another world. A world of soap bubbles" (91). Despite her ostensible desire to find a connection to these new surroundings, then, Véronica articulates instead a persistent state of *décalage,* a gap between herself and the lives around her.[11]

Because the protagonist's self-interrogations are turned both inward and backward, this *décalage* disturbs also the chronological plane of the narrative. As Gayatri Spivak has noted, Condé sets the protagonist's inner world against the temporal setting of the novel: Véronica's absorption in her own psyche peppers the narrative with frequent incursions into her past, flashes of events, conversations, or reflections that seem to haunt her so persistently that her interactions with the present are discontinuous, in a constant state of struggle with the hold of the past.[12] The temporal orientation of Véronica's "identity quest" parallels this conflict, as she is seeking not to understand her contemporary African setting, but to discover the ancestry severed by the slave trade: "That's mainly why I'm here. To try and find out what was before" (12). Pushing aside the present in search of a past that has long since disappeared, pursued by her own unresolved history, Véronica moves through the narrative frame in her own personal state of jet lag, participating at best tangentially in the events and actions unfolding around her.

The soap bubble in which Véronica isolates herself not surprisingly creates an acute disengagement from the concrete reality of the place she has chosen to inhabit. This distantiation is manifest most immediately as a linguistic one: Véronica's failure to learn any of the African languages that might be useful to her in her contemporary daily existence is a frequent subject of discussion, contributing both to her inability to participate concretely in sociopolitical movements and to her deepening sense of alienation.[13] Symbolically, this linguistic barrier points to Véronica's general ignorance concerning her environment: she is unable to read the cultural and political landscape, and thus is ill equipped to act with any kind of social conscience. Despite the persistent confluence of the personal and the political implicated in her romantic involvement with Ibrahima Sory, the minister of defense; her friendship with Saliou, a central figure in the opposition movement; and her position as a philosophy teacher at the local university, Véronica seems to guide her actions entirely by her internal reading of her own needs and desires. Protected by a temporal, linguistic, and cultural distance, Véronica resolutely situates herself on the sidelines of contemporary African politics, positing this world as opaque and impenetrable.

Due in part to this ethic of noninvolvement, the novel traces out a situation of mutual opacity, in that Véronica too is subject to the ignorance, preconceptions, and misreadings of those she encounters. In her isolation, Véronica seems as incomprehensible to her acquaintances and colleagues as they do to her: in their eyes she is devoid of social or political function and thus unrecognizable as part of the community. Véronica's sense that she is a sexual object for Ibrahima Sory extends to a general impression of inactive presence in a strange land: "I'm an arum in a vase. I say arum because the plant is exotic like me. It doesn't grow here" (104). While this problem of mutual opacity could be read allegorically as a commentary on the severed lines of communication between Africa and the Caribbean, evoking an orphaned New World no longer acknowledged by its ancestral continent, Condé's novel highlights above all the question of recognition as a problem of linguistic and epistemological exchange, as a reflection on the stakes of translation. While this tension is most apparent in Véronica's failure to translate her own language into one coherent with her setting, the impasse between French and Malinke is ultimately a signpost pointing to the problem of translation from thought to language. Arguing with Saliou, for example, about Sory's corrupt role in the political arena, Véronica refers to the link she hopes to uncover through Sory to "her people." Saliou's outraged response reveals the radically different lens through which he views her situation:

> "Him? Him? It was the blood of the people that got his family rich."
> Somewhere we are mixing our references and any dialogue is impossible. For him, the people are an exact, concrete notion. For me . . . (67)

Here the impasse stems not from a confrontation between two languages but from an incommensurable set of worldviews, converging around the use of the phrase "the people," which for Véronica connotes a transcendent notion of timeless collectivity whereas for Saliou the concept is firmly situated in a concrete contemporary circumstance. The use of a common language thus provides little resistance to the interpretive clash between Véronica's personal journey toward the past and Saliou's politically engaged assessment of the future. Later on, Véronica encounters a similar incoherence with Sory, when their exchange diminishes to silence: "I accept his silence because there is nothing to say. To be more exact, I've understood there is nothing we can say that doesn't end up dividing us" (157). To the extent that language offers no adequate means of translation between her interior perspective and her present reality, dialogue for Véronica serves only to expose points of difference.

Condé's innovative formal strategy in *Heremakhonon* underscores the interdependence of Véronica's social alienation and the uncertain divisions within her own psyche. The insularity of her narrative is reinforced visually by a disconcerting shift in graphical discursive markers: whereas phrases uttered by Véronica's (past or present) interlocutors appear in quotation marks, Véronica's own utterances are on the whole transmitted without quotation marks, so that the distinction between her private unspoken thoughts and the sentences she articulates aloud is not always clear. The result is a kind of free indirect discourse in reverse, where both the protagonist's inner thoughts and her spoken discourse are expressed with a sense of detachment, a remove that signals her epistemological separation from her surroundings. As a number of critics have noted, Véronica's voice seems somewhat trapped behind this hermetic seal, and for the reader too the impression is one of being imprisoned inside Véronica's perspective.[14]

While the story is very much Véronica's, however, and while we do see its characters and settings through Véronica's eyes, the bounds of this perspective are not as fixed as she attempts to make them. On the contrary, the dissonance between Véronica's elocutions and those of other characters is a telling expression of the extent to which her closely guarded psyche is in fact subject to frequent interruptions from a multiplicity of conflicting perspectives and worldviews. Véronica's discourse is fundamentally characterized by the uncertainty provoked by such incursions from the contemporary world around her, underscoring in its very friction with that world the existence of details, events, and sentences that do not appear explicitly in the narrative.[15] Véronica's thoughts, whether spoken aloud or not, often respond to words we can only assume were uttered by someone in her immediate setting, while these interactions also provide the impetus for her frequent flashbacks, suggesting a constant oscillation between past and present based on small, unexpected resonances. Despite her reluctance to confront the concrete realities of life around her, the narrative indeterminacy of her discourse confirms and even insists upon the existence of a world beyond her private soap bubble.

Paralleling the referential shifts of the novel's title, the proper name emerges in Véronica's narrative as the primary site of these incursions. The unusual proliferation of proper names she invokes testifies to an uncannily broad cultural lexicon: demonstrating what Vèvè A. Clark has called "diaspora literacy," Véronica makes reference at turns to classics of the French literary canon, Creole proverbs from the French Antilles, jazz musicians from the African American tradition, and the major figures of the *Négritude* movement.[16] Her discourse thus suggests a cultural dexterity that bears witness to the variety of intellectual and geographical settings she has, despite her self-proclaimed isolation, incorporated at least nominally into her understanding of the world. At the same time, however, the insistent multiplication of these names emphasizes the extent of Véronica's local illiteracy by pointing to the irreducible nature of the diverse world that escapes her linguistic and cultural purview.[17]

The proper name signals a particularly forceful disturbance of Véronica's worldview because of its situational impetus: proper names are attached to a specific locality, a spatial or temporal point of reference, or, in the case of human names, a certain system of social classification.[18] Like the sets of restrictive rules that Condé condemns in her essays, these signs of community-based projects function as threats to Véronica's individual voice. It is thus not surprising that her struggle for expressive autonomy would take place on the stage of the proper name. Indeed, one of her most persistent reappropriative maneuvers in this respect attempts discursive control over a designation from the life she left behind in Guadeloupe: her unnamed father. Véronica withholds her father's name from the narrative, irreverently replacing it with the appellation "Mandingo marabout," a nickname established in the novel's first scene when, upon her arrival at the airport, Véronica is questioned by a policeman who reminds her of her father: "The police officer . . . [is] the thin, nervous type. Somewhat distinguished. Surely from that part of the coast that produced my father's ancestors. He too was somewhat on edge and somewhat handsome. He reminded me of that Mandingo marabout I had seen in my history book when I was seven" (3). Ironically, this encounter also marks an initial attempt on the protagonist's part at a culturally informed reading of this new landscape, a reading that asserts an insider's knowledge of the ethnic and geographical heterogeneity of the continent. Within the recurring framework of the flashback anchored by a similarity between past and present, this moment allows Véronica to imagine a link from her new setting to her father, and to encode that link in a general assertion of ethnic origin. The fact that this claim of ancestry is justified by knowledge gleaned from the pages of her history book adds a poignant absurdity to the scene, evoking a recognition of concrete reality based on the geographically remote institutional experience of a child.

The moment serves as a narrative baptism of Véronica's father, as from that moment on he will be designated almost exclusively by the phrase "the Mandingo marabout." Along with the Lacanian anxiety inscribed in this gesture, the protagonist's renaming of her father accomplishes an intriguing grammatical substitution: Véronica's discourse replaces the proper name that might otherwise designate her father with a hybrid name (proper noun + common noun) that connotes, instead of a given function within a familial structure, an ethnic specificity (Mandingo) and a socially defined role (marabout). Despite its cultural specificity, the nickname imposed by Véronica evacuates the collective inscription carried by her father's name, evoking instead a generic existence unattached to any particular familial domain. Véronica's refusal of her father's proper name thus offers a means of envisioning an immediate connection to a universalizing symbol of the African, interchangeable with other Africans she encounters and unfettered by concrete individual existence.[19] This gesture is in many ways emblematic of Véronica's misguided identity quest, as her distorted view of her surroundings stems from an effort to impose a universalized vision of the past onto the discrete and indeterminate events of the present. Taken one step further, Véronica's renaming of her father can be seen as the substitution of a single African for the entire continent.

In counterpoint to Véronica's temporally confused replacement of her father's name, Condé posits another revealingly absent proper name: the setting of her novel, as numerous critics have noted, is a nameless African country. While the refusal of this name would seem to resonate with the notion of interchangeability suggested by Véronica's paternal nickname, Condé's paratextual commentary on the novel's setting complicates the gesture. Again, the question of recognition is central: cultural and geographical knowledge will provide a more informed reading of various *other* indicators of place besides the national designation. When pressed about the novel's setting in an interview, Condé asserts the priority of an insider's reading:

> I.C. —The novel is deliberately not situated geographically. In what part of Africa does it take place?
>
> M.C. —That is a question that Antilleans may ask, but all Africans recognize it. (*Parole des femmes,* 128)

While Condé's response here is provocatively divisive and simplistic, she has in other interviews and in the preface to the novel's second edition discussed the historical events in Guinea that inspired her writing of *Heremakhonon*, lending greater transparency to this aspect of the text.[20] Nonetheless the discussion surrounding the absent country name highlights the multiplicity of details and connections in the novel that offer up the reading of its setting as Guinea, and the wide range of cultural insights with which its readers might be equipped.

Juxtaposed against the proliferation of such geographically and culturally specific signs, the absence of this proper name in the narrative seems also to put into question the national *as* a potential category of geographical space. While the emphasis on the local and the particular precludes the facile use of the name "Africa" to designate the novel's setting, the implication of its namelessness is that a specific national appellation would be similarly reductive; to refuse the name of the nation is in this respect to refuse an overused, overloaded system of classification—one that, moreover, evokes an external European imposition of geographical boundaries. In this sense the absent proper name provides a freedom from the spatial designations that collapse difference, defying at once the "continent-think," as Spivak terms it, that would read the setting as "Africa" and the reduction of arbitrary colonial boundaries.[21]

Implicit in these absent names, then, is a critique of the evacuation of meaning effected by usage. Condé's novel suggests that in this sense the proper name can function much like the cliché, as an exaggerated example of erosion through repetition, of locution that refers as much to previous usage as it does to intended meaning. The narrative offers an extended commentary on the cliché, tracing out a self-conscious critique of stereotypical imagery and language that dramatizes the tension between individual and collective interpretation. *Heremakhonon* opens with an implicit denunciation, for example, of the trendy interest in all things African as a European cliché, while in the same gesture positing Véronica's journey as a unique and individual project:

> Honestly! You'd think I'm going because it is the in thing to do. Africa is very much the thing to do lately. Europeans and a good many others are writing volumes on the subject. Arts and crafts centers are opening all over the Left Bank. Blondes are dying their lips with henna and running to the open market on the rue Mouffetard for their peppers and okra.
>
> Well, I'm not! (3)

Although Véronica draws this contrast ostensibly in order to claim authenticity, her fervent protest also suggests an awareness of how closely her journey resembles the clichéd narrative of the "return" to the continent in search of African roots, a resemblance compounded by the fact that the claim of authenticity has itself become something of a cliché in such contexts.

Véronica pursues this interrogation of the cliché throughout the narrative, however, not by avoiding stereotyped images but on the contrary by evoking them insistently as a potential consequence of her reflections. This treatment sets up a discourse that turns back on itself, articulating phrases only to destroy their functional significance in the same sentence. Upon meeting Saliou, for example, Véronica remarks almost distractedly upon his smile: "He has a lovely smile, rounded teeth, very white. Careful! Beware of clichés: the nigger with flashing white teeth. All the same, his teeth are very white" (8). The sequence employed by Condé allows for Véronica's imperative warnings to be directed simultaneously at herself and at her addressee, mounting a kind of preemptive strike at the instinctive link that might be made between her "neutral" observation and the image of racial caricature. Having articulated this cliché as a reading that is uncomfortably close to the description she has given of Saliou, however, Véronica then recuperates her original observation—"All the same, his teeth are very white"—as if by addressing the racially stereotyped reading of her reflection she were then free to restore the image to a previous state of "authentic" and literal meaning.[22]

Subsequent references to racial stereotypes implement a kind of discursive shorthand, where Véronica needs only to refer back to the possibility of cliché to make room for her intended meaning. A description of one of her students allows her to make a general commentary on a revealingly undefined "they" even as she seems to protest the essentialized reading: "Birame III slips into the room. They have a silent way of moving. Beware of clichés! No. That's how they move" (16). The self-corrective gesture accomplished in such moments underscores the discursive tension underlying the whole of Véronica's narrative: the passages read as a power struggle between the collective reading of words that have been repeated beyond recognition and Véronica's individual use of language to describe the concrete world she sees before her. The indeterminate discursive space of her narrative, melding inner thoughts with spoken words, exterior voices with private reflections, also points to the tenuous nature of the very lines of distinction she seeks to draw between her own "objective" observations and the racial stereotypes with which her social surroundings—and her own psyche—are saturated. Véronica's "No" can thus be seen as a protest against such incursions of externally appropriated meaning, an effort to recuperate language and reclaim it for the purposes of her own internal perspective.

Véronica's protest also signals a more general frustration with language as the unreliable translation of ideas. But the frustration locates itself only partly in the space between thought and word, pointing more forcefully to the co-optation of words that withholds them from her claim to foreignness, impeding her ability to reprocess the "contaminated" words and recover their unfamiliar meaning. Noting that the cliché offers a particularly illuminating instance of the distance between word and meaning, Véronica posits this phenomenon as a locus of cynical detachment: "Cliché? What does that mean? That you are hardened, inured to major ideas and the words that translate them. That you are ashamed of them" (134). Véronica's evocation of shame here suggests that the constant vacillation in her own discourse between irony and sincerity emerges from a self-critical awareness of her own inability to offer an accurate translation of her experience. The novel's initial claim of protest thus implies that her entire narrative demarcates a struggle between individual and collective meaning, a confrontation with the imprints of usage that defy her efforts to assert an original articulation of her experience. Translation for Véronica is a source of shame because, as she indicates with her attempted replacement of her father's name, she is implicated in these collective repetitions, in the very clichéd images she claims to refuse.

In this light, the temporal friction in *Heremakhonon* illuminated by Spivak suggests the possibility of a more nuanced reading of Véronica's identity quest. For the protagonist's discursive struggle can also be read on a temporal axis as an effort to reach backwards through time toward an "original" language that might offer a translated world untainted by the distortions of overuse and reductive images.[23] While this projected state of originality echoes the idealism of the mythical African past Véronica claims to seek, the impulse nonetheless suggests a desire to restore a conceptual complexity to the very mythology she has imagined: "The idea I have is so vital and yet so vague, so blurred. What is this idea? That of an Africa, of a black world that Europe did not reduce to a caricature of itself" (77). The implication here is that language is responsible for the stereotyped visions of the African continent, and that while the protagonist's attempt to return historically to the past may participate in such reductions, the effort to return discursively to an earlier use of language comes out of an effort to restore the complexities and ambiguities of meaning lost to centuries of usage. In this sense the novel mounts a critique of translation that bypasses Véronica's hermetic preoccupations, in that it is not only the protagonist's personal psyche that is at odds with the reality of her present surroundings, but the reductive use of language that produces this disjuncture. Her vision of an untainted language, "unhardened" by translation, thus operates in much the same way as the absent geographical designation: the isolation of her epistemological framework proposes a refusal of the repetitive power of language. Véronica's narrative, necessarily self-destructive in its attempt to recover its own history, posits nonetheless the alienated subject as a site of discursive liberation from the distortions of collectively driven ideology.

Solitary Missions: *Une saison à Rihata*

Despite the discursive plurality of *Une saison à Rihata*, Condé's second novel does little to mitigate the stark disaffection of her first. Instead, its multiply inflected narrative elaborates a study in alienation, a series of portraits of solitary, displaced figures. Like Véronica, these characters are at odds with their surroundings, effecting a lack of engagement that stifles the possibility of political change in the small post-independence West African town of Rihata. But here Condé focuses less on the linguistic manifestations of such impasses than on the ways in which narratives of the self might fail to match up with collectively crafted scripts of political action. Whereas Véronica's was a resolve to return to uncontaminated language, the impulse on the part of these Rihatans is to maintain a lucidity concerning the individual deviance of their own experience. In an innovative reworking of familiar literary forms that foreshadows her modification of the gothic, the fantastic, and the historical novel in later works, Condé explores this tension between individual and collective narrative in *Une saison à Rihata* by revising the thriller genre. In fact, Condé's incorporation of the classic thriller ingeniously links the genre to the question of political action: by positing one of its characters as a presumed and ultimately failed thriller hero, her novel presents a forceful critique of political engagement as the false construction of a collectively transparent morality.

FOR THE characters in *Une saison à Rihata*, as for Véronica, opposition to the narrative framework manifests as a state of temporal *décalage*. Marie-Hélène, the Guadeloupean wife of an assistant bank manager of noble African descent, couples her cultural status as "celle qui vient d'ailleurs" (12) (the woman from elsewhere) with empirical vacillations between past and present, as she is haunted by the loss of her mother in Guadeloupe and by the destructive love affairs she had as a younger woman in Paris and in the capital city of N'Daru. For her husband, Zek, too, such trying memories constantly tear him away from his daily life and work, so vivid as to disturb his temporal perception: the face of a rival, for example, "loomed so close and so lifelike that he could hardly believe they had met seventeen years ago" (10). Their nephew Christophe, meanwhile, is obsessed by unanswered questions concerning his mother's suicide and imprisoned by the isolation this secret brings: "How could he get at the truth? Who would tell him? He felt hemmed in by a wall" (66). As in Condé's first novel, the characters are paralyzed by a fixation on the past, but here this temporal division does not play out, as it does in part for Véronica, along cultural, linguistic, or geographical lines.

The physical space shared by Marie-Hélène, Zek, and their family, instead of providing a foundation for exchange, further reflects its internal friction. The opening lines of the novel describe a house that is temporally and spatially "off," or *décalée,* teetering like its inhabitants on the edge of some gesture toward belonging: "The house stood somewhat askew in the middle of an immense, unkempt garden that had more guinea grass than actual lawn. . . . Twenty years earlier, before independence, it had been built by the local magistrate and his wife. . . . When the French left, the house had remained shut for years and had slowly fallen into disrepair. Its architecture was too reminiscent of colonial times for the tastes of the new leaders of the one party's regional secretariat" (1). The characters are thus unable to find an ontological anchor in this landscape even as they inhabit it with their personal anxieties, mirroring in these self-interrogations the situation of their house, a misplaced structure out of step with history.

Indeed, Marie-Hélène's perspective suggests a causal relationship between the characters' *décalage* and that of their setting, as her own confused perception of present reality seems to threaten the very existence of the house: "Marie-Hélène opened her eyes wondering where she was. Every morning she felt foreign when she woke in this pretentious yet decrepit bedroom with its varnish-flaked chests of drawers and trunks, its threadbare drapes and the smell of must that even the sun could not dispel" (13). Marie-Hélène's hovering between dream state and consciousness in this scene underlines the problem of recognition that parallels, or perhaps generates, the temporal distance traced out in the novel: these characters have difficulty recognizing their surroundings, their family members, and themselves, inscribing a persistent sense of foreignness within the repetitive grammar of daily life.

As critics have noted, the town of Rihata is characterized by a relentless sense of paralysis, a sense that no change or definitive movement is or ever will be on the horizon; Marie-Hélène's anguish arises in part out of the confinement and imprisonment she feels in the small "bush town" of Rihata where "nothing ever happened" (4).[24] Bernard Mouralis, however, has identified an intriguing contradiction associated with the theme of immobility in Condé's novel: that this lack of movement is a curious texture to give a work that might in other respects be classified as a thriller. He writes: "One cannot help but be struck by the extreme rigor with which the author directs and organizes her narrative in a perspective that recalls the best thrillers. . . . But at the same time . . . this narrative in which events rush forward is also a novel in which nothing happens" (25). The thriller narrative in *Une saison à Rihata* hinges on the actions of Victor, a member of a northern rebel group, who pursues and ultimately assassinates the minister of rural development. As Mouralis points out, however, the shifting boundaries and climactic moments that characterize this thriller motif ultimately have little effect on everyday political life in this setting, as if the immobility of the place had suffocated any catalytic impulse that the thriller model might otherwise provide.

In fact, closer consideration of the thriller genre suggests that its incongruity extends beyond the problem of immobility to the unstable disaffection of the novel's would-be thriller hero. At first glance, the conventions of the thriller genre seem entirely coherent with the aura of alienation with which Condé's novel is infused: the thriller invokes the image of the loner—the superior, even condescending, and above all self-sufficient hero who defies seemingly insurmountable odds of survival. As Ralph Harper has noted, solitude is critical to the framework of the thriller, in that the hero must experience a separation, either forced or voluntary, from his usual surroundings, thus shedding himself of the protection of society (53–54). Thanks to this isolation, the hero is poised to confront experiences with a heightened potential for risk and danger and to embark into unfamiliar moral territory. The thriller, Jerry Palmer points out, thus hovers on a Manichean brink, forcing the hero to flirt with the boundaries between good and evil, to act in a way that is "just barely tolerable" to his implicit moral community.[25]

Ultimately, however, this flirtation with an opposing moral universe is necessarily no more than a flirtation. In order to carry out his mission successfully, the thriller hero must maintain the collective morality within his sights at all times; despite the titillating ingredients of solitude, alienation, and moral corruption, the hero's ultimate goal must in fact be the *restoration* of the world order he has left behind. The separation of the thriller hero from the community is inevitably temporary, its subsequent resolution the required outcome of his solitary status, and ultimately the only means of justifying his moral transgressions. The very concept of justice upon which the thriller narrative turns is in fact defined by that resolution, by the reunion of the hero with his underlying moral universe. An implicit collective project is thus central to the successful thriller, even if its narrative unfolds principally within the temporal outline of his alienation from the community.

It is on this point that the thriller motif in *Une saison à Rihata* disintegrates: while he successfully posits himself as a risk-taking loner, Victor achieves no subsequent resolution of this transgression. Here the division between hero and community is far more consequential, as Victor draws further away both physically and morally from the collective movement that instigated his journey. Initially, despite the fact that he leaves behind the locus of the resistance movement in the north, Victor continues, like the conventional thriller hero, to see himself as part of a greater cause, a "mission of the highest importance" (46). But later he becomes separated from his friends and begins to digress more and more from the plan they had agreed upon. The subplot's climax, Madou's assassination (the account of which is tellingly absent from the narrative), is in fact the outcome of Victor's mounting sense of alienation, a state of moral and epistemological confusion in which he suddenly and somewhat inexplicably loses sight of the collective project that initially motivated him. Instead, his own individual impulses take over, as subsequent events continue to widen the gap between himself and his community. After an early blunder, for example, in which Victor throws himself a little too enthusiastically into his presumed role, accosting and drugging Madou's chauffeur instead of simply gathering information as instructed, he acknowledges his mistake: "Head lowered, Victor saw himself confessing his failure to his leaders and companions who had chosen him for this difficult assignment. He had to admit he had let himself be distracted from his objective and had not been able to resist the temptation of playing a trick on a dogsbody without getting a scrap of information in return. What a disgrace! How could he look them in the eyes?" (52). The shame Victor expresses here conveys the tenuous nature of his identification with the collective project. His fear of confronting his collaborators, of "looking them in the eyes," signals the loss of that connection which would have allowed him to see himself synecdochically, as the reflection of their collective will.

Failing to learn from this initial mistake, however, Victor aggravates his isolation through this breach of the collective project, since his thoughtless assault on the chauffeur makes him a fugitive from the most redoubtable security forces in the city. Meanwhile, his guilt over the imprisonment of Muti, a loyal friend and member of the resistance who was linked to his impetuous crime, further provokes his preoccupation with his own concerns. Out of this narcissistic confusion emerges his final inexplicable act: "[Madou] got into the car and for a brief moment Victor caught a glimpse of the face he hated. Yes, hated! When had this hatred started? He had probably always had it in him, like a sick person not knowing he has cancer. Perhaps it had started the day before, when he had heard of Muti's fate. Perhaps it was starting right at this moment. In any case, it was there, burning, depraved and famished like a wild animal. . . . He had always known there was no other way out. Madou had to be killed" (107–8). Victor thus co-opts the mission, completely losing hold of his representative status as a stand-in for his comrades, and instead displacing their project with his own personal vendetta.

Victor's failure is in essence an epistemological one, in that he finds himself unable to sustain a conscious apprehension of the collective mission, or more crucially of his role in that mission, as he acts. His betrayal is significantly not intentional: he is in fact not sure of how his individual motivations match up with the goals of the rebellion, and consequently has no idea how to interpret his own actions in the greater context of political justice. Initially hopeful that his assassination attempt might indeed be of some benefit to the resistance movement, Victor eventually must acknowledge the possibility that his choice has no collective meaning, that it might not be reproducible on the collective stage: "'I have not brought about justice. I'm an executor like them,' he repeated to himself with his head between his hands" (160). As before, his concern turns toward the reaction he imagines his collaborators will have upon learning of these events: "And his comrades back in camp, what would they think of him? Would they consider him a traitor for setting himself a solitary mission and carrying it out without orders? Without thinking of the consequences for the others? Or would they look on him as a hero?" (161). This set of questions articulates the reason Victor may have repeatedly failed to take on the representative dimension of his heroic role as an inability to read himself through the eyes of the group. Victor is at a loss before the multiple interpretations that might be attributed to his actions, and is thus unable to read with any certainty his "solitary mission" as the collective one. Victor's failure thus highlights a crucial element of the conventional thriller: that this collective self-reading is exactly what the thriller hero successfully enacts at every instant. The underlying premise of the thriller genre is the synecdochical relationship between the hero and his implicit moral community: the lone hero stands in for the (lost or threatened) collective moral framework until he is able to successfully restore its existence.

Ultimately, then, Victor's failure emerges as a source rather than a result of the ostensibly incongruous immobility of the novel's setting: despite the potential momentousness of Madou's assassination, its opacity to any collective investment in political action smothers its capacity as a force for change. Instead, Victor's incoherent private mission effects a paradoxically wide radius of stasis in the various circles of life in Rihata and even in the country as a whole. For Zek and Marie-Hélène, Madou's death means that Zek's hoped-for promotion will not be a reality, that they will be forever condemned to their mediocre existences: "Madou was dead. So that meant that life was not going to change" (183). Their daughter Sia, meanwhile, characterizes their condition as one of repeatedly broken promises and unfulfilled hopes: "All those promises that would never be kept. Never. Never. Never" (186). Rihata's purview emerges here as one of constantly projected change, a projection whose repeated failure makes the town's stasis all the more oppressive.

VICTOR'S EPISTEMOLOGICAL shortcoming—his inability to reproduce a convincing reading of his actions in a collective framework—stops the thriller narrative short in its tracks. As his intransigent and ultimately illegible personal demands definitively sever his connections to the collective mission, his actions fail to realize the reunion of loner and community critical to the thriller genre—and, as Condé points out, to political solidarity. Similarly, Véronica's resistance to the repetitive power of linguistic heritage precludes her participation in the political landscape of the present. In their own often misguided ways, however, these characters attempt nevertheless to arrive at some kind of clarity regarding the possibility of political action; antisocial and unsympathetic as they may be, they thus cannot be characterized as disengaged tout court. Their refusal of contemporary political visions emerges out of an extensive and invested exploration of the traps and incoherencies of the linguistic, social, and political worlds they encounter. Articulated in Victor's inability to act as a stand-in for a collective vision and in Véronica's withdrawal from the concrete circumstances of her surroundings is a demand for the recognition of that failure as necessary, for terms of political action that might not operate on the premise of unconditional transparency but rather in the reclaimed vocabulary of the individual. Similarly, Condé's examination of the interdependence of political solidarity and the essentializing burden of representative status in her critical essays points to the reappropriation of language as a crucial site of resistance to clichéd readings of her texts and to exoticized visions of unfamiliar literary landscapes.

2 Fixing Tituba

Imitations of the Marginal

MARYSE CONDÉ'S fifth novel, *Moi, Tituba sorcière . . . noire de Salem,* has garnered by far the most critical attention of all of her works. Its place in her literary oeuvre is also notable in that the quantity of articles, essays, and reviews focusing on the novel is matched by an equally unprecedented range of theoretical and disciplinary concerns: Condé's Tituba has been taken up by critics not only in Francophone Caribbean studies but in African American studies, women's studies, history, religion, and American studies. This bridging of the gap between Francophone and Anglophone criticism owes its success in great part to the publication of the novel's English translation in 1992; but it is also the subject of this text that has secured its place in a diverse set of critical dialogues.[1] *Moi, Tituba sorcière . . . noire de Salem* reimagines events surrounding the infamous Salem witch trials through the eyes of Tituba, a Barbadian slave who was among those accused of sorcery. For the first time, as noted by Ann Scarboro in her afterword to the English translation, a Francophone Caribbean novel evokes a setting linking the Anglophone Caribbean to the colonial United States (187). The terrain of Condé's text is thus not only linguistically familiar for her U.S. audience but also tied to a formative historical and cultural moment in the narrative of American nationhood.

Tituba's tale also has particular relevance to current debates in feminist and postcolonial theory because it brings up questions of unofficial histories, subaltern voices, and colonial authority. In many ways Tituba could be seen as the quintessential portrait of a marginalized subject: she is a slave and a woman, victimized by a colonial economy and seemingly overlooked by historical record. Condé's assertive first-person narrative, signaled at once by the "Moi" of the novel's title, suggests a reversal of the dynamics of colonial power by according discursive authority to an otherwise voiceless subject. Given the resonance of this shift from margin to center in current critical discourse, the novel has not surprisingly inspired comparative studies with traditional slave narratives, contemporary fiction on the colonial United States, and so-called Third World testimonies.[2]

While the resolute defiance of Tituba's marginal status is a compelling postcolonial move, however, I am also interested in the commentary that emerges from this newly authorized subjectivity: Tituba's *prise de parole* offers a privileged viewpoint from which to portray the dynamics of New World colonial exchange, and presents a provocative reading of the category of the marginal itself as it functions in this context. Particularly in her interpretation of the Puritan community of Salem, Tituba exposes the extent to which this society's self-definition hinges on the distinction between center and margin. The social function she holds as voiceless, invisible, and ultimately condemned is critical to the Puritans' ability to successfully invent their own collective identity narrative. In light of the theoretical and critical discussion generated by Condé's text, it seems worthwhile to consider also how Tituba's critique of the marginal might extend to the interpretive assessments of the novel in recent scholarship, particularly to the role it has been assigned in these discussions. As I hope to show here, Condé's use of parody uncovers the reductive quality of much of the critical reception her novel has provoked, both inscribing and critiquing the apparent need to read this character unilaterally.

Manifestations of Evil

Although the marginal status of Tituba Indian, the historical figure who served as the inspiration for Condé's novel, has been a subject of some debate, it is explicitly as a marginalized subject that Condé evokes her fictional re-creation of Tituba.[3] While the character faces the most ostensible forms of social exclusion in the racist communities of colonial New England, she is no less an outcast in her native land of Barbados or even among fellow slaves. Indeed, her very origins are marked by rejection, as her mother, unable to look at her child without being reminded of the white sailor who raped and impregnated her, withholds any sign of affection or love (6–7). Initiated by Man Yaya into an expertise in the healing powers of herbs, the hidden forces of nature, and the possibilities of communication between living and dead, Tituba discovers with surprise that her powers provoke fear among the slaves in the nearby plantation communities (11–12).

Tituba's experience of alterity is thus already firmly established by the time she arrives at the home of Susanna Endicott in Carlisle Bay, having accepted slavery as the price of her relationship with John Indian. Here, subjected to the disdainful gaze of her owners and their society, Tituba offers lucid descriptions of the dehumanizing effect of her marginal condition: "They were talking about me and yet ignoring me. They were striking me off the map of human beings. I was a nonbeing. Invisible" (24). Sold to the Parris family who eventually settle in Salem, Tituba learns that her subjugated position will ultimately mean her condemnation in the eyes of Puritan society, as one of those accused of sorcery and removed from the public sphere. Upon her imprisonment, Tituba reflects also on the fact that even within the viciously attacked group of accused witches, her own experience will bear the additional insult of an erasure from historical record:

> It seemed that I was gradually being forgotten. I felt that I would only be mentioned in passing in these Salem witchcraft trials about which so much would be written later, trials that would arouse the curiosity and pity of generations to come as the greatest testimony of a superstitious and barbaric age. There would be mention here and there of "a slave originating from the West Indies and probably practicing 'hoodoo.'" There would be no mention of my age or my personality. I would be ignored. As early as the end of the seventeenth century, petitions would be circulated, judgments made, rehabilitating the victims, restoring their honor, and returning their property to their descendants. I would never be included! Tituba would be condemned forever! There would never, ever, be a careful, sensitive biography recreating my life and its suffering. (110)

Through this overtly prescient vision of her own fate, Tituba underscores the distortions to which her identity will be subjected, effecting a definitive state of invisibility in Western historiography.

The passage also marks a self-referential moment in the text, in that Condé's novel embodies a reversal of Tituba's erasure, inscribing itself as a corrective gesture that restores complexity and subjectivity to a neglected victim of history. As numerous critics have noted, Condé confers an absolute authority to the first-person narrative of the novel, melding subject and author in the text's first epigraph: "Tituba and I lived for a year on the closest of terms. During our endless conversations she told me things she had confided to nobody else."[4] This stamp of discursive authority allows Condé to put forth a Tituba who speaks for herself, across the centuries, to rectify the injustices of her marginalized position. As a consequence of this *prise de parole*, Tituba's narrative takes the privileged viewpoint of a cultural outsider, casting a quasi-anthropological gaze upon this closed community.

In this respect, Condé's evocations recall the work of Ivorian writer Bernard Dadié, whose 1959 novel *Un nègre à Paris* (*An African in Paris*, 1994) is a particularly acerbic reversal of the Western travel narrative: Dadié's African protagonist observes with uncanny objectivity the unfamiliar and often unfathomable practices of the French, asking with thinly veiled irony the kinds of comparative philosophical questions that typically characterize the European adventurer's exoticist discourse on the other. Similarly, Condé inscribes a distancing effect that affirms Tituba's point of view: the members of the Puritan community in Salem are culturally and physically remarkable to Tituba, a point she underlines through repeated mention of the color of their eyes, their pale skin and unfamiliar bodies, their odor (34, 39, 78, 81). The passages set in Salem suggest a kind of *roman d'apprentissage,* describing the "enlightenment" afforded by this travel to an exotic land: "I had not realized the full extent of the ravages that Samuel Parris's religion was causing nor even understood its real nature before coming to live in Salem. Imagine a small community of men and women oppressed by the presence of Satan and seeking to hunt him down in all his manifestations" (65). Like the European explorer in the New World, Tituba invites the reader to witness through her eyes the behavioral practices of a culture she alone has penetrated.

As a subversive element, Tituba's privileged perspective exposes the extreme hypocrisy of this world, the cruelty and violence of a community that claims to uphold the highest ideals of moral rectitude. She is a firsthand witness of the treatment of women in Puritan society, of the repression of children, of the zeal with which this community eliminates its outcasts. Precisely because of her marginalized position, moreover, she holds the town's most horrifying secrets. The search for Satan in Salem, Tituba explains, leads automatically to her because of her race, her dark skin being read as a visible and unquestionable sign of her collusion with evil. Thanks to this conflation between race and morality, Tituba and the few other black members of the community of Salem become not only the victims of this society but its confessors, vehicles through which tales of repressed desires and sentiments can be liberated: "All of us were not simply cursed, but visible messengers of Satan. So we were furtively approached to try and assuage unspeakable desires for revenge, to liberate unsuspecting hatred and bitterness, and to do evil by every means. He who passed for the most devoted of husbands dreamed of nothing but killing his wife! She who passed for the most faithful of wives was prepared to sell the soul of her children to get rid of the father! Neighbor wanted to exterminate neighbor, a brother, his sister. Even the children themselves wanted to be rid of one or the other of their parents in the most painful way possible" (65–66). Tituba is thus in possession of a privileged insight into the untold horrors of this morally self-righteous people, an insight that is entirely dependent upon her marginalized status.

The *prise de parole* effected by Condé in this novel reveals also the functional importance of the protagonist's marginal position, in that the self-defining moral rectitude of Puritan culture can only be maintained if its cruel desires remain invisible. As the release of these "unspeakable" traits is a necessary operation, the voiceless witness provides a valuable epistemological space where the unavowed narratives of this society may be articulated and confined so as to maintain the illusion of purity. Without the existence of a structure delineating such a space, without the impenetrable division between center and margin, Puritan culture would be unable to conceal the duplicity of its own narrative.[5] Attributing a lack of humanity to these voiceless figures allows the Salem community to create a concrete manifestation of evil, or, as Cassuto puts it in his study of the inhuman, to "force the grotesque . . . to occupy a fixed place in a category system of shared belief" (xvii). Tituba and her fellow victims act as the necessary—and necessarily silent—products of this manipulation, the physical form taken by this externalization of immorality.[6]

Tituba's gaze thus sheds an informative light on the sociological function of the accusation of witchcraft in seventeenth-century Salem. The appellation *witch* serves as an all-purpose designation of any figure upon whom the rejected elements of Puritan culture have been expunged, outstepping its semantic boundaries and supplanting human reality with a preconceived and collectively understood image of malevolence.[7] Each marginal figure encountered (or invented) by this society is efficiently absorbed into the default category of alterity. In Tituba's case, this mechanism is particularly useful in that it allows Puritan society to bypass the question of her race, thereby concealing the role played by racism in her condition. While it is her racial difference that secures her link to Satan in the eyes of the Puritans, in other words, Tituba is explicitly not accused of being black, but of being a witch. The authority conferred upon the culturally inflected use of the term *witch* thus facilitates a crucial lexical substitution and a dissemblance of contemporary racism.

A critical component of Tituba's narrative, then, is the extended interrogation of the semantic stability of this term. Critics have noted that
Condé's reappropriation of the offhanded historical rendition of Tituba
as a West Indian slave "probably practicing 'hoodoo'" sets up an opposition between culturally different conceptions of witchcraft. Jeanne
Garane, for example, points out that instead of refusing any association
with the supernatural, Condé's Tituba "embraces the accusation" (157)
of witchcraft by affirming the powers of healing and communication
with the dead.[8] Garane's and other readings further identify an interpretive confrontation in the novel between Western Christian conceptions
of witchcraft and Afro-Caribbean beliefs in the supernatural. While it
seems the suspicion with which Tituba is viewed by the community of
slaves in her native Barbados should serve to complicate this binary division, Condé also seems to go beyond the dismantling of dominant con-
notations of witchcraft to question the functionality of the center/margin
dichotomy it supports. Indeed, Tituba contemplates on numerous occasions the meaning of the word as if it too had acquired an exotic quality
as a result of her appropriation by this foreign society.

In an early interaction with some of the Salem children who will help
to condemn her, for example, Tituba unpacks the semantic instability of
the word *witch* in a way that ultimately exposes the arbitrary *interpretive* categories erected by Puritan ethics. Having attempted to comfort
the youngest Parris daughter by assuring her that she will cure and heal
her using her unique powers, Tituba experiences an early example of the
distortion to which she will later be subjected by the entire community:

> One day things turned sour. Fat Mary Walcott was hovering around me
> and finally said: "Tituba, is it true you know everything, you see everything
> and can do everything? You're a witch then?"
>
> I lost my temper. "Don't use words whose meaning you don't know. Do
> you know what a witch really is?"
>
> "Of course we do," intervened Anne Putnam. "It's someone who has made
> a pact with the devil. Mary's right. Are you a witch, Tituba? I think you must
> be." (61–62)

Later, Tituba scolds her young confidant for having repeated her reassur-
ances to her friends, explaining, "You see how they change the meaning?"
(62). But what is intriguing about the exchange, beyond the semantic
debate over the term itself, is the extent to which the meaning of Tituba's
behavior has been distorted by the young girls. At issue is not whether
Tituba is "really" a witch, or what a witch "really" is, but how to assign

moral value to the mystical powers she claims to possess. Tituba herself hesitates between the use of these abilities "for good" and "for evil," acknowledging the difficulty of attributing a single ethical reading to her link to the supernatural.

Given the rigid binaries of the Puritan worldview, Tituba's interrogation of the accusing term reveals the extent to which such ethical ambiguities represent an anathema in this cultural setting. Close to the end of her narrative, Tituba, upon being asked by a maroon revolutionary if she is a witch and can therefore offer him superhuman protection from harm, expresses with the canny insight of experience the inevitable trap of answering this persistent question: "I sighed. 'Everyone gives that word a different meaning. Everyone believes he can fashion a witch to his way of thinking so that she will satisfy his ambitions, dreams, and desires'" (146). While this reflection evokes the semantic control that allowed the community of Salem to condemn her, Tituba also points out the sociological function of the term in the context of Puritan society: that the word *witch* provided a means of distinguishing good from evil, a catch-all designation for the repressed and clandestine elements of this culture. By questioning this unified vision of evil through her faux-naive traveler's gaze, Tituba destabilizes not only the assigned meaning of the term that banishes her but also its function in Puritan society as a means of self-purification.

A Race for Tituba

The racial identity of Tituba has been the subject of animated debate, both in historical research and in the analysis of her literary manifestations. Condé, as she herself indicates in her historical note at the novel's conclusion, was not the first writer to bring Tituba to the fictional page: Ann Petry's 1964 novel *Tituba of Salem Village* also creates a narrative around the central character of Tituba, while other works dramatizing the events of Salem, most famously Arthur Miller's *The Crucible*, feature Tituba as a minor character. In a 1974 article in the *New England Quarterly*, Chadwick Hansen traces the various appearances of Tituba in seventeenth-century court documents and in subsequent fictional narratives, expressing profound dismay at the fact that these diverse visions of the character effect a shift in her racial description. Asking the reader to keep "the fact" that Tituba was a Carib Indian woman "firmly in mind," Hansen deplores the alteration from this definitive Amerindian identification to later historical and literary renditions of Tituba that describe her variously as mixed race, "half-Indian," "half-Negro," or "Negro." Had

Condé's novel been published at the time of his writing, Hansen would no doubt have added it to the list of egregious and historically inaccurate distortions of Tituba's true racial origins, since Condé's Tituba claims African and European but not Indian heritage. Indeed, subsequent critics have taken up the question of Tituba's race in *Moi, Tituba sorcière . . . noire de Salem* as a recent example of the historically transformative properties of fiction.[9]

If such a shift from the conception of Tituba as Amerindian to African does exist, the path of this transformation would seem to offer some insight into the various cultural and historical lenses through which the relevant texts were reading this elusive figure. Bernard Rosenthal proposes, for example, that the various renderings of Tituba's race reflect contemporary manifestations of racism in the United States: while seventeenth-century colonists in New England perceived the predominant threat of violence from native Indian populations, he argues, in subsequent centuries the demographic shifts brought by slavery and its aftermath ensured that the white majority would more immediately recognize an association between African origins and a potentially threatening presence.[10] As Rosenthal notes, the shift in attention is also symbolic, in that the decimation of the Amerindian people left conceptual room in the American mind for the substitution of a more current version of racism: "The romanticized Indian of the nineteenth century having been virtually eliminated or removed to reservations, the feared 'Negro' survived. In popular culture's unrelenting effort to shape history by elevating heroes and punishing villains, an identity was forged for Tituba, and it is not at all surprising that that identity should be racialized, that Tituba should be classed with others like her who inspired fear. Now fixed in popular imagination as a black woman, Tituba retains her usefulness only if she remains so" (202). For the twentieth-century U.S. audience, Tituba would indeed be more "useful" as a black woman, as a ready incarnation of a denigrated people supplying a more accessible condemnation of contemporary racism. Condé's choice, in this sense, incriminates the particular conceptual form racism has taken in twentieth-century America in much the same way that Tituba's voice denounces the prejudices of her own community.

Perhaps even more than this shift in attention from racism against Native Americans to racism that targets those of African descent, the debate surrounding Tituba's race reveals a contemporary sociopolitical concern about race itself. What emerges above all from the extensive historical and archival research that has been conducted on Tituba is a premium placed on the resolution of the race question: the ostensible impulse driving these studies is the need for certainty, for a clearly defined racial identity that can be unambiguously assigned to Tituba. As Veta Smith Tucker aptly suggests, the controversy exposes the notion of racial purity as a specifically twentieth-century preoccupation: "In the absence of incontestable evidence indicating a precise racial identity for Tituba, contemporary readers rely on today's racial categories and import 20th-century notions of racial exclusivity into their racial reconstructions of Tituba. . . . Contemporary scholars seem to be unaware that the myth of racial exclusivity enabled by a corollary racial myth, the myth of racial purity, lies at the unexamined core of contemporary scholars' insistence that as Indian, Tituba could not also have been African" (631). By signaling Tituba's biracial origins in the opening lines of her novel, Condé seems to echo this sentiment in her own conception of this figure, refusing the suggestion of racial purity and, on a secondary level, reminding the reader of the particular historical circumstances of colonial miscegenation. Ultimately, it seems an even more telling commentary on contemporary sociological considerations that underlying the presumption of racial purity is the conviction that racial identity can be known: in the case of Tituba, the problem of historical accuracy highlights the fact that, much as it is impossible to recover the unrecorded details of the events surrounding the Salem witch trials, the "true" racial identification of Tituba remains obscured—by conflicting evidence in historical record, by linguistic and orthographic variation, and by the differing criteria for racial categorizations inscribed in contemporary documents. The epistemological challenge posed by history also suggests a parallel to the conception of race as a means of social categorization: contemporary readers of Tituba, in their efforts to "fix" her racial identity, endorse a belief in the existence of race as a functional category of identification.[11] The debate concerning Tituba's historical and literary manifestations thus suggests that determining a single, definitive racial identity for this figure would presumably bring us closer to historical "truth," while at the same time resolving a number of other questions about how to read Tituba. Much as the term *witch* in seventeenth-century Salem provided an efficient means of maintaining the Puritan dualism of good and evil, the definitive knowledge of Tituba's race would offer the possibility of reading her narrative—of assigning positive or negative value to her behavior—through the lens of the culturally constructed category attributed to her.

The Perversions of Parody

A considerable source of tension in critical readings of Condé's Tituba has been the question of the novel's seriousness. In two well-read interviews (one of which appears as part of the afterword to the novel's English translation), Condé contends that the text contains an intentionally parodic dimension often overlooked by readers. The examples she mentions in these interviews refer to some of the most frequently cited passages from the novel, the "first-degree" readings of which form the basis of a considerable amount of successful postcolonial argumentation. On the empowering epigraph establishing a mystical unity between speaker and author, for example, Condé proclaims, "Tituba's spirit did not come to me. The epigraph was just for fun" (Pfaff, 59). When asked by Ann Scarboro about the importance of the oral tradition among different generations of women, she elaborates on the intentional use of clichéd images in her novel: "The question of grandmothers telling stories and thus teaching their granddaughters how to become writers is one of the biggest clichés of black female writing. I repeat that the element of parody is very important if you wish to fully comprehend *Tituba*. . . . If one misses the parody in *Tituba,* one will not understand, for example, why she meets Hester Prynne in jail and why they discuss feminism in modern terms. Similarly, the presence of the invisible (the conversations with the mother and with Man Yaya) is deliberately overdrawn. Do not take *Tituba* too seriously, please" (212). In a few sentences, Condé effectively undermines a considerable number of critical responses to her text, suggesting that such readings have either misunderstood key scenes in the novel or that they have participated in reinforcing tired clichés about black women.

The prescriptive quality of these comments has not surprisingly created a certain amount of hesitation among critics in the very fields that have embraced Condé's Tituba as an important site for rethinking history, feminism, and cultural criticism. Ann Scarboro herself gives an account of her reaction to Condé's admonition, describing a process of rereading and revision: "I myself was embarrassed to realize that I had missed the element of parody on first reading because I was so eager to celebrate Tituba's heroism and her Caribbeanness. Wanting to honor the novel for its 'ethnicity,' I ended up missing part of the point, as Maryse herself helped me discover" (225). Jane Moss has also written eloquently on what she sees as a collective misreading of the novel by "good feminists" who praised Condé's subversive and counterhegemonic discourse: "I was not the only good feminist to hail the novel as a perfect example of how women writers challenge hegemonic discourse by unearthing lost heroines, subverting masculinist notions about the feminine, and valorizing women's knowledge. Like many others who share my politically correct, theoretically informed views, I fell into a very clever trap, seduced by both Tituba and Maryse Condé. I ignored obvious signs in the text itself and warnings by the author" (6–7). The "trap," as Moss describes it, is that of reading Tituba selectively, of seeing in her the earnest portrayal of a "Third World" or "subaltern" heroine, speaking directly to us from the forgotten pages of history.[12] The trap is an interpretive one, and consists not only of reading Tituba through a particular lens but more importantly of reading her through *only* one critical lens. As Moss suggests, Tituba's story seems poised to fit a certain mold in current critical discourse; it "fulfills the desire for a first-person narrative by a strong Third World woman" (5). But this role can be successfully played only if the parodic dimension of Condé's novel is overlooked.

Because the deceptive reading is in particular one proposed by postcolonial and feminist theories, this question of reading Tituba unilaterally is a pointed one. As Carolyn Duffey points out, the novel speaks implicitly to the criticisms raised by Third World women writers concerning their reception in the dominant Western market (101–3): while the welcome may ostensibly be a warm one, it is often predicated on a specific set of expectations concerning the subject matter and ideological orientation of the text or texts in question. Literature written by women outside the dominant culture falls under a general formula according to which the reader anticipates a reversal of power dynamics between dominant and subordinate cultures, an investigation of gender politics within and outside of their particular culture, and some smattering of regionally or nationally specific history. What is especially problematic about such readings is not only that they reduce literary texts to a formula but also that they apply the same formula indiscriminately to all instances of Third World women's literature. In essence, the operative (and thus solely determining) attribute of the text is its marginal relationship to the dominant readership. The reductive gesture of such readings thus occurs on both thematic and functional levels: the text written by a subaltern voice carries its marginal category as the only available means of interpretation.

In this sense the element of parody in Condé's novel poses a particular threat to such problematic "First World" readings because it undermines the possibility of reading unilaterally. Parody elaborates a split narrative and demands a "second-degree" interpretation based on a concurrent awareness of the genre that is being imitated and of the imitation itself. As Henry Louis Gates has demonstrated, the polemical properties of this rhetorical strategy have inscribed parody as a valuable tool of subversion in African American literary history, allowing writers to distort the meaning of earlier texts or to create a critical dialogue between texts.[13] While Condé's *Tituba* (and indeed her fictional oeuvre as a whole) certainly reflects such a project, her use of parody is uniquely complex in that its critical target is less a particular text or genre than a particular literary *reading:* instead of targeting an existing literary predecessor, what Tituba's story mockingly imitates is in a sense a false text, a nonexistent narrative created by preconceived notions of Third World women's writing. The imitative gesture offers a comment on the very creation of its (false) original, on the discursive ideology that assures the existence of such a text in the minds of readers. It is thus not simply the use of parody but, more important, this metacritical dimension of Condé's novel that has provoked the reactions of self-doubt and hesitation among recent critics: Condé expertly subverts reductive interpretations of the novel by pointing to those critical misreadings themselves as texts to be perverted by parody.

One wonders, moreover, if the self-effacing reactions of critics "guilty" of misreading Tituba are not also tied to the condemnation of misreading elaborated by the novel as a whole. For the central dynamic of Tituba's story—of her survival—is the question of parody: Tituba's guilt in the eyes of the Puritans turns upon her confession—resting, in other words, on her ability to produce a successful parody of the identity that has been imposed on her. The character of John Indian is emblematic of this performative strategy; he is the novel's trickster figure who offers the master a caricatured vision of the subservient black man in order to appease him. Tituba's crucial decision upon being accused of witchcraft is whether or not to follow this distressing example by "confessing" and thus conforming as John did to the image set before her. Ultimately, encouraged and instructed by Hester, Tituba does accept this performative task as a necessary means of survival, providing a testimony that Condé renders in her text through the reproduction of excerpts from Tituba Indian's trial deposition. The novel thus contains an embedded historical document, yet situates it in such a way as to dictate its content as an invented narrative. Tituba de-authorizes the transcription further by abruptly cutting it short to proclaim that "it went on for hours" (106) and to signal the element of parody in this scene: "I confess I wasn't a good actress. The sight of all these white faces lapping at my feet looked to me like a sea in which I was about to drown" (106).

Although this image of the "sea of white faces" evokes most immediately Tituba's sense of intimidation before her accusers, it also signals the reception of Tituba's "text" by her Puritan audience: having given them the required confession, having fulfilled their collective desire, Tituba will see her identity appropriated and subsumed by the "sea" of Puritan ideology. The text imposed on Tituba responds to a preexisting narrative on the part of this community, the desire for whose fulfillment is so forceful that it renders the event itself all but irrelevant. Tituba herself confirms this emptiness by implying that the performance was not even a convincing one; rather than listening critically in a way that might reveal a disconnect between Tituba and her words, her audience "read" only the functional meaning of her confession. As if to acknowledge the community's participation in this elaborate performance, Samuel Parris congratulates Tituba on her successful deception: "Well spoken, Tituba. You understood what we expected of you" (106). As a result of this successful parody, Tituba's lived experience recedes behind layers of invention, "drowned" by the imitated narrative of a pre-scripted desire.

Condé's novel thus incriminates this Puritan society by exposing their collective reading of Tituba as an illusion, a performance that they consumed wholeheartedly. The narrative accomplishes this condemnation in part by insisting on the parodic aspect of Tituba's confession—by insisting, that is, on the gap between text and imitation. In this sense the entire novel can be read in juxtaposition to Tituba's false confession, as an ever-accumulating collection of evidence pointing to the performative element of that historical document. Each moment, each event as related through Tituba's eyes displaces the narrative of her confession into more insistently relative territory.

The novel's conclusion dramatizes this interpretive gap in a strikingly condensed form, when Tituba, having returned to her native Barbados only to be accused of participating in a slave revolt, is led to the gallows as a double punishment for her present crimes in Barbados and her past trespasses in Salem. Again, the entire narrative of Tituba's lived experience takes on a reduced and distorted form: "A man dressed in an impressive black and red coat read out all my crimes, past and present. I had bewitched the inhabitants of a peaceful, God-fearing village. I had called Satan into their hearts and turned them one against the other in fury. I had set fire to the house of an honest merchant who had decided to disregard my crimes, but who had paid for his lack of judgment with the death of his children. At this point in the inquisition I almost screamed out that it was all untrue and nothing but vile and cruel lies. Then I thought otherwise. What was the point?" (172). Tituba's interior commentary in this passage makes the falsehood of the accusations patently clear, underscoring an unequivocal refusal of this distorted version of events.

Condé goes beyond this thematic tension, however, to evoke through the formal presentation of Tituba's final moments a parallel tension between text and narrator. The sentences relaying the crimes of which Tituba is accused appear, intriguingly, in the first person, in a discursive move that echoes the affirmative "Moi" of the novel's title. Instead of presenting this critical scene as a third-person narrative or direct discourse relation, Condé chooses to implant Tituba's perspective into this false account, as if to echo the performance she so successfully mounted in Salem. The appropriation is not complete, however: Condé uses not the present perfect tense but the pluperfect, effecting what would grammatically be characterized as free indirect discourse but reversing the subject shift customary to this mode. Where the "original" direct discourse locution might have been, for example, "She has bewitched the inhabitants of a peaceful, God-fearing village," the modified free indirect discourse version shifts the subject from third-person to first-person (instead of the usual first- to third-person modification) and signals through the shift in verb tense the indirect status of the discourse. As a formal innovation, this gesture appears to support the notion of an assertive narrative authority accorded to Tituba, but what Condé also suggests in these final passages of the novel is the distance articulated by Tituba's voice between truth and illusion, between event and narrative, between text and imitation. The "original" text of her accusation is thus typographically absent and, much like the parodied Third World woman's narrative, must be reconstructed by the reader.

Temporal Disturbances

The visibility of Tituba's parodic intention within the context of the Salem witch trials denounces the unilateral reading of individual experience, suggesting allegorically that readers of Condé's novel, much like the Puritan readers of Tituba's confession, might accomplish a parallel suppression of Tituba's voice by overlooking the novel's performative element. The signs pointing to the novel's parodic dimension are not, however, limited to this embedded example or even to the paratextual comments made by Condé in interviews. Much as the text of Tituba's confession inscribes its own performative status, Condé's novel indicates through a number of formal disjunctures the ironic distance at which it holds the heroic scope of its narrative. As Jane Moss notes, the novel contains its own "obvious signs" of parodic intent (7).

The most visible of these rhetorical manifestations is the persistent use of anachronisms in the novel, anachronisms that have in fact been the subject of considerable discussion in critical scholarship on *Tituba*. While the use of the term *anachronism* makes certain assumptions about the prescribed parameters of historical fiction—parameters it seems Condé is specifically trying to undo—Condé's evocation of seventeenth-century settings and subsequent historical moments through the voice of Tituba seems worth examining more closely. As we have seen, for example, Tituba makes predictions about her own place in history, about the way her story will be rendered in future court documents. At the novel's conclusion, she also evokes future incarnations of American racism through suggested images of the Ku Klux Klan and urban ghettos, predicting that in America, the "vast cruel land" she has come to know, "they will be covering their faces with hoods, the better to torture us. They will lock up our children behind the heavy gates of ghettos. They will deny us our rights and blood will beget blood" (177–78). These anachronisms allow Condé to mount a condemnation of the long history of racism in the United States, pointing out, as she contends in her interview with Ann Scarboro, that "in terms of narrow-mindedness, hypocrisy, and racism, little has changed since the days of the Puritans" (203).[14]

In what is perhaps one of the most frequently cited moments in the novel, Condé also suggests a temporally palimpsestic setting with the introduction of a character called Hester, a young woman accused of adultery and imprisoned in the same jail cell as Tituba. This conspicuous allusion to Hawthorne's *The Scarlet Letter* imagines a link between two figures oppressed by Puritan society, a leap across fictional time to elicit a common tale of ostracism. In fact, the perceived anachronism in this scene stems not only from Condé's placement of a character from a nineteenth-century novel into a seventeenth-century setting but, more controversially, from the presence of the word *feminist* in this transtextual dialogue. It is Hester who provides the lexical disjuncture, as she attempts to convince Tituba of the unfailingly destructive role that men play in society and describes her utopic vision of a world governed entirely by women. When Tituba protests that men might still be necessary in such a society, at least for the purposes of procreation, Hester chastises her by suggesting an incoherence between such desires and her political ideology: "You're too fond of love, Tituba! I'll never make a feminist out of you!"

(101). Tituba's response, "A feminist? What's that?" (101), highlights the anachronism of the term in the setting elaborated by this scene while at the same time suggesting a cultural separation between the two women: Hester's vocabulary—and to an extent her political vision—is foreign to Tituba. Despite the alliance formed by a common ostracism, then, Hester seems in Tituba's eyes to remain part of a world that excludes her.

Critics have read this striking exchange as a critique of twentieth-century feminist theory, establishing an allegorical correspondence between Hester and Tituba's ideological differences and the intellectual and theoretical tensions between "First World" and "Third World" women concerning the question of feminism. Hester, according to these readings, represents the condescending bourgeois white intellectual attempting to "enlighten" her poor undereducated sister, while the lexical impasse between these characters signals, as Manzor-Coats puts it, "the untranslatability of the experiences of black women vis-à-vis white women" (744).[15] But the fact that Tituba's "What's a feminist?" query points specifically to a semantic problem also has a particular resonance *within* the novel; here Tituba seems to echo the extended reflection she articulates on the meaning of the word *witch*. By asking for a definition of *feminist* (a definition that, moreover, Hester does not supply), Tituba draws an implicit link between the semantic indeterminacy of this term and that of the multiply appropriated term by which she has been censured.

This moment of incomprehension between Tituba and Hester seems to suggest that the term *feminist* in its twentieth-century context, much like the term *witch* in the novel's seventeenth-century setting, is most problematic when defined unilaterally. Hester's teasing reproach of Tituba implies an incoherence between sexual desire for men and the precepts of feminism, and thus an incoherence that bars Tituba's ideology from being defined as a feminist one. By withholding the definition of the word when pressed by Tituba, she performs a further reduction to its referential field, preempting the discussion that might expose its multiple meanings. Much as the Salem community affirmed a single social function to the word *witch*, Tituba's fellow outcast allows for only one possible behavior to merit description as feminist.

The culturally inflected ways of defining feminism have, moreover, formed an underlying debate in conflicts among theorists of different racial and geographical experience. Condé herself has raised the question in interviews, either refusing the term altogether or wondering about its universal applicability.[16] In her discussion with Françoise Pfaff, for example, Condé notes the frequency with which the question of her own alignment with the tenets of feminism comes up, and confesses to be at a loss as to how to respond to such questions:

FP   Are you a feminist?

MC   I have been asked this question a hundred times, and I don't know what it means exactly, so I must not be a feminist. If you ask people in the United States, they probably will tell you that I am not.

FP   Perhaps being a feminist means to demand equal status for women and a valuation of their position in society, literature, politics, and everyday life.

MC   That depends. I know a Caribbean women writers' organization that meets every two years. Each time they glorify themselves: "What we do is sublime." It is not because you are a woman that you write good books or have essential things to say. There is a danger in believing so. (29)

Condé's responses in this interview trace out a direct interrogation of how definitions of feminism shift locally and regionally, revealing the ideological complexities of the concept that are glossed over by the seemingly straightforward question of her own relationship to feminist thought. In a striking parallel to Tituba's seventeenth-century predicament, Condé suggests further that the term *feminist* might be imposed upon her by an external audience, and that the attribution might vary in both meaning and functional significance depending on the context.

The use of the term *feminist* thus creates a temporal disturbance in the narrative that signals an array of twentieth-century preoccupations. What is distinctive about this particular instance of anachronism is that instead of establishing a confrontation between two different historical moments, or even between two literary texts from different moments, Condé's novel juxtaposes a setting from one historical period and a critical *discussion* from another. The "text" that creates the anachronism, in this case, is in fact a metatext, an interpretive debate around the applicability of a temporally specific term. If we read Condé's numerous anachronisms in this novel as so many signs pointing to its parodic intention, it seems that here again the gap created by the imitative play of parody is one between text and reading. The use of the term *feminist* means to interpellate not a preexisting text but the very reading that might seek to create such a text, in an effort to erroneously (and anachronistically) impose its First World intellectual twentieth-century preoccupations onto a culturally and historically distinct setting. The parody mounted by Tituba, then, is a parody of a *mis*reading, a parody of what is lost in translation.

Commensurate Readings: Tituba and Billie Holiday

The critical desire to see Tituba as the representation of marginality itself imposes a unilateral reading of this figure: she is, through this interpretation, the very embodiment of the marginal voice, the subaltern subject, the suppressed narrative. Much as the Puritans established a single social function according to which they defined Tituba's identity, such narrow readings of the novel posit an ideological filter through which the character can function only as a reflection of a preconceived subjectivity. Condé's inter- and paratextual indications of parody thus undermine these reductive interpretations by tracing a split narrative, a text that refers to its own distorted readings. What is intriguing about the critical response to these parodic revelations, however, is the instinct to abandon entirely the "seriousness" of Condé's text: to acknowledge the character as a parody of reductive postcolonial or feminist visions seems to suggest an incommensurate understanding of the novel, a self-destructive gesture that precludes taking Tituba seriously.

In fact, while Condé certainly critiques readings that ignore the signs of parody in the novel, it does not necessarily follow that the understanding of the text as derisive imitation is the exclusive lens through which to read Tituba. Condé has herself expressed a hesitation concerning this dimension of the text, stating in her interview with Scarboro that her motivations shifted during the creative process: "I really invented Tituba. I gave her a childhood, an adolescence, an old age. At the same time I wanted to turn Tituba into a sort of female hero, an epic heroine, like the legendary 'Nanny of the maroons.' I hesitated between irony and a desire to be serious. The result is that she is a sort of mock-epic character" (201). What Condé articulates here, then, is a more palimpsestic vision of the text's parodic function, implying that certain moments in the novel might be read differently as either ironic or serious, or that some parts of the text might carry a simultaneous impulse towards parody and heroism.[17] The hesitation suggested by such a characterization proposes a hesitation not just between text and imitation or between single and split narrative, but among a multiplicity of layers of serious, semi-serious, and self-mocking readings, a complexity that itself varies during the course of the narrative. In this sense, the clichéd image of Tituba as a subaltern heroine is egregiously reductive, but the replacement of such a reading with a notion of "purely" parodic narrative would ultimately seem to offer an equally simplistic understanding of the novel.

To return to the question of feminism in Condé's text, it is informative that in this respect also there arises an interpretive impasse concerning this character. As we have seen, it is Tituba's sexuality that, according to Hester's ideological orientation, precludes her from attaining the worthy status of being a "feminist"; it is because Tituba expresses a sexual desire for men that Hester sees her case as politically hopeless. This sexuality is in fact at issue throughout Tituba's narrative, a tragic flaw that seems to doom her to the life of slavery, betrayal, and ultimate execution that she recounts. In the context of seventeenth-century Salem, moreover, Tituba's sexuality traces a direct confrontation with the social mores that surround her. In a world where sexual relations between a man and a woman are expressed as a "hateful act" betraying "Satan's heritage in us" (42), Tituba's desires suggest a demonized state that even she begins to consider: "I wondered whether this was not a blemish in me, a fault that I should have tried to cure myself of" (170).[18] Given this dynamic, the incoherence Hester identifies between Tituba's sexuality and feminist ideology is revealing in that it echoes the exclusion she suffers in Puritan society. Much as her depiction of seventeenth-century New England underscores the persistent force of racism three hundred years later, Condé's juxtaposition of Tituba Indian, Hester Prynne, and twentieth-century cultural debates suggests that in terms of the perception of female sexual desire, little has changed since the days of the Puritans.

BEFORE A brief epilogue recounting Tituba's posthumous form as an "invisible" presence in Barbados, Condé closes the main body of the narrative with the description of Tituba's death by hanging, evoking in the final sentence of this passage an unexpectedly connotative image: "I was the last to be taken to the gallows. All around me strange trees were bristling with strange fruit" (172). The inevitable connection, especially in its English translation, between this final phrase and the song made famous by Billie Holiday traces yet another anachronistic reference to a twentieth-century American setting.[19] The anachronism is an intriguing one in that it points at once to the contemporary circumstance of lynching and to the contemporary *reading* of that circumstance, to the twentieth-century cultural vocabulary that identifies the link between image and song.

While this closing rhetorical gesture participates in the novel's sustained critique of contemporary American racism, however, the particular choice of this final image also suggests a comment on how we read Tituba more generally. For the specific song called up by these last words is one that produced a considerable amount of interpretive tension surrounding its most famous performer. As Angela Davis argues in her study of female blues singers, *Blues Legacies and Black Feminism,* Billie Holiday's performance of "Strange Fruit" brought the question of political consciousness to the fore in a repertoire that had for the most part been dominated by the love song. The public perception of Holiday as a sensual, uneducated, weak female whose path to success had been carefully maneuvered by powerful white men thus came sharply up against a song that evoked in 1939 the horrors of lynching in the American South. What Davis identifies and condemns in her study is the critical impasse arising from this perceived contrast: that Holiday's public, not to mention her managers and business associates, was incapable of reconciling the singer's sensuality with a serious political agenda.[20] For them, the two were incommensurate, much as Tituba's sexual desire seems to resist coherent reading through Hester's conception of feminist ideology. With this parting image, then, Condé seems to assert a parachronistic denunciation of racist violence as a final plea to read Tituba on multiple levels simultaneously: as a sexually desiring, ethically complex character who both embodies and derides the heroic readings of postcolonial feminism.

3 Imperfect Genealogies

Traversée de la mangrove and
La migration des cœurs

As a reparative impulse in the postcolonial text, the search for origins suggests allegorical import as a collective balm for the ruptures wrought by colonialism. Condé frames this quest as an epistemological project, as an attempt not only to gain knowledge or to fill in gaps but also to realize interpretive consensus. For her, allegory and genealogy are linked in that the collective search for origins posits a quest for the reproduction of knowledge from one generation to the next, envisioning a utopic victory over illegibility, incoherence, and temporal discontinuity. In *Traversée de la mangrove* and *La migration des cœurs*, Condé suggests a critical distinction between the search for genealogical *identity* and the search for genealogical *knowledge*, revealing the desire for self-knowledge as the inherent but problematic motivation for the quest for origins. To fix identity through genealogy, she points out, is to conflate physical and epistemological resemblance, founding an impossible condition of mutual transparency between ancestor and progeny on an equally exaggerated vision of physical replication. By positing death in each of these novels as an irreparable epistemological rift, Condé frames the desire for genealogical transparency as an absurdly narcissistic project, and reveals further the temporal and perceptual distortions that emerge from the collective search for origins.

Because *Traversée de la mangrove* is set entirely in a small village in Guadeloupe, it has been read as a symbolic "return" on the part of its peripatetic author to the landscape of her native island.[1] The novel's focus on the figure of the stranger, however, maintains the spaces beyond this insular setting as a constant preoccupation for its characters: Francis Sancher is the outsider par excellence, appearing suddenly and mysteriously in the small town and exuding the exotic aura of one whose travels have inscribed a privileged and inaccessible knowledge. The character's uncertain origins only add to this exotic status, and in the deliberately multicultural microcosm of Rivière au Sel suggest a compelling stage for the allegorical reading of a Caribbean search for ancestry.[2] And yet the novel's insistence on illegibility, in part through the interpretive incoherence generated by its multiple narrators, and more pointedly through the enigmatic death of Francis Sancher, underlines the limited scope of allegorical reparation.[3] In *La migration des cœurs*, meanwhile, Condé presents the imperfect status of family resemblance as the site of yet another torturous experience of illegibility. This New World transposition of Emily Brontë's *Wuthering Heights* skillfully weaves anxieties concerning incest and miscegenation as twin loci of troubled genealogies, revealing the extent to which the search for ancestry connotes an otherwise problematic impulse toward sameness. By foregrounding the potential undesirability of physical resemblance, Condé's novel opens up the possibility of resisting the collapsing of difference through the recognition of these imperfect repetitions.[4]

The Father's Wake: Allegory in *Traversée de la mangrove*

Traversée de la mangrove accomplishes a brilliantly complex *mise en scène* of the practice of allegory: Francis Sancher elicits allegorical interpretation both on a thematic level—thanks to his indeterminate origins—and on a structural one. The novel's setting is the wake that follows Sancher's mysterious death, offering a series of characters the opportunity to reflect in turn upon this stranger. Condé posits these reflections as so many readings of Sancher, playing out the characteristic extratextual doubling of allegory repeatedly in multiply generated forms. Through this attention to the reader's voice, Condé thus foregrounds the allegorical text's precarious dependence on interpretation: that in order to produce both an "outside" meaning and an "inside" meaning—to follow de Man's formulation—the reader must actively engage a preexisting system of interpretation. For this doubled meaning to articulate a coherent narrative, moreover, that interpretive system must be a shared one, and the individually generated readings must faithfully inscribe themselves into a collective one.

Condé's novel shifts the grounds upon which allegory is built to underline the epistemological demands such a framework places on a temporally and interpretively discontinuous community.[5] On the one hand, the novel's structure dismantles the reliability of the reader as the source of allegory's doubled meaning: thanks to the device of the wake, the characters in *Traversée de la mangrove* ostensibly gather to reflect upon

Francis Sancher's life in some way, to ask the question "Who was Francis Sancher?"; but in a striking *mise en abîme* of the self-referentiality of allegorical reading, Condé demonstrates in each chapter that this question must in fact be more precisely "Who was Francis Sancher *for me?*"—which inevitably becomes "Who am I?" Like Barthes's Sarrasine, whose reading of Zambinella proves to be a fatal *mis*reading because it is a self-referential one, each character in *Traversée de la mangrove* tells his or her own story, and the "inside" text of Sancher recedes ever further into obscurity.[6]

Beyond the disruptive gap between text and reader, moreover, interpretive authority in the novel comes up against the second impasse of discordance. In the short space of a single night, nineteen characters clamor for their right to tell Sancher's story, the setting of the wake offering a singular moment of spatial proximity in the small village: "You don't lock the door to a wake. It remains wide open for all and sundry to surge in" (12). The performance of interpretation gives rise to heady claims of exclusive knowledge of Sancher; Moïse the Postman, for example, proclaims: "'I was the first to know his real name,'" and repeats the words to himself, "as if they gave him a right to the deceased, a right he was unwilling to share with either of the two women who had loved Francis or with the two children he had planted in their wombs" (13). Meanwhile, Léocadie Timothée declares: "That corpse is mine. It's no coincidence that I was the one to find him. . . . I have become his mistress and his accomplice" (111). Each character's story is an authoritative gesture, asserting the priority of his or her reading of Sancher and suggesting a profound suspicion of the interpretations of others. Moïse incorporates this skepticism into his story as he tells the accepted version of events in Sancher's life, then discounts that version, explaining that "people will say anything" (18, 26) and that he alone knows the true account of what happened. Interpretation is thus articulated in the novel as a defiant, hermetic activity that denies the possibility of a shared understanding of Francis Sancher.

The apparent lack of any authoritative unity behind the "text" of Sancher himself further complicates the interpretive project in *Traversée de la mangrove*. The novel is shot through with a cynical disempowering of the role of the author. Not by chance, Sancher figures as a writer, and the people of Rivière au Sel express a profound mistrust of this mysterious occupation that involves "sitting and doing nothing." His "authority" is in fact a radical failure, as Vilma describes: "He wrote pages upon pages on the veranda. When he was tired of tearing them up, he went off into the woods" (159). Sancher is thus cast more accurately as an anti-author, whose work consists primarily of the destruction of writing. He articulates this irony himself to Lucien: "For me, writing is the opposite of living. I confess to impotence" (183).[7] Similarly, as text, Sancher gives no directives to his readers, functioning socially as an illegible script. His appearance in the village, his habits, his intentions, his identity, are mysterious to everyone in the community. Vilma expresses this opacity in topological terms: "When he returned he lectured me in a hollow and meaningless way. He told me about towns, he told me about all sorts of places, and I tried to find my way through his words without a guide" (160). Even Sancher's dead body remains blank, sealed shut: there is no blood, there are no wounds to tell the story of how he died; this too is left to interpretation. This illegibility is not to imply that there is no text to be read; on the contrary, Sancher implies that he has "seen the world" and knows the truth, but refuses to tell his own story. At the village bar, for example, everyone's attention is caught by the word "Cuba," and all is silent as they wait to "drink in the words of Francis Sancher." But he denies them those words: "You won't like what I'm going to tell you about Cuba! You lot only like stories round and juicy like California oranges. All you want is sugar to sweeten your dreams. All I know are sad stories to make you cry, sad stories to make you die!" (149). Similarly, he tells Mira, "If I told you the truth, you'd run a mile" (193). The conception of Sancher's "truth" as allegorical text brings an important implication to his words: he suggests that, much like Barthes's Sarrasine, the readers prefer their own self-referential reading of the text to the "truth" of the text itself. The "truth" of these "sad stories" is thus perpetually receding, connoting, as Sancher's warning implies, a mysterious connection to death. In this sense Condé posits allegorical interpretation as an activity doomed to a certain hollowness, forever imposing false readings onto the text.

This gesture of self-referential rewriting clearly has resonance in the postcolonial context. As Stephen Slemon points out, the imperialist enterprise can be seen as an allegorical gesture, in that colonial conquests "reread" and rewrite spatial boundaries, historical meaning, and cultural identity.[8] Such projects impose a literal and ideological renaming of colonial spaces according to an exterior set of understandings of those spaces. In Condé's novel, even the xenophobia of the natives of Rivière au Sel reflects this rewriting of the Other. As Dodose Pélagie puts it, "The people of Rivière au Sel hate strangers. They hate them so much they'll say anything about them" (175). The impulse to interpretation thus comes out of hatred, a desire to annihilate the other's story. As this defiant reversal of the imperialist gesture demonstrates, moreover, a crucial component of such projects is the ability to name, which is precisely the license of allegory.[9] In this sense, Francis Sancher's illegibility effectively subverts such colonialist efforts, as his refusal to be rewritten extends to his very name: he explains to Moïse the Postman, "My name is Francisco Alvarez-Sanchez. If you receive letters addressed to that name, they're mine. Otherwise, for everybody here, I'm Francis Sancher. Got it?" (17). Similarly, Sancher tells Man Sonson that when he was a doctor he was called "Curandero," essentially emptying his name of any potential connection to his life. The interpretations of each of the villagers who encounter Sancher are thus attached to an empty sign.

Slemon proposes a notion of postcolonial allegory that would build on the evasion of an exterior, imperialist naming and engage in a project of renaming. This project would simultaneously articulate a new collectivity founded in the postcolonial condition itself: "The colonial encounter and its aftermath, whatever its form throughout the post-colonial world, provides a shared matrix of reference and a shared set of problems for post-colonial cultures. . . . Post-colonial allegorical writing suggests . . . that a shared typology grounded in the real world of cultural and political relations does exist and does provide a cultural thematics upon which allegorical communication can take place" (165). Postcolonial allegory would thus present the renovation of a collective consciousness founded in the very circumstances of its destruction: a shared code of understanding based on the experience of colonial conquest.

It is here, however, that Condé's narrative diverges from such models of postcolonial allegory: the contradictory readings of Sancher, although articulated in the context of a community and shared *experience,* fail to align that common ground with the conception of a shared *interpretive* system. The characters of *Traversée de la mangrove* share a temporal and spatial condition, but it is precisely as readers that they are divided; the multiplicity of voices whose stories conflict thus denies the reappropriation of allegory as a basis for unified understanding. Although the postcolonial suspicion of the name is a subversive and empowering move on the part of Sancher, then, the shared cultural context of his readers does not enable them to rename him with one collective voice: Sancher remains unnamed, and his readers' stories remain in profound discord.

Sancher's evasion of the interpretation of others thus renders his death a moment of radical loss. Vilma expresses this emptiness at the wake: "I wanted to ask him questions. . . . He never told me anything about himself, and I wouldn't know what truth there is in all those stories the people of Rivière au Sel tell" (160). Once Sancher is gone, the false re-writings of him are all that is left; in a sense, his identity has been utterly subsumed by the interpretations of others. Angus Fletcher remarks in his study of the allegorical mode that "allegorical stories exist, as it were, to put secondary meanings into orbit around them; the primary meaning is then valued for its satellites" (220). Since the stories about Francis Sancher, these satellites of secondary meaning, are always at a distance from the presumed primary meaning, Sancher's absence precludes the possibility of closing the gap, leaving the elusive "truth" of his existence definitively out of reach.[10] Indeed, the entire text points playfully to its own absence: Sancher tells Vilma that he is writing a book called "Crossing the Mangrove" that he is certain he will never finish. The title itself is discounted as illogical and impossible, since "you don't cross a mangrove. You'd spike yourself on the roots of the mangrove trees. You'd be sucked down and suffocated by the brackish mud" (158). Like Sancher, the novel within the novel is illegible to the point of being virtually nonexistent.[11]

The loss that is mourned by allegory can be conceived of not only thematically but also on temporal parameters, as the loss of the past. The distance traced by allegory is a temporal one in that the allegorical sign refers to a sign from the past, and allegorical interpretation is a reconstructive gesture that attempts to connect these signs in order to effect an impression of temporal continuity. The desire to recover the past, however, is an ambiguous one in a context where a colonial presence has imposed its own exterior versions of temporality and history. The triumphant reappropriation of the past suggested by allegorical reading is problematic when the original status of that past is uncertain, when, as Édouard Glissant has shown us in the Antillean context, "History" has little to do with "truth" or with lived experience. The obliteration of the past, or of the loss of past, is thus of a significantly different quality from the kind of absence typically evoked in allegorical texts.

Although the allegorical genre does suggest itself as a powerful tool in the reclaiming of lost or stolen history, then, and implies the possibility, as Slemon proposes, of "reappropriating allegory to a politics of resistance" (163), it would be difficult to claim that *Traversée de la mangrove* endorses such a project. While Sancher figures as a *loss,* his text is not *lost,* in the sense of being something that was once there and is no longer there. Francis Sancher was never at any point a cohesive presence for the inhabitants of Rivière au Sel; thus the various readings of him are not rereadings but simply readings—or predominantly misreadings, as we have seen. The stories told by the villagers and their outcasts do not come out of an ideological effort to reappropriate a lost story and thus incorporate it into a new collective understanding. In this sense, it is not really the *re*interpretive aspect of allegory that is evoked in this novel: the mourning over the death of Sancher is not due to the loss of a previous presence, but rather to the absence of any such cohesively defined existence.

The ambiguous status of Francis Sancher as lost/not lost reveals an essential point: that the temporality essential to allegory is based on a linear time frame. Condé's novel illuminates the allegorical mode by displaying the inscription of the temporal axis in theories of allegory that articulate a clear separation between past and present, a necessary disjunction between what is no more and what is. Revision, reinterpretation, reappropriation of the past require a distance between subject and object, a prior separation that enables the designation of the past as such. Both the form and the content of *Traversée de la mangrove*, however, foreground a nonlinear conception of time. While the narrative frame of the novel echoes the unity of the classical tragedy, this outer unity of time does not correspond to a unity of voice or interpretation; instead the narrative winds through several tales, constantly reversing and diverting its direction.[12] This temporal entanglement is equally evident thematically, particularly as evoked by Francis Sancher. His passionate desire to "put an end to his race," for example, involves a conception of himself as already past, which is further complicated by his effort to keep his children from being born in the future. When Mira wakes to find Sancher attempting to abort their child, he tells her: "I have come here to end it all. To come full circle. To put the finishing touches, you understand. Return to square one and stop everything" (83). This paradoxical future project of destroying the past connotes the circular logic of Sancher's aesthetic, emerging in reverse in his enterprise as a writer, as he tells Lucien, "I'm more or less a zombie trying to capture with words the life that I'm about to lose" (183).

Sancher's death at the heart of the narrative also intensifies this confusion, since thoughts of him in the past are expressed in a narrative present. Comprehending death, as Vilma implies, represents a logical impasse within any single temporal sphere: "And now he's dead! All I have left is the memory, cold as ashes, of a little pleasure and a lot of pain. I confuse the past and the present" (161). The loss of Francis Sancher thus does not accord him a coherent reading as a fixed identity confined to the past.

Indeed, this is precisely the argument that could be made against post-colonial theories of allegory, which assume a past that, if hegemonically appropriated, is nevertheless definitive enough to be reckoned with.[13] Condé's novel suggests that the imperialist imposition of History upon the spaces of the colonized world was not simply the wrong name for a content that one can now attempt to recapture and rename, but rather a name *without* content. This is a radical absence that cannot be characterized as a loss, or as a past with its distinct position on a time-line. It is for this reason that Sancher says his novel will never be written: "I'll never finish this book because before I've even written the first line and known what I'm going to put in the way of blood, laughter, tears, fears and hope, well, everything that makes a book a book . . . , I've already found the title: 'Crossing the Mangrove'" (158). Here, the premature naming of content is paralyzing, and obliterates the very existence of that content; in a sense, it is always already too late. Condé's novel thus reveals and disputes a fundamental assumption of linear time: that past moments were at some point present. In this sense, the allegorical activity of engagement with the gap between present and past is exposed as somewhat meaningless in this context of radical absence and nonlinear temporality.

Despite the cathartic consequences of Sancher's death, then, with the collective if not coherent *activity* of storytelling it generates, the search for origins emerges in this novel as a futile attempt to establish temporal continuity. In its final pages, Condé suggests further that this quest implies an exaggerated dependence on transparency. Quentin, Francis Sancher's fatherless son, foreshadows a new allegorical figure, destined, as his mother imagines it, to seek tirelessly an understanding of his heritage:

He'll set off like Ti-Jean and travel the world on horseback, stamping the ground with his hooves of hatred, stopping at every cabin, every hovel and every Great House to ask:

"Ou té konnet papa mwen?" (Did you know my father?)

He'll hear and get all sorts of answers. Some will say:

"Oh my, he was a vagabond who came to bury his rotten self here. We don't even know whether he was white, black, or Indian. He had every blood in his body."

Others will say:

"He was crazy and talked out the top of his head, out the top of his head!"

And yet others will say:

"He was a malefic man who bewitched two of our loveliest maidens. A ragamuffin, I'm telling you!" (191–92)

This passage offers a condensed version of the novel's dynamic of interpretive instability as a whole, but underscores here through Quentin's bilingually rendered question that knowledge necessarily displaces identity in such journeys: Quentin's projected question is significantly not "Who was my father?" but "Did you know my father?"[14] For him, genealogy is uncertain not because of a lack of information but because of a more insurmountable epistemological shortcoming. The overlapping and contradictory narratives Quentin will "hear and get" point to the process of translation as fundamental to the search for origins: the father's identity must be fabricated through the multiple—and entirely subjective—readings of others, and thus will fail to cohere around any single narrative if the mutual opacity of these readings is to be preserved as it is in Condé's novel. Quentin's "hooves of hatred" thus pound out the futility of such gestures of allegorical meaning, while at the same time illuminating the demand for consensus that inheres in the search for genealogical knowledge.

The Father's Wish: Troubled Genealogies in *La migration des cœurs*

The circle that seems to form around the passionate couple of Catherine and Heathcliff in the final passages of *Wuthering Heights,* enclosing them in a transcendent union of souls beyond the grave, signals a dynamics of containment in play throughout Emily Brontë's novel. The explosive force of the text is in many ways a product of these many enclosures: characters are constantly being locked into or out of rooms, entry into isolated spaces is violently forced or refused, while gates, doorways, and windows signal the tense boundaries upon which the novel's fatal ignorance and secrecy are built.[15] The relatively sparse cast of characters points to the isolation of the text's narrative world as a whole, underlining the extent to which the Earnshaw and Linton families remain cut off from the outside world. As numerous critics have noted, the tangled patterns of marriage and reproduction articulate this dynamics of enclosure in genealogical terms: Leo Bersani characterizes the relationships between these two families as a "claustrophobic inbreeding" that both mirrors and produces the endless psychological repetitions at work in the novel (199), while William Goetz notes the "closed or ingrown quality" of this tiny society (362). The impenetrable quality of this closed world is made particularly apparent by its resolute exclusion and rejection of Lockwood, the principal narrator of *Wuthering Heights,* who, as Goetz puts it, "remains *de trop,* an outsider incapable of entering into a genuine alliance with anyone" (362). The narrative world of the novel draws taut lines of demarcation between inside and outside, between knowledge and ignorance, just as the Linton-Earnshaw kinship defines itself through the assimilation or rejection of what stands beyond it.

One of the most striking modifications brought to this English classic by Condé, then, is her reversal of this rhetoric of self-containment. Instead of the claustrophobia of Brontë's tale, Condé's *La migration des cœurs* enacts an opening out of space, of geography, of social spheres, creating a world whose boundaries are difficult to define, much less preserve. The action of the novel moves through various linguistic and cultural settings in the Caribbean archipelago, while major and minor characters outline a network of interconnected families and histories. The misfit narrator Lockwood is significantly absent from Condé's tale, and without his emblematic failure to penetrate the walls of Wuthering Heights, the outside world seems free to come rushing in, disturbing and renegotiating the boundaries of this narrative and social space. Despite the potential claustrophobia of its island settings, Condé's novel refuses to maintain the isolation of the Linton-Earnshaw families, insisting instead on exploding its walls of demarcation along social and epistemological lines.

The opening pages of *La migration des cœurs* announce the thematics of disorder that will characterize the novel as a whole, inscribing the loss of clear boundaries that inheres in the New World setting into the particular historical circumstances of nineteenth-century Cuba. Melchior, the priest who leads the procession at Epiphany in this opening scene, highlights his island's position at the crossroads of European and African religious affiliations, and seems to embody the consequent blurring of distinctions between and among cultural identifications.[16] Given his ability to read the future, Melchior also occupies a privileged position between two temporal frameworks, valued by those who consult him precisely for his ability to move from one space of cultural or spiritual knowledge to another. His is an expertise that is particularly well suited to this "age of chaos and calamity," at home with the array of legacies that have collided with explosive force in the New World (5). Even Melchior, however, confronts the rebellious dimension of this chaotic setting, as the very procession he so carefully directs, initially a beautifully perfected performance with its participants grouped according to ethnic affiliation, disintegrates into a free-for-all: "After the Mandingos . . . the procession broke up. A motley crowd of women and children of all the colours of the rainbow, from Congo black to pass-for-white, cavorted in any old fashion. The children, boys and girls alike, showed off everything Nature had given them at birth" (4). Despite the "angry looks" Melchior turns to cast in the direction of this disorderly crowd, he is unable to maintain the carefully drawn lines established at the head of the procession, his culturally diverse expertise powerless before the exuberant force of these multitudes.

As the narrative shifts to the point of view of Cuba's captain general José de Cépéro, we are given a first hint that this New World disorder is also tied to a profound sense of anxiety, particularly for those whose power depends upon the preservation of social hierarchies. Watching the dancing crowds below, de Cépéro turns his thoughts instinctively to the mounting independence movement that threatens his position on the island; the transgression of boundaries exhibited by the procession is simply one more sign of this reversal of power, of the growing presence of non-Europeans in Cuba's political arena. For the general, the "chaos and calamity" is linked to a specific historical moment: "Under pressure from other European nations, Spain had finally abolished slavery. Now the illiterate barbarians fleeing the plantations were crowding into the hovels and gambling dens in the towns" (5). Through de Cépéro's eyes the abolition of slavery marks a shift in spatial boundaries, an opening up of these divisions that allows an influx of previously confined populations. The disruption of Brontë's carefully constructed borders and containments effected in Condé's novel thus coincides with a historical circumstance of disorder, syncretism, and revolution.

In yet another nod to this new historical and geographical setting, Condé envisions a cast of characters that far exceeds the tightly knit circles of Brontë's tale. Melchior is the first of many peripheral characters woven into the central narrative, and the crowd he attempts to direct seems to foreshadow the multiple voices to be heard in the novel, from powerful political figures and plantation owners to young servants and their families. The importance of movement in this novel, signaled by its original French title, further fosters such multiplications, as with each "migration" comes a new geographical setting and a new cast of characters. Given the densely knotted question of genealogy in *Wuthering Heights*, it is of particular interest to note that the patterns of reproduction in Condé's novel are also a source of this extended character list: members of each of the two principal families have numerous offspring, some who die in infancy but others who live on to reappear, if peripherally, at later points in the narrative. The novel closes on the image of what is perhaps the most striking example of this genealogical revision: instead of a final rumination on death, Condé's text focuses its last passages on the future life of Anthuria, the infant descendant of Cathy and Razyé (Condé's modified Heathcliff). As Vinay Swamy argues, the family tree, resolutely closed off in Brontë's text, is here opened out toward the future in an unfinished gesture of potentially infinite expansion.[17]

The appearance of these new faces, both within and outside of the principal families, generates a narrative structure much like that of the polyphonic *Traversée de la mangrove*, shifting from first- to third-person narrative, from center to periphery and back. Thus, Nelly's is not the only privileged servant's perspective onto the central action, as we hear also from *Mabo* Julie, the former slave who cares for Razyé's wife, Irmine de Linsseuil; from Sanjita, the Indian woman whose family also works for the Linsseuils; and from Ada, the fishwife who befriends Cathy II in Dominica. Thanks to this plethora of perspectives and insights, knowledge and information concerning the principal families circulate with considerable freedom in the communities of each setting. In marked contrast to the constrained secrecy of *Wuthering Heights,* Condé's novel emphasizes the forceful dynamics of rumor and speculation at play in the daily interactions of its characters. Without the tight limits put on family secrets by the forbidding doors of Wuthering Heights, the tireless efforts of Nelly Dean, or especially the exclusive list of those who have any exposure to such secrets, information in *La migration des cœurs* is accessible from numerous vantage points, and travels along a variety of conduits. As a parallel to (and consequence of) the dissolution of boundaries and the multiplication of characters, Condé thus posits an expansion rather than a suppression of knowledge, shifting from a rhetoric of enclosure to a rhetoric of disclosure.[18]

Among the secrets divulged in *La migration des cœurs* is the narrative of Razyé's three-year absence following Cathy's devastating decision to marry Aymeric de Linsseuil. Indeed, this "missing piece" of Brontë's novel is not simply unveiled in Condé's text but posited at its very opening, as the inaugural moment of its narrative.[19] By framing the novel as Razyé's story—and specifically as his previously untold story—Condé takes her point of departure not from inside Brontë's text but from outside it. The choice of Razyé seems a fitting one for this initial gesture of shifted boundaries, moreover, since his referent Heathcliff, as Frank Kermode has argued, has a critical position *between* many of the primary forces at play in Brontë's novel: between two families, between poverty and wealth, between culture and nature (123–30). Given this liminal stance, we can also read Heathcliff as a figure whose existence articulates the very borders that define this narrative world; it is his hesitation between the various states and forces of this novel, in other words, that makes them visible as such. In this indeterminate capacity Heathcliff is of course also a threat to the preservation of those boundaries, and as such he embodies the potential disorder against which the hermetic family dynamics must protect themselves.

By opening her novel with Razyé's narrative—with the disclosure of an untold portion of his story—Condé thus establishes this disruptive figure not as an outside force whose incursions into the inner world of the narrative define its boundaries, but as the signature force for the narrative. Razyé is no longer a threat to the forces of demarcation at work in the novel; instead, the disruption he represents is the very space of the narrative. Even the slight modification in nomenclature suggests this shift in narrative focus: in Brontë's text Heathcliff receives his name from a deceased member of the Earnshaw family, while Condé's "Razyé" refers exclusively to the landscape where the character was discovered (9). Whereas the significance of Heathcliff's name can be read either as an assimilation into the Earnshaw family through the use of a dead child's name or as a failure to achieve this normalization indicated by the lack of family name, Razyé's designation seems to assert that he is very much of this narrative world: not an inner assimilated world of cultural and economic power, but a revised world of blurred boundaries and disclosed secrets.[20]

To return to the historically specific anxiety connoted by the disorder foregrounded in Condé's text, Razyé's stamp on the narrative also suggests a revealing tie to the particular social configurations of its colonial setting. Indeed, Heathcliff too signaled the importance of colonial power in his earlier European circumstance: Susan Meyer has argued that the threatening energy of Heathcliff's presence in the novel is not only a matter of class difference but, more forcefully, the manifestation of an anxiety concerning British imperialism. Heathcliff's dark skin, linked to an array of possible origins from India to China to Africa to the West Indies, situates him outside the space of the narrative in a culturally and historically specific way; as Meyer suggests, his presence is threatening in that it points to a world "beyond the margins of England" (102), a context of colonial power and racism that otherwise remains safely outside the walls of Wuthering Heights. In Condé's novel, then, the repositioning of Heathcliff/Razyé from border to center parallels the shift from Old World to New, from slavery to post-abolition, thereby unveiling the colonial anxieties of the British text. The political and historical context that hovered threateningly outside the bounds of Brontë's tale bursts through the margins of Condé's novel to become its central focus: as the character of José de Cépéro reminds us in the first pages of the text, the guilty conscience of imperialism takes palpable form in nineteenth-century Cuba, no longer a border figure but articulated in plain view.

In opposition to the enclosure and secrecy of Brontë's novel, then, Condé proposes a narration where boundaries are destroyed, where disorder predominates, where repressed knowledge is visible. But this is not to say that the opacity of the British classic is lost, for ignorance continues to hold a critical role in Condé's variation. What has shifted here—inevitably, perhaps, given the dissolution of the physical and human constraints on what is accessible to the novel's principal characters—is the *locus* of that ignorance. In Condé's text the boundaries of knowledge, instead of being erected by walls, doorways, or human interference, are internal: individual characters create and maintain their own divisions between the self and the outside world.

One of the suspicions that circulates through rumor and gossip in the Guadeloupean community where the Linsseuil and Gagneur families live, for example, is that Cathy's daughter, Cathy II, is not the genetic offspring of Aymeric de Linsseuil. But as a conversation with *Mabo* Sandrine reveals, the young Cathy II, despite a vague awareness of these rumors, simply prefers not to know the truth. "I shall never try and find the name of my true papa," she declares. "It was my maman's secret and I respect that. And after all, I don't want anybody else except the man who has loved me since I was a child." When *Mabo* Sandrine begins to protest, Cathy interrupts her, saying, "I have two eyes to see what nobody wants to see" (200). This paradoxical declaration is a gesture of willful ignorance: the young Cathy is aware of knowledge that is being hidden from her, and yet affirms a clear refusal of that knowledge, thus aligning herself with those who "don't want to see" the truth. Later, as an adult, when rumor and suspicion suggest more specifically that Razyé is her father and that her love for Razyé II is thus an incestuous one, Cathy II expresses the fear that lies at the heart of this denial: "I am the daughter of tainted blood. Maman? Better not speak of her. As for my real papa, . . . I'm so frightened I'd rather not know" (326). In a similar gesture of fearful refusal, Razyé II throws Cathy's diary into the sea without reading it, unwilling to witness whatever "monstrosities" it might expose (334).

These moments of self-imposed ignorance thus create a striking parallel to the dynamics of containment in Brontë's novel, where tension is created by the constant repression of what is known but cannot be acknowledged, by the forces of assimilation and rejection that determine what will be accepted into the tightly enclosed world of its narrative. In Condé's text this filtering occurs at the level of each character, as an attempt to shut out a world that relentlessly makes its presence felt, to push this world beyond the borders of consciousness. It is as individuals rather than as members of a collectively narcissistic society that the characters of Condé's novel are haunted by knowledge they are unable to confront.

In this novel, then, the fear of the unknown translates as a distrust between and among individuals, and the principal characters of *La migration des cœurs,* like characters throughout Condé's oeuvre, are lonely and isolated beings, often living a self-imposed exile from the communities or family members that alienate them. If we look more closely at Razyé II's defiant refusal to open Cathy's diary, the particular source of this instinct toward self-isolation becomes more apparent. Razyé's motivation for this dramatic rejection is ostensibly the desire to remain ignorant of the truth, to allow Cathy's secrets to remain secret. But since one of his own secrets—the possibility of incest—is wrapped up in this silence, the gesture is in a number of ways not without self-interest. As he contemplates reading the diary, a childhood memory surges up, a foundational moment from the untold secrets of his own past:

> He took the diary out of his pocket again and gazed at it. The truth was there. Written in these few pages. All he had to do was turn them and he would know.
>
> But when the time came to make this apparently simple gesture, he couldn't bring himself to do it. He felt uncomfortable, as if he were about to do something wrong. When he was little he used to creep along the landing of his mother's bedroom and through the keyhole watch Irmine undress. After having coveted this forbidden body he stood ashamed, swearing he would never do it again and convinced that he was a godless child. (333)

Razyé (or his disorderly memory) draws a parallel between the reading of Cathy's diary and the childhood desire for his mother's naked body, the connection between forbidden desire for the mother and the taboo of incest presumably provoked by the suspicion of incest articulated in Cathy's secret thoughts. But beyond the multiple Freudian possibilities of this moment, it is as a fear of *shared* experience that Razyé's refusal of the diary is particularly revealing: Cathy's secrets are frightening above all because they might mirror his own. It is an unspoken shame they both carry that would be exposed in her written words, and thus her testament that would announce his forbidden desire. Razyé's fear, then, is essentially a fear of reciprocation, of seeing the other laid bare and thus confronting his own hidden vulnerability.

This critical gesture of denial creates an unexpected echo of Brontë's text. Razyé's instinctive withdrawal in this scene forms an uncanny parallel to that exhibited by the British novel's narrator, Lockwood, who, despite his fascination with the mysteries of Wuthering Heights, and in particular with the young Catherine, remains firmly shut out of the Linton-Earnshaw microcosm. As Martha Nussbaum has pointed out, Lockwood's gaze upon this society is that of a man who has specifically sought out a space of isolation, and this because of a natural disposition toward social alienation. Lockwood himself explains that this "peculiar constitution" rises out of a youthful failure, an erstwhile inability to respond in kind to an expression of love. The moment now forms, as he describes it, a shameful memory: "She understood me at last, and looked a return—the sweetest of all imaginable looks—and what did I do? I confess it with shame—shrunk icily into myself, like a snail, at every glance retired colder and farther" (Brontë, 27). Nussbaum's reading of this passage argues that what frightens Lockwood above all is the exposure of his own true feelings as mirrored in the eyes of another: "To him the reciprocation of love is more terrifying than its non-reciprocation. . . . The gaze of desire, seeing into his own desire, makes him passive and ashamed of his own softness, the snail without its shell" (368). Lockwood retreats within himself—and thus fails to penetrate the walls of the Linton-Earnshaw narrative—not because he is without passion, but because he cannot bear to acknowledge his own vulnerability. As is the case for Condé's Razyé, the Other represents the potential reflection of this vulnerability and therefore must be rejected. In this sense it is Lockwood who best captures the tragic isolation of *La migration des cœurs:* while his equivalent narrative function may be absent in her revision, Condé has in a sense created multiple Lockwoods, an array of characters trapped within their own self-imposed boundaries of fear and mistrust.

In the case of both Lockwood and Razyé, moreover, the fear of reciprocation is also a fear of resemblance, of witnessing a disturbing similarity between the other's vulnerability and one's own. The barriers of willful ignorance thrown up by the characters of *La migration des cœurs* are in part an effort to escape this potential mirroring in the other's gaze. In this context it is interesting to note that this resistance to repetition also emerges at the level of the nominal: in Condé's novel the use of first and family names, although relatively faithful to the patterns established by Brontë, inscribes slight variations that reflect an impulse away from rather than toward resemblance.

Irmine de Linsseuil, for example, in an attempt to deny the genetic link between Razyé and their first child, decides to christen the boy Aymeric, after her brother. Razyé's hatred of his son is only exacerbated by this nominative link to his lifelong enemy, and, in a gesture that seems to evoke the preoccupations of Brontë's novel as much as it does Razyé's, the community resolves this tension by replicating the father's name: "Nobody was allowed to call him Aymeric, and everyone, even his schoolmistress, called him Razyé II out of fear of offending the cruel father" (128). This Brontëan duplication will have only a temporary status in Condé's novel, however, as Razyé's son will himself refuse to carry his father's name. Having left his home for the island of Marie-Galante, he elects to call himself "Premier-né," or "First-Born," to which he later adds a new family name: "He realized that his father would have difficulty finding him under his borrowed name, First-Born, to which he had added Sabrimol, a name he had devised just like that out of his head" (237). So not only does his father Razyé fail to repeat or take the place of a previous family member as Brontë's Heathcliff does but the son also refuses the duplication of either his father's name or his family name. Accompanying—and even solidifying—Premier-né's physical separation from the family, then, is a refusal to engage in a system of nominal repetition, an affirmation of autonomy and difference: "Razyé II, or First-Born as he had chosen to be called, had made up his mind to lead quite a different life" (237).

In her own modified repetition of a British classic, Condé thus imagines characters who refuse the internal dynamics of family resemblance and instead insist on their individual and incommensurable identities. In this respect *La migration des cœurs* points out the extent to which the hermetic quality of the Linton-Earnshaw microcosm depends upon an effect of internal resemblances. The repetition of names in *Wuthering Heights*, so extensively studied by critics, signals an excessive desire to construct a self-enclosed unity of identification. Numerous experiences and relationships follow this ethic of repetition, closing the gaps between parent and child, brother and sister, past and present, and elaborating a hall of mirrors in which individual identity seems all but obscured.[21] As William Goetz has argued, the disconcertingly redundant patterns of appellation in Brontë's novel also point to the possibility of incest that haunts the narrative: the doubled names "reinforce the sense of an unhealthy proximity or likeness between characters who should remain different; they insist upon that general threat of incest that overhangs this society, the threat of a union between characters who are *too* 'alike'" (365). In Dorothy Van Ghent's analysis as well, the incest motif is inscribed in the preservation of boundaries, in the rhetoric of assimilation and rejection that determines those borders: "The incestual impulse appears as an attempt to make what is 'outside' oneself identical with what is 'inside' oneself" (169). The self-isolating impulses at work in Condé's novel, however, posit instead a desire for difference and distance between individuals, thus underlining the surplus of resemblance in Brontë's text as its symbolic expression of incest.

As we have seen, Condé's treatment of the incest anxiety is given specific form in her novel, and brought sharply into focus at its close, with the question of the infant Anthuria's filiation. Here Premier-né confronts the possibility, filtered through a childhood memory, not only that Razyé and Cathy were lovers but also that they had produced an offspring. Since this possibility is posed as a series of questions ("Who would ever know the truth behind this sombre love story? Who would know the fruit it had borne?" [348]), the final sentence of the novel seems to frame Premier-né's thoughts as a response to these questions: "Such a lovely child could not be cursed" (348).[22] In this final expression of hope, the desire is once again for a *lack* of repetition, for a failure of the genetic link that would enclose the child in ingrown patterns of familial duplication. Premier-né's hope for Anthuria is that her existence will refuse that insular resemblance, and that in the same gesture it will refuse incest.

This hope, of course, is only that: a hope that Premier-né has no possibility of fulfilling or confirming. As he had done days earlier upon contemplating Cathy's diary, Premier-né simply rejects any other narrative, refusing to allow the suggestion of incest to take explicit form in his thoughts. The gesture of denial upon which the novel closes is thus all the more intriguing in that Premier-né's hope is ostensibly founded upon the physical appearance of the child: the fact that the child is "beautiful" should guarantee that she will not be cursed. Given the subtext of incest in these final passages, though, Anthuria's "beauty" would also refer to the fact that she offers no visible evidence of her doubled ancestral ties to Razyé. Indeed, in this respect Premier-né's hope is entirely reasonable: resemblances can only be approximate, in that the body of the child never provides a precise visual mapping of its genealogical history.[23] Anthuria, like all of the characters in the novel, will offer instead an imperfect reference to a multiplicity of ancestors, known and unknown, legally or socially sanctioned and illicit. And like her mother before her, she will be at the mercy of social perception, treated and judged according to the varied interpretive readings of her appearance.[24]

Ultimately, then, Premier-né's forlorn hope points to the impossibility of perfect resemblance. His refusal of his father's name also asserts that genealogical repetition, if a powerful force, is only partial: that the individual cannot stand in for the family, but can only refer to other individuals in a series of elusive approximations. In this sense Condé's novel as a whole undermines the symbolic mechanisms of *Wuthering Heights,* insisting that the world beyond its borders also exists, that the narcissism of the Linton-Earnshaw family is necessarily metaphorical. Similarly, Condé rewrites the romantic union of Catherine and Heathcliff by evoking death as the essential dividing line, the "migration of no return" that definitively separates one person from another: as she signals with her epigraph from Beauvoir's *La cérémonie des adieux* ("Death has separated us / My death will not reunite us"), death represents the impossibility not only of union between dead and living but also of a subsequent reunion among the dead. Within the novel, this morose message is delivered most explicitly by Cathy herself, in a short passage where she announces her own death in the first person. "I am gone," she begins, then shifts to the second person: "You must realize we shall never see each other again, for death is nothing but the night. It is a migration of no return" (90–91).

Although both *Traversée de la mangrove* and *La migration des cœurs,* in a nod toward Tituba's otherworldly powers, raise the possibility of communication and exchange between the dead and the living, Condé's novels stop short of advancing a romantic notion of union through death.[25] The voices that reach the text from beyond the grave may be heard and juxtaposed with those of the living, but they do not offer the possibility of transcendent alliance. In this context Condé's revision of one of the most frequently cited lines from Brontë's novel is telling: Cathy's climactic "I am Heathcliff" translates here as "While I was on earth, I had the feeling you were inside me, always there, in my head, in my heart and in my body. I even got the impression I was you" (92). The romantic claim of passionate substitution is downgraded to a feeling, an impression; and while the sentiment may be no less strong in the Caribbean Cathy's case, the union it suggests is nevertheless an explicitly imperfect or approximate one.

The incomplete coincidence of these star-crossed lovers thus serves as a reminder of fears surrounding the exposure of racially or socially problematic genealogies through physical resemblance. At the same time it points to the rhetoric of substitution upon which genealogical knowledge is founded: the separation hewed by death reveals the expectation of recovered ancestry as one of an impossible epistemological conflation. Unlike *Traversée de la mangrove, La migration des cœurs* does not worry over uncertain origins but rather over undesirable ones, pointing out in its resistance to *Wuthering Heights*'s narcissistic family patterns that such absorptions of alterity are in fact fundamental to genealogical history. Successfully resolving the search for origins in a way that would satisfy the collective desire for history thus suggests through Condé's lens an excessive dynamics of resemblance, an insistence on hyperlegible duplication that leaves no room for approximate or polyphonic knowledge. In this sense *Traversée de la mangrove*'s Quentin, with his hateful stomping hooves, seems to both foreshadow and revise the angry son of Razyé, whose refusal of nominative repetition lashes out against the allegorically driven demand for genealogical transparency.

4 Breaking the Compact

The Limits of Trauma in *Desirada*

LIKE THE INTRANSIGENT heroine of Condé's first novel, *Heremakhonon*, *Desirada*'s protagonist, Marie-Noëlle, maintains a state of confrontation with her surroundings. As is the case for Véronica, spatial displacement is both the symptom and the consequence of this disjuncture: Marie-Noëlle's frequent migrations across the Atlantic and between the Caribbean and the United States are at once a sign of the character's restlessness and the result of her efforts to establish a spatial and temporal stability that has persistently eluded her. While in *Heremakhonon* Véronica's trajectory follows a more overtly symbolic arc toward the promise of pan-African unity, *Desirada*'s driving question is the secret guarded by Marie-Noëlle's mother and obfuscated by her family and acquaintances: the identity of her biological father. Given the historical context of severed genealogies in Marie-Noëlle's native Guadeloupe, however, the symbolism in which this question of paternity is steeped suggests in this later novel too the scope of an identity quest narrative: Marie-Noëlle's individual desire for concrete information about her father's identity points allegorically to questions posed on a collective scale concerning the historical condition of a deracinated Caribbean population. Given that among the possible narratives of her origins is the rape of her mother by a white man, Marie-Noëlle's personal trajectory also calls up a transgenerational history of sexual violence as it is inscribed in the legacy of the Atlantic slave trade.

This imbrication of temporal rupture and sexual violence in *Desirada* connects Marie-Noëlle's experience to the framework of the trauma narrative that has been engaged to assess the large-scale psychological effects of the slave trade, the Middle Passage, and plantation economies on the inheritors of this history in the African diaspora. Indeed, Condé's novel traces an extended interaction with the principal preoccupations of trauma studies by returning repeatedly to the tropes of memory, epistemology, and witnessing. Marie-Noëlle's search for paternal identification is thus infused with readings of historical experience through the lens of trauma theory wherein catastrophic violations of humanity perpetrated against a group of people can have an effect on the collective scale analogous to that of the individual trauma victim. By staging this dialogue with trauma studies in *Desirada*, Condé inflects the reading of Marie-Noëlle's personal search for information as a Caribbean identity quest, but in doing so she points at the same time to the interpretive conflations and assimilations that necessarily underpin such a reading. To the extent that Marie-Noëlle's quest fails to reach a definitive conclusion, the alternative vision of cultural identity proposed by Condé's novel suggests a reassessment of both the allegorical scope of the individual search for origins and the universalizing precepts at work in the field of trauma studies.

Traumatic Landscapes

In two seminal works published in the mid-1990s, Cathy Caruth elaborated the incidence of spatial, temporal, and epistemological distancing associated with traumatic experience.[1] Drawing on Freud's notion of latency, Caruth's work examines trauma as an "unclaimed" event, an event that is defined by its inaccessibility to the conscious mind and therefore remains suspended in a perpetually unassimilated state. As such, the traumatic experience can present itself repeatedly to the traumatized subject through hauntings, flashbacks, or nightmares, in a return that is in fact the very domain of the traumatic event: "Trauma is not locatable in the simple violent or original event in an individual's past, but rather in the way that its very unassimilated nature—the way it was precisely *not known* in the first instance—returns to haunt the survivor later on" (*Unclaimed Experience*, 4). Trauma thus describes a fundamental rift in temporality in that its unnarratability prevents it from acceding to the status of a past event in a linear temporal progression.

As Caruth's work reveals, this problem of representation associated with the experience of trauma has made its study relevant not only in psychology but also in literary studies, cultural studies, sociology, and history. Because the rise in interest in trauma theory in the 1980s and 1990s coincides with the formal recognition of post-traumatic stress disorder by the U.S. medical and scientific community in the wake of the Vietnam War and the emergence of Holocaust video testimonies, moreover, work in the field has primarily addressed the large-scale traumatic events of the second half of the twentieth century.[2] Recent work in African American theory, however, has shifted the spatial and temporal scope of such approaches to the transatlantic slave trade to consider how psychoanalytical and literary studies on inaccessible narrative might inform the assessment of marginalized or silenced stories through the history of slavery. While the debate surrounding the comparability of the Holocaust makes clear the necessity of methodological vigilance in this regard, the foregrounding of notions of "transgenerational" and "cultural" trauma in the field of trauma studies has offered salient frameworks for considerations of slavery, genealogy, and memory in the context of the African diaspora.[3] Since, as Michael Rothberg notes, the logic of trauma "seeks an origin or event that would account for the suffering of the present" (502), the epistemological and historical gaps that mark the legacies of slavery and colonialism have been found to resonate with critical work on traumatic experience as well as with the postmodernist and poststructuralist interrogations of representation that informed trauma theory.[4]

Condé invokes this critical discussion in *Desirada* by linking the protagonist's "search for origins" to the possibility of her mother's rape. The fact that this possibility is presented as an unspeakable narrative, moreover, further underscores the relevance of discussion on trauma to the epistemological disturbances and the spatial and temporal *décalages* that permeate the novel. Reynalda's secret is necessarily entangled with the question of genealogy because its revelation would presumably identify Marie-Noëlle's father. But, as Ronnie Scharfman and Johanna Garvey have pointed out, this untold story also calls up a multigenerational legacy of sexual violence: Scharfman notes that Marie-Noëlle's unsympathetic grandmother Nina replaces the narrative of her daughter's rape with that of her own, drawing out a "genealogy of rape" ("Au sujet d'héroïnes péripatétiques," 146) that scars the mother-daughter relationship, while Garvey suggests that Reynalda's traumatic experience "shadow[s] the text as a reminder of the original rape of Black women in the slave ships" (171). Given that Reynalda, pregnant with Marie-Noëlle at fifteen, threw herself into the sea in a suicide attempt, the silence surrounding her story is infused with the shame that apparently marks her pregnancy. This pairing of silence and shame inscribes Reynalda's narrative—and Marie-Noëlle's—in a lineage of what Toni Morrison terms "unspeakable things" in the history of the transatlantic slave trade.[5] The inaccessibility of the narrative that forms the objective of Marie-Noëlle's search is thus implicitly linked to the traumatic past of the Caribbean, to the inexpressible events that have affected multiple generations and form a crucial but unassimilated present condition.

Indeed, Condé suggests that many of the elements of traumatic experience are at work in this protagonist's journey of self-discovery. Marie-Noëlle's enchanted childhood in the care of the woman who saved Reynalda from drowning, for example, is brutally cut short when she receives a summons to join her estranged mother in Paris. As if to recall the trauma invoked by her mother's silence, the ten-year-old Marie-Noëlle develops a sudden and intense fever upon receiving this news, is seized with convulsions and falls into a coma. Regaining consciousness a week later, Marie-Noëlle has been dramatically transformed by the experience:

> The Marie-Noëlle who left the General Hospital one morning in July in the arms of Ranélise was not the same Marie-Noëlle who had gone in almost a month earlier. The chubby, mischievous little girl, temperamental and tender, who had been the delight of Ranélise's heart, was gone. In her place a great gawk of a girl, nothing but skin and bone, with a glazed look, staring at people in a way that made them feel ill at ease, for she seemed to be looking through them to pursue some personal obsession. Once so imaginative, a real chatterbox filling Ranélise's head with fantastic stories, she now said virtually not a word. She sat for hours on end without moving, staring straight in front of her; then she would rest her cheek on Ranélise's shoulder while tears streamed down her face. (17)

The silence, the vacant gaze, the mental absence all speak to a rift with temporal and physical surroundings that has exceeded Marie-Noëlle's ability to apprehend the empirical event.

The protagonist's "personal obsession," moreover, manifests itself in her life as a persistent and unassimilable repetition of the experience, connoting the haunting that characterizes trauma: "Marie-Noëlle still carried these images and sensations deep inside her. Without warning they would surge up and take possession of her. Time would stop. Right in the middle of a sentence or a gesture she appeared to fall into a trance, go numb, and her eyes glazed over" (22). These possessions also take form through a specific connection to her mother's trauma, as when Marie-Noëlle imagines imitating Reynalda's suicide attempt as she swims in the ocean, tempted "to kick her way down to eternal peace" (19), while her persistent "absences" prompt the people she encounters in La Pointe to draw the comparison themselves: "They . . . thought her a bit cracked. Like her mother before her" (22). Rendered nearly unrecognizable by the devastating end of her tranquil childhood in Guadeloupe, Marie-Noëlle seems condemned to repeat the traumatic history of her female lineage. By invoking the vocabulary of trauma in describing Marie-Noëlle's physical and psychological response, Condé posits this turning point as a paradigmatic Freudian moment of maternal loss, while at the same time revising its precepts by overlaying the separation from the affective maternal figure and the reunion with the biological mother.[6]

IN HER attempts to put together the events leading up to her birth, Marie-Noëlle encounters the obstacles of faulty memories, conflicting accounts of events, and self-interested deceit. Compromised by these human failings, Marie-Noëlle turns instead to the physical spaces of her trajectory, investing them with seminal power in the belief that they might retain some clue to her story. Passing by Il Lago di Como, the jeweler's shop where Reynalda lived with her mother, for example, Marie-Noëlle expresses an apprehensive reverence, as if the past she seeks is preserved in its very walls: "She sensed that this shop, which did not look like much, nothing more than a dark, narrow passageway, where the electric light was left on day and night, held the secret of her birth" (12). Later, in Paris, Marie-Noëlle attributes a similar force to one of the key sites in her mother's life: "The taxi drew up in front of 305 boulevard Malesherbes, and Marie-Noëlle inspected the tall stony façade. It had sheltered a fifteen-year-old Reynalda. Perhaps it knew her secrets but was not telling" (225). In her efforts to "decipher the indecipherable" (24), not only in the elusive narratives of her mother's relatives and acquaintances but also and more urgently in the spaces and buildings linked to her mother's past, Marie-Noëlle posits landscape as a repository of memory, a text that might hold a unique and definitive response to her question if only she could attain the necessary epistemological orientation to unlock its secrets.

Marie-Noëlle's spatial interactions thus recall studies linking memory and place by such critics as Pierre Nora, Geoffrey Hartman, and Simon Schama, whose work examines, particularly in the context of the Holocaust, the cultural and historical significance with which collectively read spaces can be infused, while also responding to the disconcerting experiences of loss and betrayal delineated by topographies that seem to bear no trace of the horrific events they encompass. Here the cultural meaning of sites imbued with collective memory is one that must be socially constructed, demanding an excavation, as Simon Schama describes in *Landscape and Memory*, "below our conventional sight-level to recover the veins of myth and memory that lie beneath the surface" (14). In confronting the missing narratives of slavery, Toni Morrison makes a similar call for retracing and digging through the past to uncover the unspoken. She writes in an essay on eighteenth- and nineteenth-century American slave narratives of the disparity between the volume of production and reflection on slavery and the "veil" of silence drawn by authors across descriptions of the most extreme instances of colonial violence. Since, Morrison writes, "popular taste discouraged the writers from dwelling too long or too carefully on the more sordid details of their experience," the pace of these narratives would often change suddenly to pass through or omit certain events: "In shaping the experience to make it palatable to those who were in a position to alleviate it, they were silent about many things, and they 'forgot' many other things" ("Site of Memory," 109–10).

Morrison describes here the project of unveiling absent narratives as a process, essential for any member of a marginalized category who has historically been excluded from discourse, that undertakes a reading of the past sensitive to its gaps, to its silences, and to the traces of unheard narratives. Like critics writing on the Holocaust, Morrison posits the relationship to memory as an archeological one, but here uses landscape metaphorically as a methodological framework for the particular reading stance she adopts in this project: "It's a kind of literary archeology: on the basis of some information and a little guesswork you journey to a site to see what remains were left behind and to reconstruct the world that these remains imply. What makes it fiction is the nature of the imaginative act: my reliance on the image—on the remains—in addition to recollection, to yield up a kind of a truth" ("Site of Memory," 112). Morrison's archeological metaphor thus offers an epistemological link between space and memory, a spatially conceived methodology of reading that attempts to work through and around the silence of traumatic loss.

The textual investment that Marie-Noëlle places in the "sites" of her mother's past, however, comes sharply up against the same obstacles of opacity and loss that characterize her human interactions. Rather than offering the material for archeological investigation, the physical structures Marie-Noëlle approaches aggravate the severed link with her genealogical past. Condé situates this illegibility in part in the context of urban renewal, elaborating, as Dominique Licops has aptly demonstrated, a pattern of destruction and replacement in this novel that underscores the particularly urban settings encountered by the protagonist.[7] The shop where Reynalda and her mother worked for the jeweler Gian Carlo Coppini, for example, is gone when Marie-Noëlle returns to it as an adult: "The old upstairs-downstairs house, hunched over its secrets, had been replaced by a building in the ubiquitous concrete that was all balconies and striped awnings" (132). Modernity also makes a personal attack on Marie-Noëlle's Guadeloupean roots, as her placenta has been dug up by property developers and supplanted by a "city of concrete" (221). The connection to the past that these spaces seemed to promise is thus suppressed by urban renewal and industrialization in a way that undermines Marie-Noëlle's efforts to read them archeologically, while the symbolic investment she has made in the permanence of her native landscape proves as deceptive as the numerous conversations she has had concerning her mother's adolescence.

The inaccessibility of the novel's spatial configurations of narrative is encapsulated in Marie-Noëlle's subconscious as a recurring nightmare, a trope that reinforces the inscription of her experience in the discourse of trauma studies. Here Marie-Noëlle finds herself alone at night on a bare plateau: "She had no idea where she was. It was nighttime. The moon was on its back in a cloudless, luminous sky. Its beams lit up a pitted, vermiculated limestone plateau that ran down to the sea she could hear screaming with the voice of a madwoman. Not a house in sight. Only a cabin bathed in moonlight. . . . Marie-Noëlle knew she had to draw closer and go in. But her legs refused to carry her as if weighed down by an enormous swelling. After a while the door creaked open. Nobody came out, and it remained ajar on a darkness as terrifying as the starry void. Then it creaked shut again, offering up its hard wooden face" (131). The authority with which Marie-Noëlle invests this gothic vision is revealing: her apprehensive desire articulates a fixed, stable, and above all unique narrative that will at last put her uncertainties to rest with a definitive explanation of her origins. The "hard wooden face" of the cabin door, however, underscores her failure to engage in an archeological reading of her landscape, either, as the dream suggests, because the knowledge has receded beyond her reach or because she is paralyzed by the fear of discovery.

Later, when the cabin ["la case" (153)] takes form in Marie-Noëlle's conscious reality as her grandmother Nina's home in Désirade, the site seems to present a possibility that might overcome previous obstacles to the excavation of memory: its far-flung location (a satellite island to the already marginal space of Guadeloupe) suggests an immunity to the destructive forces of urbanization, and the moment of contact between Marie-Noëlle and the site marks a climactic expression of discursive authority. But while, unlike the jeweler's shop, the cabin is indeed still standing in its forsaken setting when Marie-Noëlle finally ventures to confront her grandmother, its interior yields a narrative that is critically *inconclusive,* in that what Marie-Noëlle learns within its walls fully undermines the narrative she had been carefully piecing together up to that point. Having sought out as many accounts of events from as many family members and acquaintances as she could find, Marie-Noëlle has gleaned her mother's accusation that she was raped by the jeweler Gian Carlo Coppini, and, in a gesture that marks the convergence of her search for knowledge and her search for identity, announces herself to her grandmother as "the daughter of Reynalda and . . . and Gian Carlo" (164). Upon hearing this bold claim of Gian Carlo's paternity, Nina unleashes a vicious and terrifying laugh, a laugh that "in one blow wiped out Marie-Noëlle's convictions and hurled her back to that realm of uncertainty and anguish that she thought she had left forever" (165). The physical violence with which this laugh is attributed thus connotes a direct refusal of Marie-Noëlle's idealistic vision of landscape-as-truth: through Nina's laughter, the space she enters rejects her, "hurls her back" in a mocking dismissal of her hope for a conclusive answer to her questions.[8] Like the dwellings, streets, and spaces that trace out the trajectory of Marie-Noëlle's search, this nightmare cabin fails to provide either the permanence or the certainty she attributes to its physical form.

The narrative that would put an end to Marie-Noëlle's errant displacements is thus expressed only in its unrealized—or unrealizable—form. The fact that the site of Marie-Noëlle's crucial moment of (non)recognition is the island of Désirade, moreover, connects the unrequited desire elaborated by Marie-Noëlle's relationship to landscape to the colonial history signaled by the novel's title. Condé's use of the Spanish *Desirada* instead of the French *Désirade* to evoke this desolate satellite island of Guadeloupe recalls the colonial act of linguistic appropriation that is evoked explicitly in the narrative by Reynalda, who claims to share this appropriated image of her native land with the original colonial gaze: "For me, as a little girl, it *was* really 'Desirada', the desired island, looming up out of the ocean in front of the eyes of Christopher Columbus's sailors after days and days at sea" (51).[9] Through the semiotic chain from Marie-Noëlle's nightmare landscape to her grandmother's rejection of narrative certainty to the colonial genealogy of the New World, Condé expands the scope of Marie-Noëlle's identity quest to the collective assessment of the Caribbean's traumatic past, while at the same time resolutely closing epistemological inroads to the region's urban and rural landscapes.

Mnemonic Floodings

The scene of grandmotherly rejection falls just past the midpoint of Condé's novel, and while it encapsulates the barriers of memory, landscape, and maternal separation that drive the protagonist forward, the moment ultimately seems to act as an embedded catalyst toward less linear modes of inquiry in Marie-Noëlle's quest. Woven through the protagonist's frustrated search for the truth is the simultaneous articulation of a more indirect relationship to memory, a sense of personal narrative that might not be tied to the absolute revelations of human interactions or the stability of a fixed landscape, but that envisions instead a fluid, redirected notion of time, space, and knowledge. The river, for example, figures prominently in the novel as a space that hovers between permanence and impermanence, as a locus that might allow Marie-Noëlle to circumvent the apparent impenetrability of the structures and people she encounters. In Paris, Marie-Noëlle juxtaposes the center of the city with other urban spaces whose terrain has been transformed by modernization. The heart of Paris, she says, "doesn't change": "However much they stick a fast-food restaurant here, a home electronics shop there, a pyramid of Plexiglas, sex shops, and pizzerias just about everywhere, they can't manage to disfigure it. Under the Mirabeau Bridge the Seine still flows" (218). While the description ostensibly identifies this site with an unchanging and even lifeless landscape, the offhanded reference to Apollinaire's "Pont Mirabeau" nevertheless suggests a hidden countercurrent to this stasis; for the 1913 poem notably evokes *both* the infinite repetitions of the river's form and the irrecoverable loss of time signaled by its constant movement. Similarly, the apparent timelessness of the area surrounding the Seine in this passage is one that seems to resist transformation by incorporating physical change rather than by rejecting it.

In the otherwise uninspiring landscape of Newbury, where Marie-Noëlle lives while she holds a teaching position at a local university, another river offers a site of unexpected dynamism: "Newbury has one saving grace: the Charles River. Runners in colored tracksuits jogged along its winding banks, working their elbows against their bodies. When the weather permitted, mothers pushed their babies along it. Sometimes you even passed old couples tottering along amorously. The river itself changed the color of its mantle to reflect the season: a blank shimmering gray in the fall, a thick white wool in winter, a tender green velvet in the spring, bright green in summer" (208). The Charles River thus offers a fixed site that is at the same time a literal reflection of the passage of time, while its borders become the locus of a "saving grace," the singular suggestion of happiness among the desolate spaces of Marie-Noëlle's trajectory.[10]

The emphasis placed on fluid spaces in Marie-Noëlle's landscapes recalls the spatial metaphors employed by Morrison in her evocation of literary archeology: while the model of excavation suggests solid earth as the creative project's metaphorical text, Morrison frames her description around the image of the Mississippi River. Like Marie-Noëlle's peripatetic trajectories, the indeterminate spatial configurations of water call up for Morrison an ethics of both permanence and instability: "They straightened out the Mississippi River in places, to make room for houses and livable acreage. Occasionally the river floods these places. 'Floods' is the word they use, but in fact it is not flooding; it is remembering. Remembering where it used to be. All water has perfect memory and is forever trying to get back to where it was. Writers are like that: remembering where we were, what valley we ran through, what the banks were like, the light that was there and the route back to our original place. It is emotional memory—what the nerves and the skin remember as well as how it appeared. And a rush of imagination is our 'flooding'" ("Site of Memory," 119). Here memory acts as a catalyst for a rereading of landscape, whereby the "traces" left by the river's "true" path become visible. Since the markings of the river's previous location are not only ignored but covered by the construction of houses and farmland, the floods present a literal threat to the existence of these constructions, and at the same time expose the boundaries of the straightened river as not outer but *inner* spaces: during these floodings, the straight lines of the synthetically formed river indicate not its limits but its distance from the river's earlier form. Instead of neatly separating fact from fiction, or truth from falsehood, these official lines are reread as entirely relative, arbitrary points within the now visible traces of the past.

The shifting reflections and boundaries of the rivers evoked in *Desirada* are in this sense emblematic of Marie-Noëlle's search: she must work to encompass impermanence and instability in her assessment of what might appear to be fixed. Following Morrison, we can read the emergence of Marie-Noëlle's story as a kind of flooding: an attempt to weave together various accounts of the past and to read them "archeologically," pushing aside the boundaries and fixed sites she encounters. Condé inscribes this approach formally in the novel by using narrative perspective to evoke the interplay between overlapping versions of events, between memory and impression, between direct and indirect knowledge. As in such earlier novels as *La migration des cœurs* and *Traversée de la mangrove*, Condé moves in *Desirada* from third-person to first-person narrative so as to cede discursive authority to various characters in turn.

While the conflicting accounts of Marie-Noëlle's origins are most directly shaped by this strategy, Condé also inscribes epistemological uncertainty within the overarching third-person narrative centered on Marie-Noëlle. Particularly in its engagement of memory and knowledge, this voice is subject to many of the same ambiguities as the conflicting stories of the different characters. In the novel's opening passage, for example, Condé establishes a blurring of lines between memory and experience, between first- and secondhand knowledge in the description of Marie-Noëlle's birth: "Ranélise had described her birth to her so many times that she believed she had actually played a part—not that of a terrorized and submissive baby . . . but that of a clear-sighted witness, a major role, her very mother, the mother in labor, Reynalda herself, whom she imagined sitting rigid, lips pursed, arms crossed, and a look of inexpressible suffering on her face" (3). In this striking opening scene, the evocation of the protagonist's origins is a hybrid narrative: part firsthand memory of a story, part secondhand memory of the event, interspersed with audacious convictions of firsthand objective experience. Marie-Noëlle returns to the "site" of her birth *through* the story told to her by her adoptive mother, and invents an imagined perspective in order to reread the experience as a lived one.

By exposing the epistemological gaps in Marie-Noëlle's relationship to her own past and that of her mother, Condé's narrative technique thus succeeds in questioning the possibility of Marie-Noëlle's narrative authority while at the same time relegating this question to irrelevance through the production of narrative through and around that impossibility. The term "souvenir imaginaire" (imaginary memory), used to describe the above passage and a series of key events in the character's life, including Marie-Noëlle's baptism, encapsulates the strategy of mixing that generates narrative in the face of missing answers, closed doors, and uncooperative interlocutors. Even when Marie-Noëlle makes no claim to appropriated knowledge, the absence of memory announces itself in defiance of repeated narration—"Curiously enough, although Ranélise must have recounted the incident fairly frequently, Marie-Noëlle had no memory of her mother leaving" (8–9)—but produces no disruption of the novel's account of the event. Instead, the mnemonic shortcoming is incorporated into the narrative of Reynalda's departure, its acknowledgment the very fabric of this articulation.

Given the emblematic importance of the trope of maternal separation in Freud-informed trauma studies, the inscription of the inaccessible in Marie-Noëlle's narrative perspective forms an implicit engagement with the rupture in memory effected by traumatic experience. The archeological rewriting of the gap between memory and event is particularly evident, moreover, in the moment that most closely shadows the description of traumatic experience, where the crisis provoked by the anticipated separation from her adoptive mother severs Marie-Noëlle's consciousness from the event recounted:

> Years later Marie-Noëlle still retained the sensations and images that flickered through her head while she was in a coma at the General Hospital.
>
> At times she was cold, a cold that cut her to the bone. Other times she felt herself next to a blazing furnace. It seemed her skin was about to scorch, burn to a cinder, and leave her naked, an unwholesome heap of entrails. Daylight had been snuffed out. She remained in darkness. (20)

Condé's strategy here is of interest not only because of its hybrid focalization but also because it produces a narrative account of the seven days when Marie-Noëlle was unconscious, "flooding" the boundaries set by conscious apprehension. Phrases such as "elle se croyait" (she thought herself) and "il lui semblait" (it seemed to her) emphasize Marie-Noëlle's firsthand experience of these events, as if to enact the narrative she would have produced at the time had she been conscious, but at the same time preserve them as impressions rather than as objective facts corroborated by a second observer. Since the articulated memory of these events is explicitly not in Marie-Noëlle's possession, the passage suggests an effect close to what Marianne Hirsch has termed "postmemory," a form of memory whose "connection to its object or source is mediated not through recognition but through an imaginative investment and creation" (22). While appropriating an expressive ability that is unattainable to her, the passage offers a rendering of Marie-Noëlle's experience without denying that inaccessibility.

Even moments of conscious reflection enact this palimpsestic narrative voice, as we see in the ludic description of Marie-Noëlle's arrival in Paris in the novel's third chapter, where a skeptical interrogative interrupts the seemingly straightforward description:

> Outside the sky shimmered gray and overcast, skimming the rooftops. It was snowing.
>
> Was it snowing? It seldom snows in Paris. And not on November 1. In any case in Marie-Noëlle's memory big snowflakes were falling and fluttering like insects around the flame of an oil lamp. (25)

Here, rather than the impressionistic apprehension of events, Condé's narration gives discursive authority to Marie-Noëlle's memory while at the same time casting considerable doubt on its accuracy. The lighthearted

"In any case" and the exuberantly detailed description of the potentially nonexistent (or nonexperienced) snow adroitly defy the very question of accuracy or authority. The trace left by the memory of that Paris day has thus potentially lost all connection to the event itself; and yet as Condé evokes it here, she insists on that possibility as an essential part of the memory, and on Marie-Noëlle's experience as fundamentally tied to that possible snowfall.

THE SHIFT to first-person narration in Marie-Noëlle's voice at the end of the novel thus suggests the formal realization of a modulated identity quest, a self-affirmation based not on the epistemological appropriation of her mother's narrative but instead on a rejection of genealogical and spatial groundings. Implicitly opposed to the various first-person sections of the novel where characters such as Marie-Noëlle's grandmother or Reynalda's husband stake their claims on the narrative, this concluding section seems to allow for a *prise de parole* that diverges from the combined narratives that came before it rather than rooting itself in this potential network of voices. Marie-Noëlle, having cast off the paralyzing investment in authoritative landscapes, narratives, and memories, appears at last to have found her own voice.

The novel's closing eschews the triumphant, however, in that Marie-Noëlle, still mystified by the identity of her father, continues to be afflicted by profound social isolation. In this reflection, Marie-Noëlle sets up an opposition between her own situation and that of her friend Anthea, who has left for Ghana in search of her ancestral roots. Awaiting Anthea's return, Marie-Noëlle imagines the sweeping and grandiose stories that she will bring with her: "Soon Anthea will return from Ghana, her head full of her imaginings. . . . She'll tell me every detail of the story of Efua. She'll repeat the stories dreamed a hundred times of the lost paradise. Of the Middle Passage, that terrible journey we all took before we were even born. Of our scattering to the four corners of the earth and of our suffering. In exchange I shall have only my own little tales of misfortune to tell her, the real reason for my journey to Europe, and the circumstances of yet another failure. . . . Ashamed, I shall keep silent until I too learn to invent a life" (259–60). Here Condé sets up the resolution of the search for origins in Africa as an invented narrative, juxtaposing it with what Marie-Noëlle calls the "monstrosity" of her identity: "In some way or other my monstrosity makes me unique. Thanks to it I have no nationality, no country, and no language" (259).[11] Despite the evocation of shame and misfortune in these passages, Marie-Noëlle characterizes her unrequited search for "a certain kind of happiness" in terms of alternative knowledge rather than as a lack: "My path," she claims in opposition to such narratives of happiness, "is traced elsewhere" (259). Unlike the demystification of a unifying African past presented by Véronica's sudden departure for Paris at the end of *Heremakhonon*, Marie-Noëlle's closing thoughts frame her demystification as a point of departure, as an insight that will form the very material of a revised self-narrative.

In this "path traced elsewhere," the displacements, obstructions, and setbacks of Marie-Noëlle's quest take priority in and of themselves, in relationship to one another and regardless of their relevance to a larger, more coherent image. For Marie-Noëlle, to find the definitive "answer" to her question would mean the annihilation of all but one of the narratives she has encountered during her search, including her own imagined and impressionistic ones. The novel's concluding passages suggest furthermore that this "unnatural" narrative, excessive like Morrison's flooding Mississippi, signals a freedom from such collective markers as nationality and language. Unlike Anthea's triumphant claim to collective ancestry, strikingly similar to the narrative unsuccessfully sought out by *Heremakhonon*'s Véronica, Marie-Noëlle's mode is a recurrently diasporic one, drawn from movement rather than stability, built on indeterminate multiplicities rather than a unique genealogy. Instead of "waiting for happiness," Marie-Noëlle envisions an alternative trajectory that finds inroads to buried memories through more fluid archeological landscapes, skirting and reshaping the linear path of reclaimed genealogies.

Genealogical Deceptions

The explicit opposition between Marie-Noëlle's narrative and Anthea's in the novel's final pages underscores the constructed nature of self-inscription in an African genealogy: Anthea's is an "invented" life, a performative gesture of self-realization that razes the kinds of "little tales" and "failures" that form Marie-Noëlle's experience. A scholar of nineteenth-century female slave narratives whose remaining objective is to "rehabilitate her race" through her work (96), Anthea takes on the collective trauma of slavery through an abstract link to past generations and altered landscapes. The opposition between these two narratives thus implicitly critiques the reparative potential of Anthea's journey that promises to heal the very temporal, geographical, and epistemological rifts that have afflicted Marie-Noëlle. In particular, Condé's closing on the "monstrosity" of Marie-Noëlle's modulated identity quest foregrounds the congruences and abstractions that form the basis of collective frameworks of experience.

By highlighting the invented status of Anthea's triumphant restoration of African heritage, and by inscribing formally Marie-Noëlle's postnational and indeterminate form of knowledge in *Desirada*, Condé thus seems to elaborate an important distinction between Marie-Noëlle's self-conception and the narrative that might be offered up by theories of transhistorical or cultural trauma. In the description of Anthea's reading of Africa cited above, for example, Marie-Noëlle signals the very separation that makes such readings empirically impossible, characterizing the Middle Passage as "that terrible journey *we all took before we were even born*" (259, my emphasis). While the phrase points evocatively to the transgenerational effects of a traumatic past, the words rendered in Marie-Noëlle's voice connote a skeptical distance from the claims to common experience that would erase the very rifts so critical to her reading of her own past. Her words can be read as both an affirmation of the political utility of a prenatally formed "we" and a parroting of such conceptions that ridicules their mythic ambitions.

Indeed, Condé's novel signals a number of significant points of differentiation between Marie-Noëlle's narrative and the central problematics of trauma studies. While her protagonist exhibits the psychological symptoms associated with traumatic experience, and while the specters of rape and shame are intertwined with Marie-Noëlle's search for a genealogical past, the particularities of Marie-Noëlle's narrative, and the ultimate failure of her identity quest to coalesce around a unified understanding of the past, expose the numerous slippages and abbreviations that are necessary to the reading of traumatic experience on a collective level. Foremost among these slippages is the epistemological rift between Marie-Noëlle and her mother, particularly as it inheres in the primary event of Reynalda's rape. While the inaccessibility of this narrative to Marie-Noëlle references the unspeakable status of traumatic events, and while her mother's silence may indeed manifest such a relationship between victim and event, Marie-Noëlle's relationship to the event is secondhand, and its inaccessibility is a product both of its absence as narrative and of this distance between two subjects. As we see in the "imaginary memory" of Marie-Noëlle's birth, the firsthand relationship to the events recounted is necessarily invented, as while Marie-Noëlle imagines herself a "témoin lucide" (lucid witness) to her own birth, the impossible superimposition of Marie-Noëlle's perspective onto her mother's undermines Marie-Noëlle's ambitions of unified narrative. Condé thus frames the obstacles of genealogical knowledge through the specific moment of her character's birth, foregrounding the physical and empirical separation of Marie-Noëlle from her mother to expose the elision of fundamentally divided perspectives toward which the recapturing of severed lineage necessarily aspires.

In this respect Condé's novel resonates with some of the caveats concerning historical trauma proposed by Dominick LaCapra, who argues that the preoccupation with trauma often gives way to "rash amalgamations or conflations" (*Writing History*, x), particularly with respect to the Holocaust. LaCapra notes in *Writing History, Writing Trauma* the importance of distinguishing empathy from identity, evoking the particular condition of the secondary witness to traumatic events, whose "empathic unsettlement," while a necessary piece of the network of the post-traumatic, becomes problematic when "the virtual experience involved in empathy gives way to vicarious victimhood, and empathy with the victim seems to become an identity" (47). Marie-Noëlle's status as secondhand witness to a withheld event, and the explicitly constructed narrative that underwrites that status, thus refuses to enable the kind of epistemological identification that would allow her to affirm a transhistorical reading of her mother's experience. This preservation of difference in Marie-Noëlle's empathic endeavors impedes the kind of community formation *through* trauma elaborated by such critics as Kai Erikson and Jeffrey C. Alexander, whereby trauma's "centrifugal tendencies" (Erikson, 186) produce a means of defining collectivity via a notion of shared suffering.[12] In inscribing the detours and closed doors of Marie-Noëlle's quest into the narrative fabric of her novel, in other words, Condé pulls apart also the potential identification between mother and daughter as a reminder of the constructed nature of such conflations.

On a more disquieting note, the conflicting accounts woven through Condé's narrative also raise the question of reliability in traumatic experience. In this respect, the *denial* of the rape accusation by Marie-Noëlle's grandmother does as much damage to the engagement of trauma studies with this novel as it does to Marie-Noëlle's search for knowledge, bringing the inaccessible status of Reynalda's story from the abstract domain of the unspeakable traumatic to the concrete domain of meditated deception. As recent work on post-traumatic stress disorder and the legal implications of trauma theory has shown, the crisis of narratability that characterizes traumatic experience presents a highly exploitable terrain for duplicity.[13] On the one hand the constructed nature of post-traumatic narratives is embedded in the discourse of trauma itself, while on the other hand the injunction against any questioning of such testimonies is firmly couched in terms of medical therapeutic strategies intended to prevent further trauma to the victim. By articulating the rejection of Reynalda's claims through the voice of Reynalda's mother, who claims to have herself lied to her daughter about her own rape and thereby about the identity of Reynalda's father (172), Condé expresses the unspeakable accusation of dishonesty, thus exposing the taboo surrounding the posing of such questions in the discourse of trauma theory. By the same token, Nina's violent laughter destroys the possibility of an abstract reading of Reynalda's status as a victim of trauma, while in the process rewriting Marie-Noëlle's narrative genealogy as a legacy of deception.

The comparability of traumatic experience has raised questions primarily with regard to studies on the Holocaust. As LaCapra explains, the Historians' Debate of 1986 brought to light "the extent to which certain interpretive procedures, notably the comparison of Nazi crimes with other modern genocidal phenomena . . . , tended to relativize, normalize, or even 'air-brush' Auschwitz in order to make it fade into larger historical contexts and out of conscious focus" (*History and Memory,* 49–50). The moment's historical specificity is deeply ingrained in the psychoanalytically informed readings of its aftermath as the legacy of a large-scale and prolonged traumatic event and a disruption of human comprehension. To propose that the Holocaust might be seen as similar to other periods in history can thus seem as much an ethical affront to those who experienced it as the facile representation of the events themselves.[14]

And yet, perhaps to echo these reservations even as she invokes some of the work in comparative trauma studies that has been undertaken, Condé's novel points out the ethics of comparability that inhere in any assessment of traumatic experience on a general scale. To define a group by the incidence of trauma on that group is to imply a congruity between and among experiences internal to that group, regardless of the historical moment or period in question, and in this respect demands the appropriation and elision of events that are otherwise defined by their singular and inaccessible status. Similarly, Condé underlines the confusion between the attempt to repair the rupture of traumatic experience through linear narrative and the creation of collective identity *through* the identification of a common trauma. The rejection of constructed narrative upon which her novel closes thus illuminates the temporal and epistemological myths that feed collective extrapolations of the traumatic. In forging a path elsewhere, Marie-Noëlle seems in her unhappiness to claim a freedom from such mythologies and from an overdetermined investment in the other's empirical narrative, without celebrating the destructive force of her own personal history that ultimately generates that freedom. Following Paul Gilroy, we can read the protagonist's corporeal, empirical, and epistemological differentiation from her mother as the basis of a new archeology of self: "Even if forgetting incorporated memories is impossibly difficult, the decision to set aside the claims of the flesh and break their special compact with past trauma need not always be unethical or illegitimate" (255).

5   The Margins of Race

Célanire cou-coupé

CRITICAL DISCUSSIONS of race present a forbidding array of conceptual and discursive double binds. While exposing the fallacy of biological groundings for the concept of race has established its constructed status, the persistent and concrete effects of racism necessarily temper the impulse to debilitate the term unilaterally, and critiques of racism confront the catch-22 of discussing a paradigm whose discursive impact they seek to eliminate. As Henry Louis Gates notes, the use of the term has both a descriptive and productive force: "The sense of difference defined in popular usages of the term 'race' has both described and *inscribed* differences of language, belief system, artistic tradition, and gene pool" (*"Race," Writing and Difference,* 5). Hence the challenge of separating the designation and reproduction of racism: to identify, in the place of an internally determined category, a common contemporary experience that has been realized by an insidious history of social and scientific discrimination seems ultimately to present a position that, even as it rejects biological and genetic determinism, underwrites a categorical legitimacy that is no less pernicious. But for many, given the politics of visibility at work in racial constructions, to reject out of hand the continued invocation of this "floating signifier" resembles too closely a denial of its historical, cultural, and socioeconomic incidence.

Paul Gilroy's *Against Race* maintains that proclaiming the invented status of "race" is meaningless if we are unwilling to undo also its semantic and social functionality in the world. His work also points to the importance of hybridity as a framework that brings the conceptual impasse of race to the forefront. The problematic history of the term *hybridity* in the racialized scientific explorations of the nineteenth century, as discussion provoked by Robert Young's *Colonial Desire* has shown, has formed a caveat to the wide range of theorists who have employed the term to reflect upon cultural and linguistic syncretism, diaspora and migration, and popular culture and technology.[1] In fact, the very shift to the cultural in recent invocations of hybridity exposes the persistence of the underlying notions of purity that come under critique in biologically grounded discussions of race. While the term's emphasis on mixing and crossing makes it discursively useful for efforts to transcend artificial social boundaries and categories, its employment thus poses the risk of reinscribing the integrity of the presumed components of such fusions. As Gilroy asserts, hybridity presents its own discursive aporia, in that critics come up against "the lack of a means of adequately describing, let alone theorizing, intermixture, fusion, and syncretism without suggesting the existence of anterior 'uncontaminated' purities" (250).

Gilroy thus foregrounds the conceptual challenge posed to theorists of cultural mixing rather than the terminological or the etymological, pointing out that the lure of purity informs contemporary engagements with hybridity as much as it does its usage in nineteenth-century scientific discourse. To overcome the term's problematic history, then, is also to abandon its conceptual precepts: "Whether the process of mixture is presented as fatal or redemptive, we must be prepared to give up the illusion that cultural and ethnic purity has ever existed, let alone provided a foundation for civil society" (250–51). Pulling apart the semantic viability of "race" demands also that we expose the myth of purity as an invisible theoretical apparatus and that we undermine the epistemological recourse to that mythology in contemporary discourse on fusion and mixing.

Condé's *Célanire cou-coupé* presents a meditation on the transgression of boundaries delimited in racial, sexual, religious, linguistic, and metaphysical terms. Through the innovative—and irreverent—re-creation of Mary Shelley's *Frankenstein,* Condé foregrounds in particular the trope of the monstrous as an expression of the epistemological challenge presented by such transgressions. Her eponymous protagonist is a figure whose corporeal existence, in defying the laws of science, also engages race, gender, and sexuality in a way that points out how cultural theories of hybrid identity can remain confined by scientific categories of identification. Like the Swiss doctor's creation in *Frankenstein,* Célanire functions as the very embodiment of the fears and anxieties particular to her historical context, thus offering the possibility of examining the mechanics of exclusion upon which those social and cultural codes are built. Condé modifies the signature legibility of the classic figure, however, with a protagonist who is herself only partly or deceptively legible, slipping constantly out from under natural and unnatural identifications, contemporary and anachronistic preoccupations, parody and serious-ness. Condé's use of the fantastic in this novel, moreover, reveals the grounding of this illegibility in the simultaneity of incommensurate read-ings that inheres in the genre. By closing her novel with the suggestion of a censured hybrid offspring, Condé aligns racial indeterminacy with this epistemological defiance, demanding a rethinking of hybridity both in terms of the rejection of racial categories per se and as the simultane-ous apprehension of untenable oppositions. Condé's twentieth-century monster, read through the prism of postcolonial politics, exposes racial indeterminacy as a persistent phobia and legibility as a central preoccu-pation in current social categorizations.

The Garments of Hybridity

Condé stages an extravagantly gory baptismal scene to make explicit the gothic origins of her heroine and to establish the particular morphology of her own monstrous progeny—a morphology that, as we will examine more closely, departs in significant ways from that of Shelley's creation. As a newborn, Célanire is found in the street in Guadeloupe, nearly severed in two at the neck as the victim of an attempted human sacrifice. Dr. Jean Pinceau, having recently read with fascinated interest Shelley's *Frankenstein*, sets himself to the task of reconstructing her tiny body with heady enthusiasm: "I had to reconnect the severed arteries, veins, nerves, and tendons. . . . Then, I sutured the flesh. I grafted a strip of skin taken from her thigh onto the jagged suture that twisted around her neck. . . . I needed blood to irrigate my work. I transfused the blood from two chickens that I sent Ofusan to fetch as fast as she could. The whole time I felt that here I was at last emulating my hero Victor Frankenstein, and it spurred me on. I too was equal to the Creator, and when the child began to sneeze and cry I was overcome with pride" (107). In a kind of *mise en abîme* of artistic cannibalization, Pinceau appropriates the work of his fictional mentor to generate his own creation, "grafting" the supernatu-ral technologies of Victor Frankenstein's covert project onto the lifeless body before him, "transfusing" the Swiss doctor's scientific inspiration into his own craft. Célanire's physical existence thus draws on an internal act of reading as much as her fictional representation subsists on Condé's appropriation of the same English classic.

Just as corporeally Célanire straddles the natural and the unnatural, her presence read through the filter of the novel's early-twentieth-century transatlantic setting also elaborates a crossing of unaccustomed racial, cultural, and religious signals. In the novel's opening passage, when Célanire first arrives with a group of missionaries in the Ivory Coast in 1901, the particular placement of this reconstructed being generates an immediate impression of incoherence: "She stood out from the others. She hardly spoke. She did not seem curious or excited like her traveling companions, who were eager to begin their missionary work. What's more, her color set her apart, that dark skin that clothed her like a garment of deep mourning. Her features were not strictly black—rather, a hybrid of goodness knows how many races. She did not wear religious garb, since she had not yet taken her vows" (1). The passage underlines the politics of visibility at work in Célanire's "uncommon" status, moving from her exceptional behavior to the physical attributes that ensure her categorical segregation. Through the eyes of the priest who welcomes this missionary party, Célanire's race is explicitly indeterminate, but at the same time the parallel between skin and clothing suggests the contingency of this categorization, as if to signal that, like the missing religious garb, Célanire's racial identity is subject to the interpretive investments of her viewer. The character's situation at the novel's opening, moreover, is emblematic of her position at the crossroads of cultural, geographical, religious, and racial allegiances: as a Guadeloupean woman in Africa, a Christian missionary who has not taken her vows, a person of mixed race in European clothing and with a European education, Célanire represents a fusion of cultural markers that suspends her outside the order of unified categories.[2] Although Célanire's telltale scar remains hidden under her scarf, the character's scientific "monstrosity" is doubled socially and culturally by this rejection of conceptual order.

In a significant departure from the Frankenstein model, however, the creature in Condé's text is strikingly beautiful: rather than inspiring universal horror and being categorically rejected from human society, as is the case for Shelley's monster, Célanire is an object of fascination as well as fear, holding a seductive power over men and women alike. In this respect Condé employs beauty to underscore how fundamentally Célanire's gender is imbricated in her transgressive status: her mysterious sexuality is aligned with sorcery, as characters wonder if she has bewitched those who appear to have lost themselves under her influence. Célanire becomes a Medusa-like figure, dangerous to those who dare to look at her, especially if their gaze is returned. While her admirers compare her eyes to stars, diamonds, and other precious stones, this admiration is coupled with fear: "It was difficult to sustain the look in those gleaming eyes of hers" (131). Dr. Pinceau, furthermore, compares Célanire's scar to female genitals, describing it as "obscene . . . purplish as an infibulated labium" (109). The doctor's horror at his creation, mirroring that of Dr. Frankenstein, connotes a Freudian castration anxiety that is reinforced later in Célanire's story by the mysterious deaths that accompany her on her journey, as two of the men who die are castrated.[3] Célanire's physical beauty and seductive powers thus uncover a transnational inclination to read female sexual power as dangerous and unnatural, relegated to a realm outside the rational as a threat to social control.

Condé's rewriting of Shelley generates a figure who embraces this disruption of normative categories, who, refusing the passive monstrosity of Shelley's thrashing loner, takes an active role in the promotion of transgression at all costs. Célanire uses the power gained from various interpretive facets of her identity—her beauty, her religious faith, her European schooling—to claim spaces of her own and to disturb the existing boundaries of convention, also claiming for herself the creator's role in her destiny as the bane of social order. Among the principal such disturbances is the advancement of women's education and independence: upon her arrival in the Ivory Coast, Célanire takes over the Foyer des métis and transforms it into a haven for women, where girls can take classes alongside their male peers, and where young women can find protection from abusive husbands or from the practice of female excision. She is unambiguous about the ramifications of her project, explaining to one character that her efforts stem from a desire to correct the errors of African society as she sees them: "In her opinion there was only one dark side to the beauty of its civilization: the treatment of women" (24). Her project thus asserts an intentional editing of the cultural and religious norms of the region. Similarly, the physical work she is doing on the land disturbs a preexisting order: "Her plans for the Home were troubling, for the land around it did in fact belong to someone. It belonged to the Ebriés" (18). Célanire's ferocious presence asserts an indelible legacy in Adjame-Santey, as she manifestly disregards the indigenous codes of ownership and tradition to replace them with her own "monstrous" vision of society.

The racial indeterminacy signaled in the novel's opening passage and Célanire's rewriting of gender roles converge in this space of transgression to reveal the character's specific agenda of miscegenation. For at the Foyer in Adjame-Santey, Célanire has also founded a brothel, with the explicit goal of encouraging interracial love. In her mind, the solution to colonialism is to be found in the intimate relationship between the African woman and the European man: "Once the colonizer had clasped a black woman in his arms, could he ever be the same again? . . . The Home for Half-Castes would be that meeting place that was sorely lacking, a privileged place where love between the races would fructify, grow, and multiply. That was its vocation" (41). Through her Foyer, Célanire thus institutionalizes sexual practices that until her arrival had remained unacknowledged, silenced by social convention and legal sanction. At the same time, the economic shifts generated by this newly visible practice reveal the concrete corollaries of her experiment in social deviance, as the African women receive gifts from their French partners that, in combination with the education they complete, allow them to substantially shift their social status: "Relatively well off, therefore, knowing how to read and write, they married into good families and helped form a veritable aristocracy in the country" (80). Célanire's disruption of sexual convention thus signals the inseparability of racial and economic history, giving rise at once to a changed relationship between the races and to a new social class.

The heroine's own sexual practice is equally transgressive, as she has an affair with and eventually marries the French colonial officer Thomas de Brabant in violation of his own personal interdiction against physical intimacy with African women. According to several reports from those working at the Foyer, she is also sexually involved with two women, one of whom is an African woman accused of murdering the king's uncle in a refusal of his sexual advances. Célanire provokes further disturbance by allowing this intimacy to be publicly legible: an instructor at the Foyer recounts that Célanire and Tanella "drank champagne from the same glass until they were completely intoxicated. Once the visitors had left, they locked themselves in the same room. If Tanella was shy, Célanire was excessively bold. Even in public it was a never-ending serenade of 'my pet' and 'my little darling' and unequivocal caresses" (74). Later, in Guadeloupe, Célanire once again uses institutionalization as a means of reinforcing the visibility of supposedly unnatural behavior. Through her relationship with a lesbian separatist and founder of a women's association, she designates a space for this association that will allow women to live in isolation from men: "At their initiative, the innocent little island of Fajoux . . . was transformed into Lesbos" (165). The reaction of the surrounding Guadeloupean society is a mixture of shock and fear: "The fishermen, shocked by the copulation going on almost under their noses, quickly hauled in their nets, and it wasn't long before there was a shortage of fish in Grande-Terre" (166). As in Africa, Célanire's initiative, specifically because of its transgressive nature, enacts a transformation of the landscape and causes a fundamental shift in the systems of economic exchange in the region.

Condé's creature, then, parallels the disorder subtended by her unknown origins, her unnatural re-creation, and her hideous scar with a deliberate and lucid transgression in her acts—in the spaces she occupies, the partners she chooses, the politics she endorses, the institutions she builds. In each of the religious, cultural, and spiritual spheres she encounters, she exposes the limits of socially sanctioned behavior by violating those limits. Just as Victor Frankenstein's creature can be seen as the manifestation of a range of contemporary social anxieties, from Enlightenment science to maternity to revolutionary upheaval in France, Célanire embodies the fears and concerns particular to the various worlds she enters: the prescriptions against miscegenation, against the intellectual, sexual, and political agency of women, and against homosexuality.[4] Unlike Shelley's monster, however, she is in control of her own monstrosity, an autonomous instrument of social disorder with a firm hold on her public image.

Fantastic Transgressions

It is difficult to miss the parodic element in *Célanire cou-coupé*. Recalling *Tituba*'s deceptive heroine, the novel presents a chronologically disconcerting inventory of exceedingly contemporary concerns in the very reading of Célanire as transgressive: this heroine's defiant acts fit a little too neatly into the political agendas of the late-twentieth-century left as they are configured in U.S. academic discourses of women's rights, equality, and sexual freedom. Much as she did fifteen years earlier with her critically confounding Puritan-era protagonist, Condé challenges her readers simultaneously to place Célanire in her own temporal setting and to read her as a champion of American political correctness, to take her seriously as a socially rebellious figure and at the same time to allow her parodic status to undermine the force of the very political agenda her transgression endorses.

For this reason the legibility of Célanire's transgressive status becomes a critical question, for her monstrosity too is subject to contradictory interpretation, not least because Célanire can conceal her scar—the primary sign of her unnatural provenance—at will. If, as Chris Baldick has underlined in the context of *Frankenstein*, the moral function of the monster is primarily to render *visible* the results of aberration or unreason, Célanire decisively eludes this social role by controlling the visible markings of her alterity.[5] The anxiety she provokes is rarely produced by the scar itself, but rather by the uncertainty generated by the fact that her neck is covered; those she encounters are troubled not by the sight of something unnatural, but rather by the uneasy sense that there *could* be something unfamiliar or threatening concealed beneath her scarf. It is thus Célanire who determines whether or not their suspicions will be confirmed, and she who maintains the state of interpretive uncertainty in the other. Similarly, the transgressive effect of her acts is firmly under her control; Célanire is all the more threatening because those around her are not entirely sure who she is or what her true motivations are. Versions and explanations conflict, firsthand accounts of her behavior meld into rumor and exaggeration, and interpretation vacillates with shifts in audience. By maintaining this aura of mystery, Célanire keeps her public suspended in a constant state of interpretive confusion, and it is perhaps in this sense that she is most "monstrous," since she refuses even the interpretive proscriptions of a society that is constantly thwarted in its attempts to fix her identity.

In this respect the genre with which Condé chose to tell Célanire's story merits closer consideration. The novel is designated a "roman fantastique" (fantastic novel), signaling a narrative form well suited to echo Shelley's classic. But beyond the thematic link to the monster's creation, the genre mirrors the conception of this heroine in crucial ways: even in its most general definition, the fantastic narrative elicits the collision of various worlds, of the real and the unreal, the known and the unknown, the natural and the supernatural. It is thus first and foremost a transgressive genre, in that it depends upon the departure from the familiar, the escape from the normative. Linked to the fantasy, it suggests the breaking of social codes and boundaries.[6] Roger Caillois pinpoints the departure from the familiar as the fantastic narrative's defining characteristic, and notes that the introduction of the unknown is characterized principally by its destruction of narrative integrity: "In the fantastic, the supernatural appears as a rupture of universal coherence. The marvelous becomes a forbidden and threatening aggression that shatters the stability of a world whose laws had until then been considered rigorous and immutable. It is the impossible, intruding unexpectedly on a world from which the impossible is by definition banished" (9). The fantastic crumbles the boundaries between the possible and the impossible, destabilizing codes and laws that had previously seemed immutable.

Inherent in this collision of worlds is also the encounter with the other—the alien, the demon, the monster, the sorcerer, the mythical creature. The newly formed narrative world of the fantastic is thus one that inscribes multiple modes of understanding and communication; the fabric of the fantastic is necessarily a patchwork one, combining various and conflicting perceptions of reality and suggesting a context in which such perceptions might coexist. It is in this sense that the fantastic can itself be seen as a "monstrous" narrative, in that, much like Frankenstein's creature, it is an entity constructed through the suturing of materials from disparate sources.[7] Condé's novel too follows this model, not only because of the element of the supernatural but also because of its diverse cultural lexicons and multiple spheres of reference. The conflicting worlds inhabited by Célanire produce fragments of information that shift constantly and refuse to cohere around any single vision of reality. The narrative is thus "monstrous" in the sense that it does not represent a coherent whole through the lens of any particular interpretive context.

There is, however, an important substantial (in the literal sense) difference between Shelley's creature and Condé's that is relevant here: Célanire as a physical being is not a patchwork of disparate human body parts but a single human body severed in two and then reattached. In fact, the splitting of her body is (just barely) incomplete: when she is discovered in the street, her head is "hanging by a thread" ["sa tête ne tenait qu'à un fil" (116)]. Presumably it is in part this fragile remaining connection between body and head that allows Jean Pinceau to perform his miraculous operation. While the revival of Célanire's bloodless body maintains the incursion of the unnatural in this scene, Condé stages a critical morphological difference between the classic creature and her heroine: the result of Jean Pinceau's labor is, while monstrous and incoherent, the (re)assemblage of parts from a single human body.

Returning to the question of form, then, the discursive function of Célanire's reassembled body is informative. For, as we have seen, the fact that she is composed of the parts of a single human body means that Célanire can, if she chooses, *appear* to be a scientifically coherent physical form; she can appear to belong to the natural world, with only the mysterious scarf as a disturbing suggestion of other possibilities. Her monstrosity thus does not have to be immediately apparent, but will emerge depending on how she is seen by others. Similarly, the fantastic is a genre that functions crucially on interpretation: the categories navigated by the fantastic—of realism and fantasy, of possible and impossible, of known and unknown—are categories established by the reader. Depending on such factors as cultural or historical background, religious belief, gender, age, sexuality, and individual experience, a given reader will be equipped with his or her particular conception of the "natural" or the "real" and will recognize the fantastic as a disruption of that specific set of codes.[8] In *Célanire cou-coupé*, by invoking such systems of understanding as animism, Christianity, Islamic faith, and Western science, Condé allows for a culturally diverse lexicon in order to produce a potentially limitless number of "monstrous" narratives, both of Célanire herself and of events in the novel. The text thus insists on a multicultural reading, an interpretive participation in its monstrosity.

What is striking about Condé's novel is that these various possible readings coexist simultaneously. In a narrative structure that suggests an amplification of *Traversée de la mangrove*'s interpretive indeterminacy, where characters spar for authority primarily from within the confines of their respective chapters, here Condé offers multiple accounts of a single series of events side by side, conferring no priority of the rational over the irrational, the secular over the sacred, the known over the unknown. In particular, the numerous deaths that coincide disconcertingly with Célanire's presence are a source of heightened interpretive tension in the novel, as each one of them has a number of possible explanations, none of which is confirmed within the narrative.

The body of Thomas de Brabant's French wife, Charlotte, for example, is discovered deep in the forest, destroyed almost beyond recognition: "The sight was horrible. It was as if wild beasts, eaters of human flesh and drinkers of fresh blood, had done her in. All around the body the earth had been clawed into ruts. Yet no lion had been reported in the region" (52). As is evidenced by this citation, the passage describing the discovery of Charlotte's body emphasizes the limits of the possible that, through the lens of the natural, the rational, and the scientific, appear to have been severely tested. While the hypothesis of an attack by wild animals as the means of death is undermined by the lack of concrete evidence, it seems implausible that the less-than-sturdy Charlotte could have walked alone across the kilometers of dangerous terrain between the forest and her home. General opinion in the community proposes that Célanire is guilty of this murder, yet while the Europeans attempt to find a scientific explanation for how the crime was carried out, the African population sees Charlotte's death as further proof that Célanire is a "cheval," a carrier of evil spirits seeking vengeance on the living and certain to strike again. The novel offers no resolution to this conflict and, as the deaths associated with Célanire multiply, preserves the status of Célanire's culpability as a suggestion, but never as definitive. The conflicting readings of these events thus maintain an unsettling coexistence in the narrative, each representing the impossibility of the others but forced to occupy the same discursive space.

Given this interpretive instability, Condé's novel seems to correspond to the more strict definition of the fantastic genre elaborated by Tzvetan Todorov in *The Fantastic: A Structural Approach to a Literary Genre*. Here the fantastic is not simply a genre that allows for departures from the real or the familiar, but one that is characterized above all by the simultaneity of two conflicting worlds, and by the resulting uncertainty on the part of the reader: "The fantastic is that hesitation experienced by a person who knows only the laws of nature, confronting an apparently supernatural event" (25).[9] Once a choice is made between the natural and the supernatural, the narrative is no longer a fantastic one. The two (or, in the case of Condé's novel, multiple) possible interpretations must carry equal discursive weight throughout the narrative, must conflict with one another without canceling each other out. The effectiveness of the fantastic narrative as elaborated by Todorov thus rests in the power of suggestion, rather than in the power of conviction: "*'I nearly reached the point of believing'*: that is the formula which sums up the spirit of the fantastic. Either total faith or total incredulity would lead us beyond the fantastic: it is hesitation which sustains its life" (31). The reader of the fantastic can and should wonder, but must never be certain.

Much as the physical composition of Frankenstein's creature imitates the patchwork construction of Shelley's novel, Célanire's body provides a striking evocation of the fantastic narrative in this strict definition. Even without the piece of cloth to obscure her scar, the "natural" reading of Célanire's body is disturbingly coincident with the "unnatural" one: she is at once whole and divided, at once a living creature and a physical impossibility, at once known and unknown. Unlike Frankenstein's project, Dr. Pinceau's work is an effort to recover a preexisting form: Célanire's body thus refers back to the real, even as its scar points to its distance from the natural world. Like the fantastic narrative, then, this heroine's form is a simultaneous suggestion of two conflicting worlds, and her scar is the sign of that disturbance.[10] The anxiety produced by the sight of Célanire, even or perhaps especially when her scar is covered, is a sudden awareness of the unknown: Célanire thus represents at the same time a body existing wholly in the familiar world and the suggestion, necessarily inconclusive, of an unfamiliar one.

As we have seen, the transgressive nature of Célanire's existence rests to a significant degree on the uncertainty she produces in the other. In fact, this uncertainty and the simultaneity that inheres in the fantastic are closely linked: as Andras Sandor points out in his analysis of the genre, the anxiety provoked by the fantastic disturbance reveals above all the tenu ous quality of those divisions that are being ruptured. The confrontation of the unfamiliar instantly puts the bounds of the familiar into question, since the perception of that unknown object or event sheds doubt upon its position "outside" perception: "Fantastic stories establish a beyond against which the actual world can be noticed, and they project a mental field in which incomprehensible and/or only subliminally noticed aspects of the actual world can be suggested to experience" (350). The simulta neity of conflicting worlds, in other words, points to an added paradox: that to confront the unknown is in some sense to allow for its know ability. The result is a sphere of interpretation whose boundaries have shifted: the encounter with the supernatural points out the arbitrariness of the natural, and the perception of the inhuman that of the human.

Condé's novel evokes such troubled distinctions at various points in the narrative, particularly with reference to the popular knowledge of native communities in the Ivory Coast and in Peru. A reaction to the first mysterious death in Adjame-Santey, for example, proclaims that "there is no such thing as a natural death" (7), thus putting the very category of the natural into question, while in Peru a violent death yields a simi lar demand for speculation: "In our countries, where imagination reigns supreme, popular curiosity is not satisfied with a mystery. Everything has to have an explanation, preferably supernatural" (215). Here the idea of the supernatural as a way to elucidate a mysterious event redefines the concept of the explanation as a demystifying, rational process: instead of being reasoned away, the supernatural *is* the explanation for the un known. Like Célanire's scar, these passages evoke a division between two worlds even as they suture them together again, pitting the concepts of natural and unnatural against each other to expose the arbitrary quality of such distinctions.

A Good Mother: Reproducing Hybridity

In the closing pages of the novel, Célanire seems to have completed a significant chapter in her journey: if she has indeed been pursuing her enemies, the last of their injustices has perhaps been avenged. "I have nothing more to do here" (223), she announces, and demands that her husband take her back to Guadeloupe. Greatly transformed after recov ering from a nearly fatal illness, and seemingly drained of her previous thirst for revenge, she claims that she needs a new purpose, "a new reason for living" (228). Once in Guadeloupe, this newly formed ambition is made clear, as Célanire appears unexpectedly in her husband's bedroom, dressed in silk and lace and telling him she wants a child. "Please!" she pleads. "All I can do now is be a good mother" (232).

Célanire's new reason for living, then, is procreation. With this operatic conclusion, Condé would seem in a single gesture to recuperate a number of the monsters haunting Shelley's classic narrative: Célanire's claim is an assertion of female creativity, of birth, and of motherhood—a motherhood specifically characterized as "good," and thus an implied revision of the orphan's fate so frequently evoked in *Frankenstein*. But in the cross-cultural contexts of Condé's novel, it seems especially telling that Célanire also revives another monster destroyed in Shelley's narrative: the creature's bride. For Victor Frankenstein's refusal to allow his female creature to live arises out of a phobia of procreation: it is the thought of "a race of devils . . . propagated upon the earth" (Shelley, 144) that gives him pause and prevents him from granting the creature's demand. The repression of this new species represented by the destruction of the female is thus categorically refused by Célanire's final words: Condé's creature *will* reproduce herself, she will create a new race of monsters.

Although Célanire rewrites her own literary ancestor in these fundamental ways, however, the final declaration seems an aberrance in the legacy of anachronistically flaunted gender and sexual roles that the heroine has established thus far. On the contrary, this endorsement of sanctified motherhood, especially framed as it is as an exclusive role that will presumably extinguish the wild rebelliousness of Célanire's previous incarnations ("All I can do now is be a good mother"), seems an eminently normative gesture in the context of late-twentieth-century Western progressivism. Hence, Célanire slips out from under yet another socially coded reading, undermining the very criteria that might have championed her as an icon for women's equality and sexual freedom. As if to provide an eleventh-hour liberation from the parodic figure who doubles her, Célanire drives a defiant wedge between her desire for maternal goodness and the numerous attributes and behaviors that had until then traced out a coherent model of anticonformist politics. The novel's final act of seduction, then, asserts a gesture of differentiation that refuses to conform to the paradigm of nonconformity and thus reveals how paradoxically rigid the criteria for transgression can ultimately prove to be.

The promise of procreation with which this novel closes, moreover, reminds us that even a normative valorization of reproduction will fail to ensure transparency. For the "monstrousness" of her child's race is only in part the taboo of miscegenation that hovers in the colonial setting of Célanire's story and the gothic hauntings of Shelley's classic.[11] It is also the specter of racial indeterminacy that will be revived, a reference back to the mother only in its echoed illegibility. By weaving together Célanire's transgressive status and the narrative uncertainty of the fantastic, then, Condé shows us the epistemological basis of the challenge presented by racial hybridity. Célanire's illegibility is generated not only by her unidentifiable racial traits ("a hybrid of goodness knows how many races") but also by the need to simultaneously apprehend categories that have been socially constructed as distinct. Condé's fantastic protagonist reminds us that it is a mistake to think of racial hybridity as a sum of two or multiple entities, or as a Frankensteinesque assemblage of foreign body parts. Instead, hybridity expresses a simultaneity that belies the integrity of the parts themselves, an epistemological uncertainty that must be preserved.

Condé's innovative use of genre thus suggests an incisive response to Gilroy's call for resistance to the automatic endorsement of race as a stable biological or social category. Just as the fantastic destabilizes the distinction between the natural and the unnatural, between the known and the unknown, the creature that exists as a simultaneous reference to multiple origins puts into question the very possibility of establishing racial divisions. Since the individual races that presumably produced the child are not visible as such, the child's existence destroys their viability as distinct categories. Célanire's transgressively conformist desire for reproduction reveals the disruptive scope of racial mixing in that it demands the acknowledgment of this previous, preexisting indeterminacy. Condé's "ingestion" of the British gothic and the European fantastic genres, meanwhile, suggests a new vocabulary for thinking about hybridity by bringing into focus the crucial relationship between monstrosity and epistemology. The novel's intervention in critical race theory is thus to inscribe the sustained interpretive hesitation prescribed by the fantastic genre into a reflection on racial hybridity and social transgression, thereby underscoring the demand for transparency upon which such configurations can be founded, even or perhaps especially when they seek to transgress categorical boundaries.

6 The Coherence of Caricature

Reparations in *La belle créole*

THE TITLE OF Maryse Condé's 2001 novel *La belle créole*, warns Jacques Coursil, is a trap.[1] Not only does it defy expectation by referring to a boat rather than to a woman, but even in this displaced designation it proves misleading: the boat in question is not one of the small, stereotypically autochthonous variety that might come to mind for the expectant reader of a Guadeloupean novel (or, for that matter, that is pictured on the cover of the 2001 Mercure de France edition), but rather a large yacht purchased by a European family for their pleasure trips through the Caribbean archipelago. Coursil further observes that the name "La belle créole" reveals a linguistic exteriority in terms of both usage and meaning, noting that in the bilingual Antilles small fishing boats might be given the Creole name "bel kréyol," but not the French "La belle créole," and that if the name is intended as a French rendition of the more commonly used Creole name, it is in any case an erroneous one. The French expression "La belle créole," Coursil asserts, is not an accurate translation of "bel kréyol," and thus represents a "re-imported exoticism," a symptom of the European's false and externally imposed reading of an unfamiliar culture.[2]

The parallel naming of book and boat proves equally deceptive, in that Condé's narrative marks a deliberate divergence from the clichéd image of a peaceful Caribbean village suggested by its title and cover art.[3] Instead, the pages between those covers reveal a turbulent, dirty, complicated town fraught with political and personal conflict. Setting her narrative point of departure on the dramatic trial and acquittal of a young man accused of killing his mistress, Condé focuses on the twenty-four hours following the trial to demythologize not only exoticized visions of Guadeloupe but also the legal and racial politics at work in the defense strategy that sets the protagonist free. As I discuss in this chapter, Condé's novel stages what could be described as a series of distorted translations, a repetition in various forms of a substitutive gesture that erases incoherent or problematic narratives in favor of more recognizable or palatable ones, that erases difference in favor of transparency. By elaborating the process through which these permutations occur as a process of reduction and expansion, Condé identifies these distortions as various forms of caricature. Her critique thus extends beyond the exotic vision of the Caribbean to examine the ways in which caricature becomes a useful discursive tool toward multiple ends, including those that might be considered politically progressive or resistant. In particular, by scrutinizing the methodological strategies employed by the protagonist's defense lawyer, Condé offers an instructive reflection on the debate surrounding slavery reparations, suggesting that the imbrication of racial essentialism and reparations discourse that has come under critique by opponents might be usefully examined alongside exoticism and racial stereotyping as an instance of the pitfalls of representativity.

Courtroom Dramas: The Narrative of Victimhood

The courtroom setting of *La belle créole* offers an arresting dramatization of legal discursive strategy. The crime at the heart of the novel, the slaying of a wealthy white woman by her black male gardener, guarantees the heightened symbolism of the trial, providing a ready-made sensationalism upon which the prosecution draws amply. The indictment strategy is in fact made relatively simple by the class and racial differences between Dieudonné Sabrina and Loraine Féréol de Brémont and the irrefutable evidence of Dieudonné's responsibility for his employer's death: the defendant is painted as a "brute grossière et dangereuse" [vulgar and dangerous brute] (14), tapping into classically stereotyped visions of the threatening Other. Rather than addressing any of the details of the defendant's character, personal history, or his relationship to Loraine, the prosecution makes recourse to caricature, trusting in the jury's readiness to conjure up an abstracted image of depravity and to superimpose it upon a nameless defendant.

Matthias Serbulon's task, then, is to save his client from this stereotype of black male criminality. Drawing his own portrait of Dieudonné with sustained premeditation, Serbulon skillfully links together a series of details that will encourage the jury to see the defendant as a victim rather than as a criminal: his portrait is that of a poor black gardener working in the home of a *grande békée,* orphaned, illiterate, and powerless, trapped in a permanent state of oppression. Having reinforced these aspects of

Dieudonné's identity, Serbulon can then effect a link between his client's state of subordination and the island's history of slavery: "After all, everything could be summarized in a few sentences: tired of being humiliated, a lover breaks it off with his mistress. What gave the whole affair an aura of symbolism was that it was happening in a country that was just coming out of slavery (well not exactly—a hundred and fifty years already!), that the mistress was white, a *békée* to boot, and the lover was black" (40–41). According to Serbulon's logic, if the jury is willing to see Dieudonné as oppressed and marginalized instead of as a violent criminal, they will necessarily read the circumstances of Loraine's death in the context of a larger narrative of institutionalized racism.

The framework of history is fundamental to Serbulon's defense, as it allows him to transform the jury's understanding of the very concept of victimhood. Rather than presenting the crime as a conflict between individuals, Serbulon portrays it as a struggle between racial groups, so that Dieudonné, not Loraine, is the victim, and society in general is guilty of the transgression—the transgression being not Loraine's death but racial oppression. Serbulon's argument thus has significant ideological ties to a legal strategy Stephen L. Carter has examined in the context of the United States. Carter notes the ahistorical nature of the most widely accepted understandings of victimhood, premised on a "bilateral individualist" perspective that turns a blind eye to the vast network of social and historical circumstances surrounding a given crime. Such a view, he explains, "denies that all black people are 'victims' in any legally or morally cognizable sense. Whether or not there are any present day legacies of racism past, the bilateral individualist construction of victimhood denies that anyone holds a legal responsibility to alleviate them. A victim is someone injured by someone else, and only the someone else, not the society as a whole, deserves punishment" (436).

With its deliberate historical symbolism, Serbulon's defense can be read as a direct reversal of this bilateral individualism in its refusal to present Loraine as the victim in this case. By rejecting the interpretation of the events in question as a transgression between individuals, Serbulon insists on a concept of victimhood that is general and historical, and that, given the island's legacy of colonialism, can apply only to the circumstances of a member of its oppressed class. Having established the image of his client as a poor, orphaned black man, powerless before the legacy of wealth and tyranny embodied by his mistress, Serbulon is able to successfully shift the notion of victimhood from the particular to the general, from the individual to the historical, from Loraine to Dieudonné.

The socially progressive ethos of Serbulon's defense seems to fly directly in the face of the prosecution's uninventive use of blatant caricature, while at the same time saving his client from a lifetime in prison. But while its implicit contrast to the racist stereotyping of the prosecution lends a sheen of moral superiority to Serbulon's project, this perception is quickly undercut by the novel's post-trial revelations. Following the dramatic trial verdict, the gap between Serbulon's constructed image of Dieudonné and Dieudonné's actual experience grows ever wider, underlining the extent to which the lawyer took liberties with the truth in order to win his case. A key exchange between Serbulon and his client reveals that the defense narrative was built partly on the suppression of certain details or facts and often on a brazen ignorance of them. Rather than replacing inconsistencies or adding the odd nuance, Serbulon for the most part writes his defense over silence, for after several months of interviews he has scarcely heard the sound of his client's voice, eventually concluding that Dieudonné is simply incapable of articulating his own experience:

> He had resigned himself to his silences, understanding that it wasn't stubbornness, unwillingness, or impertinence. Dieudonné was trying. But he didn't know how to present facts, explain them, relate a cause to its effect. So, he had gone to work alone, constructing the real from his imagination like a novelist, patiently developing or rejecting various versions of the drama. When he was finally satisfied with one of them, he had scolded his mute client:
> — Listen! Listen to me! That's how it happened, alright? (40)

Dieudonné's narrative as presented to the jury is thus explicitly described here as an invention, a product of Serbulon's active and self-interested imagination. Given the defendant's silence, Condé leaves little room for any potential connection between the defense narrative and Dieudonné's experience, signaling instead the lawyer's excited replacement of whatever account Dieudonné might have offered with his own; the imagined drama does not just represent a legal strategy, but must actually become "the way things happened" in the minds of everyone concerned. Serbulon, it seems, needs to convince even himself (and, perversely enough, his silent client) of the "truth" of this invented account.

Paradoxically, then, it is precisely by positing him as a hero that Serbulon has effectively erased Dieudonné's role in his own narrative; it is by ensuring retribution for his disenfranchised status that he has rendered him powerless. As a result, Dieudonné faces a future plagued by the gap between this salutary persona and his own experience: "He didn't recognize himself in the image the lawyer had worked so hard to give of him, a pitiful victim" (14). This sense of alienation is reinforced by his interactions with others during the hours following the trial: while suddenly he has become a local celebrity, this recognition corresponds to someone else's narrative. His public life, invented by his lawyer and appropriated by the media, no longer seems to be under his control: "His life no longer belonged to him. It was all over the media" (130). Defeated, Dieudonné simply cedes the spotlight to Serbulon, underlining the conflation between creator and creation in which he himself can claim little part: "Let Serbulon put on airs, let him show off! This victory was his. It was the triumph of his intelligence. As for him, in the end he was nothing but a walk-on who had never had anything to say" (16). In the very gesture that hinges on giving voice to the voiceless, then, Serbulon effectively silences his rehabilitated client. While the historically responsible impulse of Serbulon's defense may be laudable, Condé reminds us here that this strategy necessarily entails the suppression of the individual.

By recounting these moments of alienation and manipulation, Condé's novel thus exposes the narrative that saved Dieudonné as a fabrication. But in mounting his defense, Serbulon does more than paint a convincing portrait of his client; he also constructs a story around that portrait. Narrative is a crucial aspect of his legal preparation, as the description of Serbulon's pretrial efforts ("constructing the real from his imagination like a novelist") makes clear.[4] If we return to this crucial scene of creative inspiration, it is evident that his defense argument demands a particular kind of narrative in order to function successfully: the story must be above all a legible one, instantly recognizable and quickly digested by his audience. Serbulon's skill is vital specifically because it enables him to do what he thinks Dieudonné cannot do: "to present facts, explain them, relate a cause to its effect." As we have seen, the suppression of Dieudonné's voice is fundamental to this coherent narrative, but Serbulon's rendition at trial, in overwriting Dieudonné's account of events, also obscures the *process* through which the narrative achieves its state of coherence. Serbulon explicitly "reject[s] or develop[s] various versions of the drama," and yet the final version is presented as definitive—no longer a version at all, but simply "the way things happened" (40). This legal discourse thus not only eliminates incoherent or ill-fitting details in favor of the coherent but also erases any trace of such prior inconsistencies, presenting the narrative as an absolute and immaculate whole. In this sense Serbulon's trial fabrication is problematic both because it presents an artificial construction of Dieudonné's identity and because it denies its own relative status as one of many facets of the lawyer's creative process, as one of many versions of Dieudonné's story.

It is ultimately the need for coherence, then, that drives the process of reduction and expansion in the creation of the trial narrative.[5] Coherence demands the elimination of the tangential, the reduction to recognizable imagery, and the subsequent expansion of that imagery to effect the appearance of wholeness. Serbulon's procedure is a substitution of the part for the whole, which, as his own self-conscious work-in-progress reveals, also demands that the part *masquerade* as the whole, that it be taken as the complete and unified account of events. Given the insistence on the creation of consumable narrative in Serbulon's strategy, Condé's novel thus suggests that, just as the prosecution projects an image of Dieudonné founded on a reductive vision of his identity in order to call up a wealth of preexisting stereotypes in the cultural imagination of the jury, Serbulon creates his image of the helpless gardener by eliminating all aspects of Dieudonné's experience that do not connote victimhood. Thanks to this reductive operation, he too is able to appeal to the jury's familiarity with a certain cultural lexicon: the story of the defenseless slave who finally rebels against his oppressor is already in place, a file that already exists in the jury's memory and needs only to be accessed, prompted by a few key images.

Referring with some irony to the field of reference that ensured the legibility of his narrative, Serbulon congratulates himself on his successful defense: "Matthias was rather proud of his argumentation, which he considered Césairean, perhaps even Fanonian. The cruel *békée* mistress. The defenseless slave. The mistress humiliates, wields the whip. One day, the slave liberates himself. By killing. Baptism of blood" (44). The references to Fanon and Césaire in this passage, to which I will return below, underscore the importance of a preexisting frame of interpretation on the part of the jury members. Serbulon rests his defense on the familiarity of these diluted theories of colonialism, as if to imply that nearly fifty years after the publication of *Black Skin, White Masks*, the image of the black man as victim had become commonplace, universally recognizable to the point of cliché.

Both the prosecution and the defense employ a process of reduction and expansion in their presentations of Dieudonné's identity: the defendant is first stripped of his specificity in favor of a simplistic image, and that image is then expanded onto a generalized and preconceived notion of black male identity. In this sense these legal strategies trace a methodology that is discursively consistent with the construction of caricature:

each lawyer isolates a single feature of Dieudonné's existence and exaggerates it so as to dominate his entire legal portrait. Indeed, synecdoche is precisely what links caricature and coherence: the replacement of the whole with the part is necessarily accomplished through a process of exaggeration.[6] While the prosecution's depiction of the defendant as a savage brute seems easily identifiable as such an exercise, the juxtaposition of the two arguments uncovers methodological similarities that implicate the defense as well: Serbulon's talent as a lawyer rests in his ability first to reduce his client's identity to a simple and legible sign, then to exaggerate that sign beyond any connection to Dieudonné's lived experience. Given Serbulon's further expansion of this simplified image onto the stage of history, his legal strategy engenders what we might term a historical caricature, in that history is the mechanism through which he obscures the particularity of his client's experience in order to represent him as a victim.

Fanon in Self-Defense

If we read Serbulon's strategy as a claim for the social utility of narrative, we can understand the appeal to history as a call for narrative coherence in temporal terms: to encourage the jury to read Dieudonné through the lens of colonialism is to envisage a unified understanding of time that repairs the rift between the history of slavery and contemporary legal practice. Serbulon's defense of Dieudonné, in other words, constitutes a plea to consider the present retrospectively so as to correct the injustices of the past: whereas the prosecution would propose a reading of the murder as an atemporal event, Serbulon insists that the present relationship between Dieudonné and Loraine is inextricable from the island's colonial history. His defense narrative thus resonates powerfully with legal arguments that inform the demand for reparations, whereby contemporary society is held responsible for the debts incurred by past generations.

Serbulon's characterization of his own legal argument as "Fanonian," then, is particularly telling, in that while its insipid and reductive representation of fundamental precepts of Fanon's thought generates a successful narrative for public and judicial consumption, Serbulon's methodology in actuality engages much of what came under critique in Fanon's temporal and phenomenological assessment of reparations. In *Black Skin, White Masks,* Fanon explicitly rejects the claim to reparations for slavery on the grounds that its insistence on temporal continuity traps the present in the very structures of racial inequality that need to be eradicated. "I do not have the right to allow myself to be mired in what the past has determined," he writes; "I am not the slave of the Slavery that dehumanized my ancestors" (230). Françoise Vergès, who takes the title of her essay from this latter citation, explains that Fanon's critique of reparations was anchored on a demand for a temporal break with the past that would enable a recovery of the body from servitude: "Fanonian reparation was about getting access to a site of freedom in which the body and the self are in conversation, a site free of the spectres and ghosts of the past" ("'I am not the slave of slavery,'" 267). Rather than imprisoning the self in an overdetermined identification with past enslavement, Fanon argued for a rejection of reparations as an act of self-liberation.

As this position makes clear, the problem with the primacy placed on history, or what Fanon terms "the materialized Tower of the Past" (226), is not only the perpetuation of untenable social and phenomenological conditions but also the imposition of a false continuity. This continuity, moreover, imposes a correlation across time from slave to descendant that at the same time underwrites constructed categories of race as both diachronically and synchronically valid. The temporal exigency of reparations, in other words, imposes a notion of shared identity across generations that is founded on the ideologies of racial essentialism that defined slavery. As Naomi Zack writes, "The discourse of reparations . . . takes place on the assumption that racial distinctions are natural distinctions that can be genealogically traced over time" (142). For Condé, this assumption has a seductive power in contemporary discourse precisely because of its temporal and conceptual coherence. As her staging of Dieudonné's trial reveals, defense and prosecution alike draw amply on biological constructions of race, and the same logic that condemns Dieudonné as a "vulgar and dangerous brute" informs the reparations argument that frees him. To push the comparison further, then, we can read Condé's critique of reparations discourse as an exposure of the element of caricature at work in this position, in that the argument for reparations demands that a social construct be taken for biology just as it asks that an individual be taken for his ancestors.[7]

Fanon turned his back on this caricatured vision of temporality and corporeality to claim his right to become "a man among other men" (112).[8] But Condé's novel, although it seems to critique the "enslavement" of Dieudonné to the rhetoric of slavery reparations, takes a cynical stand also on the possibility for self-creative freedom in fin de siècle Guadeloupe. Having been "emancipated" by Serbulon's defense strategy, Dieudonné has the chance to reclaim his particularism, to forge an identity out of the gap between his private life and the appropriated public image that so baffled him during the trial. But although he does contemplate the distance that separates him from the collective ancestry constructed by his lawyer, his break from that narrative is framed less in liberatory terms than as a perception of indifference and irrelevance. Seeing African and African American figures on television and in the movies, for example, he senses the expectation of a community but is unable to make the necessary affective leap to realize this continuity: "He knew that long ago they had been brothers and sisters, born from the same womb, before a cruel force scattered them to the four corners of the world. How had that happened exactly? He didn't know and didn't really care" (220). Instead, Dieudonné puts precedence on the complexities and ugly problems of his present existence over the abstractions of the past.[9]

Dieudonné's own personal history, however, if not his constructed past, seems to have maintained its grip on him. Having suppressed this account throughout the trial, he finally cedes to the demand to speak for himself, but even given an open floor, he falters:

> Usually, he kept everything to himself. He had let Maître Serbulon construct that lousy scenario. . . . Now, he couldn't take it any more.
> — What is there to tell? You can tell stories about misery, about tragedy. Not happiness. I was happy. (137–38)

Although he is presumably free to claim his voice and replace Serbulon's distortions with the true account of how Loraine died, Dieudonné confronts the impermeability of his experience to a publicly acceptable narrative, the incoherence of his happy yet murderous relationship with Loraine. Much like Tolstoy's indistinguishable families, Dieudonné's reflection suggests, his happiness may itself have been incommensurate with narrative.

As Dieudonné forges ahead with his story, he seems to come up against a series of such impasses, providing revelations not only about the events leading up to the infamous murder but also about his own motivations for keeping silent. While he and Loraine did, it seems, find a somewhat peaceful coexistence, this relative harmony is interrupted well before the murder by the unexpected arrival of Loraine's former lover Luc, whose revelation of his physical attraction to Dieudonné creates a treacherous double love triangle. It is a fit of jealousy on the part of Loraine that provokes the fateful confrontation between the gardener and his mistress, as she seizes her handgun and shoots twice at Dieudonné, only to be killed in the ensuing struggle. In turning himself in to the police, however, Dieudonné distorts these events out of proclaimed loyalty to his mistress:

"In her pain, in her drunkenness, Loraine would have shot him down like a dog. But to admit that would have been the ultimate betrayal. That was why, after four days of reflection, he had turned himself in at the Cadenat police station like a guilty man. That's why he had kept silent, letting the lawyer construct his absurd theories" (227). Dieudonné thus posits his silence not as a passive gesture of helplessness but as an intentional shielding of his mistress's private pain, a contorted effort to preserve an empty public image at his own expense. Given the fact that what is also shielded by Dieudonné's self-proclaimed loyalty is a homoerotic narrative, moreover, his silence can hardly be considered innocuous. By saying nothing, he exempts himself from examining his own attraction to Luc as a factor in Loraine's death, obscuring this layer of the narrative and replacing it with a vague expression of (heterosexual) loyalty to his mistress.

In the end, then, Dieudonné's handling of the event bears a striking resemblance to Serbulon's, in that he too generates an artificial portrait of the act, turning himself in "comme un coupable" (like a guilty man). Similarly, the key moment of Loraine's death is absent from his story, rendered indirectly as "a short struggle during which all he had done was to defend himself" (226), and finally encapsulated with a familiar and resonant phrase: "That's how it had happened. Self-defense ['Légitime défense'], Maître Serbulon would have argued, if he had known the truth" (227). This "truth," then, while it may be distinct from both the lawyer's version and Dieudonné's self-incriminating one, is ultimately transmitted in clichéd form. The appellation "légitime défense" would indeed be quite at home in Serbulon's strategic repertoire, not least thanks to its resonance with a key phrase of the *Négritude* movement, suggesting a cynical echo of Serbulon's evocation of Fanon and Césaire.[10] Instead of elaborating the complications of his confrontation with Loraine, or articulating the events leading up to her death, Dieudonné abruptly aborts his narrative to replace it with a simplified, easily identifiable trope of self-defense, a mocking repetition of Serbulon's vocabulary of racial solidarity. Given Dieudonné's own role in this reductive image, the parallel illuminates the fact that caricature is not always imposed from the outside, but can be intentionally generated by its subject.

INDEED, CONDÉ PRESENTS myriad instances in her novel of the propensity for self-caricature, evoking characters who, like Serbulon and Dieudonné, make recourse to fiction by projecting distorted images of their own experiences. Dieudonné's father, for example, having neglected his son during his lifetime, has a realization of profound sorrow upon learning of Dieudonné's death at the end of the novel, and sits pitifully at the funeral ceremony, "his head between his hands." In the novel's final sentence, we learn the reason for his grief: "His wife had convinced him that everything that had happened was his fault" (253). Like his son, Milo has taken on a heavy burden of guilt, a guilt exaggerated in caricature to a general responsibility for "everything" that has happened. By closing with this portrait of abjection, Condé suggests that Milo is heretofore marked by this gesture, that he will live out the rest of his life under the fixed and singular image of guilt. Not unlike some of Jean-Paul Sartre's illustrations of existential bad faith, Milo will reduce his existence to the unvarying narrative of an abstract quality: "Je suis coupable."

Even as it exposes the reductive nature of caricature, then, Condé's novel repeatedly reveals how compelling its logic can prove to be, foregrounding the instinct toward coherence as a driving force for these characters. The post-trial narrative reveals that the deception engendered by caricature, beyond its capacity to manipulate public perception, can be exceedingly useful for the individual faced with his or her own unintelligible experience. Much as Serbulon's legal caricature of Dieudonné's identity provided a coherent narrative for interpretation by the jury, Dieudonné's own use of clichéd drama provides a way for him to make sense out of the confusion of his final weeks with Loraine, a way to isolate a unified interpretation that will eliminate the disconcerting elements of the events leading up to her death. Similarly, his father can simply become guilt and nothing else, instead of reflecting upon the less transparent and potentially troubling details of his experience as a father. For all of these men, caricature cuts out the incoherent then expands to fill its discursive space, blocking out the potentially unreadable and exempting them from confronting the more disturbing aspects of their existences. Through this series of repeated caricatures, I would argue, Condé's novel also illuminates the discursive force of the reparations narrative, the pull of coherence that endorses a constructed notion of racial identity as a substitute for the ineffable.

As a character who gained his freedom at the cost of such a caricature, Dieudonné bears the brunt of such contradictions, so that his disappearance at the end of the novel suggests a defeated withdrawal from the symbolic battlefield that consumed him. In a narrative confirmation of the demythologized exoticism announced by the novel's title, his beloved boat *La belle créole* is discovered in pieces in the ocean. But even the potential act of revolt signaled by Dieudonné's presumed suicide recedes behind the appropriative chatter of Port-Mahault, for his final crime is declared to be that of caricature: "This spectacular and unusual manner of ending one's life seemed theatrical and put people off" (252). Of course, the sensational nature of this presumed suicide is only part of Dieudonné's final offense: he has more egregiously produced an event that is incoherent with the carefully mounted legal defense narrative and media image embraced by the public. Instead of being grateful for the freedom Serbulon worked so hard to secure, the people of Port-Mahault grumble, Dieudonné gave himself his own death sentence: "It was as if, in spite of his efforts, Dieudonné was proclaiming himself guilty, self-inflicting the punishment [Serbulon] had spared him" (252). Since suicide represents an incoherent event in the narrative of a liberated victim of social injustice, Dieudonné's actions are read as an audacious and unseemly rejection of Serbulon's defense. The public outcry over this betrayal of narrative points to the either/or logic of the legal courtroom, where it is precisely the selection of one version of events over another that is staged. Similarly, the inhabitants of Port-Mahault, having endorsed Serbulon's persuasive sound bite, have little tolerance for the vagaries of one man's misgivings.

To refute the postcard vision of a tranquil, uncomplicated Caribbean island, Condé thus expresses her trademark insolence in a deliberate reflection on the poverty, corruption, and despair of present-day Guadeloupe. In her cynical portrayal of the collusion of legal and media representation, moreover, she undoes the logic of caricature that not only informs exoticized visions of tropical islands but also attempts to redress the historical injustices hidden behind this exotic imagery. The argument for reparations founds temporal continuity, shared ancestry, and collective identification on a logic of false coherence that is undone repeatedly in Condé's novel. And yet the path traced by freedom from such overdetermined categorizations is less clear, as Milo's closing self-caricature and Dieudonné's apparent election of self-obliteration over the "freedom" offered by Serbulon suggest. Hovering in the background of these narrative moments, moreover, is the image of Rodrigue, Dieudonné's close friend born on the same day and in the same hospital as the protagonist. Dubbed "Public Enemy Number 1" by the police (28) and pursued for numerous crimes, Rodrigue is finally arrested several weeks before Dieudonné; unlike his doppelganger, however, Rodrigue receives a twenty-year sentence for his transgressions. Thus, Dieudonné's victory in the courtroom is shadowed by this alternate experience, the parallel fate produced by another possible narrative of his identity, and the one he would mostly likely have met without Serbulon's appeal to history. In this way Condé suggests from another standpoint the difficulty of averting the reductive methodologies of reparations, unveiling the same circular logic: just as the debt of slavery cannot be declared without recourse to its racial categorizations, the only discourse that can hope to defeat the caricature of black male criminality in the image- and sound-bite-driven exchanges of Condé's Guadeloupe may be that of another caricature.

7 Unfamiliar Cannibals

Postcolonial Readings in *Histoire de la femme cannibale*

THE CANNIBAL announced in the title of Condé's 2003 novel is a figure deeply embedded in the discourse of postcolonial studies. Its literal meaning invokes the historical context of New World exploration and thereby the seminal structures of alterity and subjugation that come under critique in postcolonial theory, while in the twentieth century the term's metaphorical value has been conscripted by anticolonial artistic movements. Condé herself has written in recent essays about this latter strategy of "literary cannibalism," identifying its emergence in Brazilian modernism via Oswaldo de Andrade's anthropophagist movement and tracing a literary history through such intellectual figures as Martinican critic Suzanne Césaire and Argentine-Chilean writer Ariel Dorfman. The revisionary impulse behind this project, as Condé describes it, draws on the nominal power of the term "cannibal": "to acknowledge and rehabilitate the appellation 'cannibal,' once a term of opprobrium, and transform it into a symbol of a new, noncolonized self" ("Suzanne Césaire," 64). Firmly situated in a New World geography, Condé's framework foregrounds the violence and incorporation associated with cannibalism as a mode of creative freedom: "For Oswaldo de Andrade and the modernists of the early twentieth century, it is not enough to simply eliminate intellectual colonization, to simply reject Western culture. Instead Western heritage must be desacralized and then ingested. We must subvert Shakespeare, the canonical European author par excellence, and ridicule his hero Hamlet so as to better appropriate him" ("Des héros et des cannibales," 31). By engaging the rhetorical force of cannibalism, this project both reactivates and mocks colonial fantasies of barbarism as it deposes Western authority.

Condé's novel offers abundant material for reflection on the unavowed anxieties, distorted logic, and ethically suspect appropriations associated with the cannibalistic mode. Indeed, her narrative appears to be shot through with instances of the violence, monstrosity, and incorporation that are encompassed by cannibalism. As Mireille Rosello puts it, "*all* the characters" in this novel can be seen as cannibals ("Post-cannibalism," 37); such are the reciprocal properties of cannibalism that those who are fascinated by it divulge its defining characteristics within themselves while those who reject it reenact its brutality in the strength of their denunciation. While the trope announced by the novel's title and copiously developed within its pages is impossible to overlook, however, the engagement of cannibalism in *Histoire de la femme cannibale* does not automatically invoke the postcolonial models of reappropriation that Condé investigates in her critical work. As Rosello astutely shows, the multiplicities of suggestions, accusations, and self-incriminations of cannibalism in the novel yield no figures that can be easily categorized according to such familiar parameters as the evil European or the vengeful barbarian. Instead, she argues, Condé somewhat paradoxically uses the plethora of cannibalizations in her novel to propose a more specific and limited definition of cannibalism, a "post-cannibalism" that "successfully reworks the difference between colonizer and colonized by remapping it over an ambiguous and reversible continuum between the figures of the one who eats and the one who is eaten, the cannibal and the cannibalized" (49).

Taking Rosello's cue, I would like to consider further this striking absence of familiar cannibals in *Histoire de la femme cannibale* by looking in particular at how Condé illuminates the epistemological machinery set in motion by cannibalism in order to mount a critique of postcolonial reading practices. By tracing parallel narratives of recognition on the part of her protagonist, who not only "discovers" Fiéla, the accused cannibal woman, but also learns unspeakable truths about her companion of twenty years, Condé foregrounds the ways in which the reflective properties of cannibalism present themselves epistemologically as a self-incriminating compensation for narrative lacunae. Drawing on critiques of colonial ethnographies and anthropological discourse that reveal the hypothesis of cannibalism as a preemptive substitution for methodologically sound accounts of anthropophagy, I consider in particular Condé's protagonist Rosélie, whose story exhibits the proclivity toward cannibalism in its various somatic, psychological, social, and artistic modes, and illustrates especially the infinite hall of mirrors generated by those inclinations. While both Rosélie and Fiéla experience hatred and ostracism in forms that implicitly and explicitly reference the codes of postcolonial discourse, I argue, the reflective and ambitiously empathic relationship drawn out between the two women at once suggests and complicates the models of cannibalism drawn from colonial history, and points further to the unavowed expectations of the postcolonial reader.

Reflections of Cannibalism

In Western discourse, cannibalism has functioned as a term of absolute alterity, as a line of demarcation between the thinkable and the unthinkable, between self and other, between human and inhuman. The figure of the cannibal provides a site of radical opposition for Western understandings of the self, encapsulating notions of savagery and moral depravity against which civilization can define itself: to consume another human represents an act of no return, the ultimate social threat that cannot be accepted into coherent narratives of community. For Odysseus facing the Cyclops, for Columbus before the *canibales*, for Clarice Starling before Hannibal Lecter, mythically or historically conjured cannibals are threatening not only in their potential violence (imagined or real) but also in that they violate the boundaries of the human.[1] The figure of the cannibal inspires both attraction and repulsion because it offers a visible manifestation of those boundaries between the human and the inhuman, a concrete representation of censored and monstrous behavior.

This combination of fascination and demonization instantaneously characterizes the public reaction to Fiéla in *Histoire de la femme cannibale*: as an accused cannibal, Fiéla quickly passes from criminal to monster in the media. Citizens demand her execution, while the police are under pressure from the *ministère public* to "make an example" of this morally appalling case (85). Before long, the accusation of "inhuman" behavior has been inscribed on Fiéla's physical form: she is pictured in drawings that circulate outside the courthouse with devilish horns on her forehead, while inside at trial her former neighbors unleash elaborate descriptions of her serpent-filled intestines and her bile-filled breasts (204). But it is Rosélie's interest that suggests a more revealing motivation for the fascination with the monstrous: Rosélie reacts to Fiéla's story not with a desire for destruction but instead with a profound sense of identification. Transfixed by the photograph that accompanies the first news coverage of Fiéla's arrest, Rosélie initially establishes this personal link to Fiéla through physical resemblance: "She's my age. She's not beautiful. She could be me" (78). As news of the trial continues, Rosélie begins to conduct an inner dialogue with this stranger, weaving their stories together so tightly that she is unable to distinguish them. When Fiéla appears to Rosélie in a dream, her words imply that this shared fate is tied as closely to her crime as it is to her identity: "I did it for you!" she says. "For you!" (231). Although the "it" ["cela" (237)] signals an abstraction that I will discuss further below, Rosélie's nightmare seems to repeat the suggestion of cannibalism that condemns Fiéla and, furthermore, to implicate Rosélie herself in this monstrous act.

At the heart of Rosélie's affective identification with Fiéla is her personal familiarity with the cruelties of social alienation, most often garnered through a constant confrontation with racism. During her twenty-year relationship with Stephen, a European academic, she experiences society's contempt as a black woman and as part of an interracial couple, or "couple domino," especially in the segregated neighborhoods of Cape Town. She navigates the various spaces she occupies braced for the uncompromising gaze of the Other, for the familiar expressions of distaste, horror, or anger. In the intellectual circles of Stephen's friends and colleagues, for example, she is at turns mistaken for a maid, treated with condescension, or simply ignored. Despite Stephen's repeated denials and reinterpretations of this behavior, it is clear to her that even the most politically correct of his friends are incapable of seeing anything beyond her race, as a vacation encounter in California painfully reveals: "Products of centuries of racism and exclusion of blacks, Lisa and Richard were incapable of looking at Rosélie in the eye and treating her like any other human being" (115). Here Rosélie explicitly frames the refusal to acknowledge her existence as a refusal of her humanity, a cruel filter that relegates her to the status of another species. As such experiences accompany Rosélie throughout her nomadic life in the Caribbean, Europe, the United States, and Africa, the phrase "Invisible Woman" becomes a persistent refrain in the narrative, reflecting a transcontinental experience of racial exclusion. With this intertextual nod to Ellison, Condé underlines the racist impulse as a refusal to acknowledge what is perceived as incoherent, and aligns racism metaphorically with the Western conception of the cannibal. Rosélie, like Fiéla, must confront a society that collectively defines itself through her exclusion.

Rosélie's affinity for the beings and existences rejected by society also emerges in her work: although after Stephen's death she earns her living as a medium, Rosélie is an artist, creating paintings populated by "inhuman" creatures and filled with images of violence, horror, and corporeal destruction. "I like horror," she explains. "I think that in a previous life I must have belonged to a pack of vampires. My long, pointed canines sunk into my mother's breast" (48). As with Fiéla, Rosélie's fascination with society's outcasts is accompanied by an identification with their monstrous world. Here her appreciation of horror suggests a further link to Fiéla's alleged cannibalism, as she evokes a Freudian moment of cannibalistic self-definition: the child devouring the mother's breast.[2] The incidence of cannibalism in her own identity is in turn traced to society's hateful treatment of her, as she imagines a student considering with disapproval Stephen's choice of companion: "What was the sordid connection between him and this descendant of cannibals?" (96). Rosélie sees herself through the eyes of others as a monster, a descendant of the cannibal race, and consequently relegated to the same demonized world as the figures in her paintings.

Cannibalism thus persists in the novel as an ever-present subtext for the hostile encounter with the Other: the figure of the cannibal is a monstrous vision of the threatening, unfamiliar being. What Condé emphasizes here, however, is the extent to which this encounter also represents a threat *to* the cannibal: that the resulting fear on the part of the dominant culture will necessarily translate into a desire for extermination. Alongside the narratives of Rosélie and Fiéla, and the devastating tales of persecution and anonymity recounted by the clients who solicit Rosélie's services as a medium, Condé sketches this particular dynamic through a recurring motif of the destructive tourist: in opposition to the nameless, anxious nomad is the pleasure-seeking traveler, a minority abroad who is nonetheless in a position of economic power with respect to the desired destination.[3] Through Rosélie's eyes the tourist is an agent of distortion and perversion, a damaging force that fundamentally transforms the historical and geographical landscape it enters.

In South Africa this transformation involves a romanticized view of the country's history of violence, stemming from a combined fascination with the horror of that violence and a desire to reach some sort of moral catharsis. As she leaves the home of an acquaintance, for example, Rosélie discovers that the friend's garden is one of the attraction sites for Africultural Tours, a phenomenon condemned by the narrative's bitterly sarcastic description: "Look, ladies and gentlemen, take a good look! Yes, you can take pictures with your digital cameras. It was on this exact spot that ten little niggers were shot during one of the ghetto's most violent revolts. Their blood has irrigated the soil that has nurtured these wonderful flowers Brenda is giving you today" (252). This account is a telling incrimination of the tourist as consumer, as a noxious presence whose insistent curiosity transforms the historical traumas of the land into aesthetically pleasing exotic keepsakes. The novel frames this visit to Brenda's garden as the outgrowth of an insatiable appetite on the part of the tourist, an appetite the tourism industry understands and indulges only too well: "What the privileged from the North want when they travel to Southern shores does not boil down to sun, sea, and safaris guaranteed to include zebras and giraffes" (252). As the North/South opposition in this passage implies, it is economic dominance that allows the tourist to emerge victorious in this intercultural encounter, imposing its fantasies of the exotic landscape in a gesture that all but erases the reality of South African history.

Similarly, Condé's novel exposes the calculating distortions at work in this tourist economy by evoking another key site of South African violence: Robben Island. This island, "once a concentration camp, now transformed into an international tourist attraction" (1), figures briefly in the novel's opening passage, then returns through the testimony of one of Rosélie's clients. Dawid Fagwela, one of the only native South Africans seeking her counsel, is a former Robben Island prisoner who, in a particularly cynical maneuver on the part of the tourism bureau, wears a refashioned prisoner's uniform in his capacity as tour guide. As tourists eagerly collect photographic images of the prisons, Dawid is forced to relive incessantly his years of torture and mistreatment: "[From] describing it down to the last detail to the inquisitive hordes in an endeavor to satisfy their curiosity, the poor guy was losing his head. It woke him up at night" (24). The relentless desire of the tourist to consume this foreign land engenders not only the distortion of history through its crass commodification but also the destruction of this South African man's life, so that he is left to question whether his torture has truly come to an end: "Was apartheid really over? Was he really free?" (24).

Tourism is thus a cultural exchange violent enough to reawaken the terrors of the past, a phenomenon that wields its destructive force through the commodification of other cultures and histories. Since this destruction occurs primarily in the mode of *consumption*, the metaphorical link to the figure of the cannibal is difficult to ignore: like the fearsome cannibal, the tourist exhibits an insatiable desire to devour all that comes in its path, consuming other cultures to the point of extinction.[4] Indeed, the figurative significance of the tourist-as-consumer model is duly underscored in Condé's narrative, with its incriminating descriptions of greed and its sustained vocabulary of consumption. In the passage cited above, for example, the tourists' demand for added stimulation on their artificial African safari emerges in gastronomic terms: "They also need thrills and chills, a new version of *panem et circenses*, a gut-wrenching retrospective scare" (252). Just as the "bread and circuses" would placate the masses of ancient Rome, these contemporary visits to the South African ghetto are a means of satiation, providing the added sustenance with which the tourist masses will feed their cultural appetites. Condé's reference to antiquity here is a telling one, as it points to the element of spectacle in the tourist's experience (a performative dimension also signaled by Dawid Fagwela's perverse costume of prison garb) and underlines the link between consumption and the spectacle of violence: just as Roman appetites could be appeased by the sight of a man being torn to pieces by a beast or by a fellow man, the palates of South Africa's tourists demonstrate a particular propensity for the bloody battles fought on this foreign soil, for the "delicious horror" ["délicieuse horreur" (258–59)] such a history might offer. The archetypal tourist thus relegates violence and destruction to the cultural domain of the Other, all the while overlooking his own violent and destructive role in the repackaging and commodification of those foreign cultures.[5]

For the particular cannibal evoked in Condé's novel, as we have seen, the fascination of discovery coexists with an equally strong destructive instinct. Repeated demands for the execution of Fiéla reveal a bloodthirsty violence that blurs the distinction between accused and accuser. Particularly when the shocking news of Fiéla's verdict—a mere fifteen-year prison sentence—emerges, public outcry reaches a fever pitch. As the solicitor general bemoans the fact that the death penalty was abolished at the same time as apartheid, a crowd gathers outside the courthouse, once again recalling the moral framework of antiquity: "An eye for an eye . . . a tooth for a tooth. Kill the murderess. Cut her into little pieces like she had done to poor Adriaan" (264). The only fit punishment for Fiéla, the crowd reasons, would be to fall victim to her own crime. Lurking unspoken behind this reasoning is the suggestion of cannibalism as a logical extension of the formula, as surely this vengeance would only be complete if the pieces of Fiéla's body were devoured. Condé thus posits in no uncertain terms the inevitable circularity of such condemnations, the instinct to destroy that is doomed to blindly repeat the behavior it incriminates.

Fiéla, then, as her name suggests ("fiel" means "rancor" or "venom"), has an accusatory function in the novel, as an emblematic figure whose fate exposes the violent capacities of the society that excludes her. Fiéla's eyes, which first draw Rosélie's attention and which she will later capture in her artwork, stare out from the pages of the newspapers as an unwavering reflection of the injustices of her social world. In this sense Fiéla's gaze suggests an intriguing resonance with the gaze that closes

Peter Greenaway's filmic meditation on cannibalism, *The Cook, the Thief, His Wife and Her Lover.* As Crystal Bartolovich points out, the shift in camera angle in the closing shot of this film implicates the viewer in the vengeful act of the wife who, having commanded her husband, the eponymous thief, to eat her dead lover's flesh, proceeds to shoot him dead while uttering a single word: "cannibal." The implication of the viewer in this epithet, Bartolovich aptly notes, is disconcertingly ambiguous, suggesting an uneasy parallel between the viewing of this spectacle of violence and cannibalism itself.[6] When violence becomes spectacle for public consumption, when violence is met with matched violence, these gazes seem to report, the notion of civilization forgoes its constitutive opposition to savagery.

Imagining Cannibalism

Perhaps the most emblematic instance of the cannibal occurs in the context of the colonial encounter, where the European explorer makes his initial contact with unfamiliar territory, apprehensive of what he might find in this frightening but fascinating (and potentially profitable) new world. In many ways the notion of cannibalism encapsulates the dynamics of this encounter, since, as we have seen, it functions as a marker of radical difference from the familiar, as the most fundamental challenge to the European's understanding of himself and of humanity. Moreover, the figure of cannibal, since it poses a physical threat to the explorer's livelihood, signifies the extreme nature of the colonial adventure itself, the risks taken, the boundaries crossed in this bold enterprise of scientific, intellectual, and territorial conquest. Much like Barthes's "Bichon chez les nègres," the French baby surrounded by Africans whose image in *Paris-Match* left a European public breathless with terrified admiration at the bravery of his parents, the colonizer raises the suggestion of cannibalism as a marker of how very far he has been willing to travel away from the comforts of home. The cannibal is the colonial discovery par excellence, definitive proof of the radical otherness of what the fearless explorer has unveiled.

Indeed, as Peter Hulme's work has shown, the term "cannibal" has its origins in the early moments of colonial encounter. The first use of the term in a European text is attributed to the 1492 *Journal* of Christopher Columbus, as a reference to the *canibales,* a native Caribbean people purported to be fearsome and warlike and to engage in the consumption of their enemies (Hulme, 16–17). In fact, Columbus misunderstood or misheard his native informants, who were actually referring to the *caribes,* members of the neighboring Carib tribe.[7] But the association between the word *canibales* and the practice of eating human flesh, having been fixed by this moment of initial encounter, would of course persist well beyond the fifteenth century, "adopted," as Hulme puts it, "into the bosom of the European family of languages with a speed and readiness which suggests that there had always been an empty place kept warm for it" (19). The term's etymology thus captures linguistically the ways in which the notion of cannibalism is inscribed in the encounter with the exotic Other, with all of its attendant distortions, misreadings, and fantasies.

As Hulme and others have pointed out, moreover, the distortion of the term *canibales* is compounded by the fact that Columbus asserted the man-eating practices among the Caribs based not on direct observation but on secondhand reports in a language of which he had at best a rudimentary knowledge. Columbus would of course not be alone in this liberal approach to scientific inquiry: recent critiques of ethnographic exploration in numerous parts of the globe have revealed the extent to which such studies may have drawn exaggerated or distorted accounts of cannibalism in native populations. This criticism points in particular to the fact that the notion of discovering cannibals typically preceded the encounters themselves. Gananath Obeyesekere, for example, surveys eighteenth-century ethnographic study in the South Seas to point out the search for evidence of cannibalism as a primary motivating factor in such journeys. In his analysis of logs and journals from James Cook's meetings with the Hawaiians, he contests that reports on cannibalism in these texts "reveal more about the relations between Europeans and Savages during early and late contact than, as ethnographic statements, about the nature of Savage anthropophagy" (630–31). The reports expose in particular the preexisting desire on the part of the British explorers to confirm their suspicions of cannibalism, a desire that fundamentally influenced the ethnographic encounter. Exchanges with the native population, for example, were shot through with repeated questions concerning cannibalism, so that Cook and others, in looking for cannibalism everywhere they went, were sure to find it everywhere they looked.

The ethnographic encounter can thus reveal an obsessive preoccupation on the part of the European explorer, a preoccupation so persistent that it seems unlikely to have left the resulting documentation unaffected.[8] Indeed, as William Arens has argued, the desire to find cannibals seems to be so urgent as to allow a considerable amount of slippage to occur in profiles of the cultures under examination, effecting a kind of methodological paralysis when it comes to the question of cannibalism. In his controversial 1979 study, *The Man-Eating Myth,* Arens proposes that the practice of cannibalism on the part of non-Europeans is essentially a Western invention. He examines an extensive array of accounts of cannibalism, exposing the unusual lack of intellectual and methodological rigor employed in such accounts in comparison to other subjects of anthropological inquiry. In particular, Arens notes that, given the enormous amount of discussion concerning cannibalism, there is a surprising absence of eyewitness accounts of humans actually in the act of consuming other humans. Even when such accounts do appear, close examination of these claims reveals that the firsthand observation was in fact confined to events that might potentially precede or more often follow an act of cannibalism, and that the link between these events and actual cannibalism thus remained pure conjecture on the part of the author. In this sense, Arens concludes, the myth of cannibalism superseded the usual requirement of direct evidence of native behavior.[9] The act of anthropophagy—the consumption of human flesh by other humans—is thus exposed as a fabrication drawn from observations of other tangentially related behaviors, secondhand reports of cannibalism, and the preexisting assumption of cannibalism.

Given this critical background, it is difficult to overlook the absence of narrative describing the accused cannibal woman's crime in *Histoire de la femme cannibale.* Indeed, the portrayal of Fiéla's relationship to her public seems to mirror the colonial encounter, in that the association between Fiéla and the act of cannibalism, while nominatively explicit, can otherwise be made only by assumption and indirect reasoning. Thanks to the novel's title, the designation "la femme cannibale" precedes the introduction of Fiéla herself, its evocation leaving no room for doubt as to the nature of Fiéla's crime; but, meanwhile, in the narrative itself the description of this pivotal crime is glaringly absent. In Fiéla's first appearance in the novel, for example, the question of cannibalism is raised without being addressed directly: "A woman was accused of murdering her husband, who had been missing for several weeks. According to her son-in-law, who had become suspicious of the meat packed in plastic bags on the refrigerator shelves, she had cut him up into little pieces and frozen them. Why would be anybody's guess" (77). The final sentence of this account is particularly disingenuous in that while "all hypotheses were permitted" ["toutes suppositions étaient permises" (87)], there is clearly one hypothesis in particular that emerges quite forcefully from the preceding information; yet the responsibility for drawing this hypothesis—even for claiming its obviousness—lies with the reader. In an intriguing echo of the temporally contorted logic of ethnographic accounts of cannibalism, the conclusion that Fiéla is a cannibal is forgone by her public tag: much like the quest of the Western explorer, Fiéla's story has been overdetermined by a prediction of what will be found in it. The information offered by the victim's son, bolstered by this prediction, points overwhelmingly to the conclusion that Fiéla consumed her dead husband's flesh. All hypotheses may be permitted, but only one will fit.

Condé creates yet another parallel to colonial "discoveries" of cannibalism in this initial evocation of Fiéla by shifting to another *fait divers,* which Rosélie recalls immediately after reading about Fiéla, and which just happens to describe a case of cannibalism: "A Japanese student had murdered a twenty-one-year-old Dutch student. He had raped her dead body, cut it up, and eaten several pieces. Declared insane, he had been extradited to Japan" (78). Here, the detail with which the act of cannibalism is described provides a striking contrast to the account of Fiéla's crime. Much like prior reports of cannibalism that spurred on the Western explorers in their quest for cannibals, this account seems intended to somehow confirm the suspicions cast upon Fiéla. Since human flesh was consumed in the case of the Japanese student, the logic presumably would go, it is entirely reasonable to incriminate Fiéla based on the presence of cut-up flesh in her freezer. In this brief paragraph, then, Condé points out the particular way in which conclusions concerning cannibalism can be drawn: the unwitnessed details of Fiéla's story can materialize, unspoken but unmistakable, through the juxtaposition of two otherwise unrelated stories.

Condé thus exposes the desire on the part of this public to find cannibalism in Fiéla's story: members of this community are willing to forgo concrete evidence, firsthand accounts, and certainly Fiéla's own testimony in their urgent quest to condemn this woman's inhumanity. Fiéla's resolute silence throughout her trial, meanwhile, followed several days later by her suicide in prison, only underlines the impossibility of gaining any direct knowledge of her alleged crime. What remains will be the "documented" account of her cannibalism, an account fabricated from guesswork, secondhand accusations, and public imagination. By withholding direct description of the act of cannibalism, Condé underscores the lengths to which a fascinated public will go in order to compensate for this lack of firsthand evidence. But of course the incrimination suggested by this lacuna extends beyond the fictional public to the novel's audience: by leaving a gaping hole in the narrative, Condé forces the reader too to fill in gaps, to make connections, to draw conclusions. The novel's provocative title creates a desire, or at the very least an expectation, so that the reader, like the colonial explorer, is already looking for cannibalism before the journey has begun. Since the description of Fiéla's deed is left out, however, this desire can only identify its object through a preexisting familiarity with cannibalism: in order to attach the novel's title to the character of Fiéla, the readers must supply the missing link by imagining for themselves what Fiéla may have done with the pieces of plastic-wrapped flesh in the freezer. Fiéla's accusing gaze thus implicates not only the violence of her public, vociferously clamoring for her destruction, but also the epistemological leaps of the novel's readers who, by imagining cannibalism, reveal both the desire for the Other's monstrosity and their resulting participation in this monstrous creation.

Presumptions of Knowledge

For Rosélie, Fiéla represents a common figure of marginalization, a sympathetic companion in her moments of anger and resentment against the racist society that surrounds her. The protagonist's interest in Fiéla is also spurred, however, by a strong desire to understand more about this enigmatic "cannibal woman." She addresses Fiéla in the second person, attempting to trace out an exchange, however one-sided, with this silent soul mate. These imagined conversations are peppered with questions, ranging from the practical ("Do you have a lawyer? Is he gifted?" [131]) to the personal ("Did you ever cheat on Adriaan?" [167]). Upon learning of Fiéla's suicide, Rosélie inflects these questions with a new urgency, demanding an explanation for this unexpected act: "Did you think you were guilty? Or did you no longer have the heart to live?" (285). Rosélie frames the relationship with Fiéla as a quest for knowledge, an effort to understand a stranger, and, thanks to the connection she senses between them, an effort to understand herself.

The fact that the startling revelation toward which the narrative builds seems to expose a critical epistemological lacuna on the part of the protagonist, then, is all the more devastating. It seems that while Rosélie was focusing her attention on Fiéla and on her own solitude, she failed to correctly interpret the moment of greatest impact in her own life: Stephen's death. Despite the insistent questions of the police, Rosélie had accepted the most uncomplicated account of Stephen's final moments: that he had been attacked and killed by a common thief in search of cash. As Rosélie discovers during the course of the novel, however, Stephen's attacker was not a stranger, but a young man he had known through his students at the university, who, aware of the fact that Stephen had had sexual affairs with his male students, was attempting blackmail. As Stephen appeared for this exchange without the required payment, the conflict turned violent, ending in Stephen's murder.

The truth behind this apparently anonymous crime thus forces Rosélie to reassess the event of Stephen's death and by extension the entirety of their relationship. Her loss takes on an unexpected second meaning, as Stephen's murder simultaneously marks the end of her companion's life and the end of her understanding of the most recent chapter of her own. The twenty-year narrative she had fabricated for herself is suddenly revealed as painfully inadequate, presenting a reductive and distorted vision of her relationship with Stephen. Ultimately, then, the revelation to which the novel builds is only superficially the explanation of Stephen's murder, the more crucial discovery being Rosélie's realization of her own ignorance, of the extent of her own blindness concerning the person closest to her in the world. As the story she must now view as incomplete is also her own, the traumatic reversal provoked by this realization is all the more severe in that she must also acknowledge the limits of her own self-knowledge.

Stephen's hidden narrative is not only adultery but also homosexuality. In this respect his secret suggests a striking parallel to Fiéla's, as a narrative that provokes intense social anxiety. By juxtaposing these two hidden narratives, Condé's novel draws on the common phobias signaled by cannibalism and homosexuality, phobias concerning the transgression of social boundaries between self and other, sameness and difference. As Caleb Crain argues, cannibalism and homosexuality subvert the function of the body as a marker of such boundaries, violating "the distinctions between identity and desire; between self and other; between what we want, what we want to be, and what we are" (34). This confusion of boundaries accounts for the combined fascination and repulsion provoked by cannibalism and homosexuality, the "unspeakable" status of these narratives obscuring unavowed desires as much as it does their transgressive nature.[10]

For Condé's protagonist, Fiéla's unspoken narrative seems to function in much the same way, as a replacement for Stephen's. Rosélie's intense engagement with Fiéla punctuates the novel as a counterpoint to her lack of involvement with the complexities of Stephen's life, underscoring the attention she offers to a woman she has never met as an attention she failed to direct to her companion of twenty years. Throughout the weeks following the murder, Rosélie avidly pursues Fiéla's story, seeking it out, incorporating it into her own, while Stephen's secret remains a stone unturned. Instead of attempting to uncover the transgressions of her companion, Rosélie directs her quest for knowledge toward another "unspeakable" narrative, another strangely fascinating unknown. Cannibalism thus replaces homosexuality in her life as an inaccessible narrative, until the final revelation that highlights their common epistemological function.

In fact, the parallel between the two narratives extends to the dubious nature of their inaccessibility; for the revelation of Stephen's hidden life is neither as sudden nor as unexpected as Rosélie might claim. The novel's narrative structure follows Rosélie's thoughts as she makes her way through her daily life of unfamiliar solitude, and thus affords frequent and extensive glimpses of the past. Rosélie's reflections on her relationship with Stephen reveal not only the anxieties inherent to the interracial couple but, more specifically, a persistent sense of disjuncture between her perception of the relationship and his, or between her perception and that her friends and acquaintances. Throughout their life together appear signs of myopic vision on her part, evidence of the fact that all may not have been as it seemed. While Rosélie's admiration for Stephen is apparently boundless, for example, nearly all of her close friends admit either before or after his death that they found him an inappropriate match, manipulative and authoritative. One tells her of Stephen's constant need to control people, while another, after some hesitation, proclaims, "He was an egoist and a despot. He prevented you from being yourself" (150). Each of these interactions seems to stun Rosélie, sending her into a spiral of self-doubt as she wonders how the impressions of these close friends could be so radically different from her own. Often her response is physical; she experiences a sudden nausea, or shivers at the awareness of an entire identity unbeknown to her.

Ultimately, these criticisms of Stephen come together to provoke a rereading of their relationship as a whole: "Dominique first of all. Then Fina. Ariel. Simone and her husband. Amy and Caleb. Alice and Andy. Olu Ogundipe. Mrs. Hillster. Rosélie made the roll call of those who had criticized Stephen as if summoning them to a tribunal. What were they accusing him of? Of hiding something, of being a despot, an insensitive, domineering manipulator, a racist even? All these accusations that drew a picture as sketchy as a police profile led her nevertheless to call into question their entire life together" (219–20). Here the long list of names functions as an accumulation of signs whose meaning Rosélie was unable or unwilling to confront individually, but whose collective force points to the question she can only now bring herself to ask: "What had happened that night?" (222).

When, after this crucial moment of interrogation, Rosélie begins to investigate Stephen's death in earnest, it becomes clear that her friends' censorious remarks were not the only signs foreshadowing Stephen's hidden identity. In fact, it seems that many of the answers to her questions concerning Stephen already exist as part of her own memory. The name of a young student in whom Stephen had taken a particular interest, for example, suddenly "springs up" ["surgi[t]" (231)] in her mind as she attempts to retrace what she knew of Stephen's intellectual relationships: "His name had remained lurking in the folds of her memory, ready to emerge into broad daylight at the slightest call" (224–25). Similarly, Rosélie's body seems to lead her to one of the crucial points in the trail to the killer: "Rosélie walked off in the direction of the Threepenny Opera without realizing it. It was as if her body were obeying orders from her brain without her knowing it" (266). The truth of Stephen's murder and hidden life is thus not as distant as Rosélie may have imagined. On the contrary, her body, her brain, her memory seem to have retained traces of this information, traces of an entire narrative that she needed only to recover.

The questions Rosélie asks during her search for the truth betray a similar duplicity. Questions are not, of course, neutral, as they point to specific potential answers to be confirmed or denied, and thus reveal a hypothesis on the part of the questioner. This subjective investment is particularly clear when Rosélie dares to approach even indirectly the possibility of Stephen's homosexuality, as she confronts Chris Nkosi, the former student whose name had inexplicably emerged from her memory. The question she puts to him, "What exactly was there between you two?" (250), attempts to say nothing while it asks everything, but as Chris ably points out to her, the pretension is disingenuous. By asking her directly, "What do you mean?" (250), or, in a literal translation, "What do you want to say?" ["Qu'est-ce que vous voulez dire?" (256)], Chris returns the meaning of her question back to her, forcing her to recognize the precise suspicion that motivated it: "She was already frightened and ashamed of her question" (250). Although Chris ultimately responds that there was "nothing" between himself and Stephen, his retort, and Rosélie's shame, underlines the extent to which preexisting information and suspicions predict the meaning of any question, and therefore of its answer. In this instance, the brief exchange between Rosélie and

Chris, ostensibly a means for Rosélie to make new discoveries, ultimately divulges far more about Rosélie than it does about Chris or Stephen.

The process of slow revelation that structures this novel thus traces less Rosélie's apprehension of facts than the realization of her *knowledge* of Stephen's double life. The truth she was most reluctant to confront was not Stephen's duplicity per se but rather her own awareness of this alternate reality. Her persistent questions, her frightening confrontations with Stephen's past, were thus strategies of postponement, part of a false search designed to obscure her knowledge of the truth: "As for Stephen, deep down inside her, in that part where the light of truth never ventures, she had to admit that she had always known who he was. . . . She had simply chosen to ignore the evidence" (273). The ostensibly unknown Other is thus not external but internal, not unknown but unacknowledged. While the path toward knowledge may appear to be directed outward toward an exterior world, here it is ultimately an inward process of self-revelation, and the unspeakable horror that is the Other is in fact the untold horror of the self.

The false premise of Rosélie's investigation is particularly apparent in the scene that is posited as its climactic moment, when Rosélie finally confronts Dido, her closest confidante, for confirmation of her suspicions about Stephen:

> "You knew, didn't you?"
> Immediately Dido's expression clouded over. As if she had been waiting for this question for days. . . .
> "What did I know?" she asked.
> "Stephen," Rosélie simply murmured. (274)

Here the simple pronouncement of Stephen's name signifies all that Rosélie wishes to ask, provoking Dido's confession, not of the information itself, but of her *knowledge* of that information, and her reasons for keeping it secret: "You never mentioned it, so I never dared bring it up. It was beyond me. . . . I said to myself she must know. So she accepts it? Can one accept something like that?" (275). Dido's passionate tears seem to signal the momentousness of this statement, as the physical manifestation of a shift from duplicity to transparency. For Rosélie too this is a defining moment, when she can finally confront the truth of what everyone, including herself, seems to have known in secret all along: "There! I've said it" (275) ["C'était dit!" (281)]. Despite this triumphant statement of catharsis, however, the dialogue itself makes it quite clear that in fact "it" has not been said at all, but gingerly implied in the most indirect means possible. The only semblance of a direct reference to "it" is through an intriguingly unspecified use of the comparative: "it" is "such a thing" ["pareille chose" (280)], apparently similar to other "things" one might find difficult to accept. What has actually been "said" in this conversation, of course, is that Dido knew of Stephen's hidden life. As before, Rosélie's question does not arise from ignorance, but reflects a knowledge she already possesses; her goal is not to hear of Stephen's infidelities themselves, but to see her knowledge of them reflected in Dido.

Without underplaying the taboo-induced anxiety that generates the lacunae in Rosélie and Dido's conversation, it seems important to note, given the mutual shadowing of cannibalism and homosexuality in this novel, that any direct reference to Stephen's sexuality is entirely *unnecessary* to the two women's exchange of information. Stephen's sexual relationships with other men, although they are ostensibly the subject of this conversation, can also be entirely left out of it, precisely because, as we have seen, the narrative already exists in the minds of both Rosélie and Dido. The status of their conversation as a "successful" and revelatory exchange of information thus betrays the extent to which the notion of Stephen's sexuality is very much preconceived. Just as Rosélie's shame in questioning Chris reveals an already well-formed suspicion, the certainty with which she seems to believe that "it had been said" in her conversation with Dido signals the fact that a preexisting knowledge replaces the need for an explicit narrative. Just as the lacunae of Condé's novel force us to acknowledge the images of cannibalism we can easily supply to fill them, the blank spaces of Rosélie's narrative signal all that she has already been able to imagine. The narratives of cannibalism and homosexuality are in this sense not necessarily unspeakable but more importantly unspoken, relegated to irrelevance, precluded by imagined notions of the Other.

Hypocrite lecteur

The novel closes on an affirmative note: Rosélie, having abandoned her artwork during her months of confusion and solitude, finally takes up the brush again. This time, she will paint Fiéla, beginning with the impenetrable set of eyes that so impressed her the first time she saw this woman's photograph in the newspaper. Uncharacteristically, she already has a title for this work: "This time, she knew what her title would be. She had found it even before she had started. It had welled up from deep inside her on the crest of a raging tide: *Cannibal Woman*" (311). While the certainty conveyed by this ability to name her work before it is complete seems a hopeful omen of future artistic fulfillment, the gesture also recalls the extent to which invention represents a fundamental dimension of Rosélie's relationship with Fiéla.[11] Much as the events and locations pointing the way to Stephen's secret "rise up" from Rosélie's cerebral depths, the knowledge necessary for completing the current artistic project seems already to exist within her. Rosélie literally invents Fiéla's story, imagining thoughts and details that correspond to her own vision of this apparent soul mate. Her insistent questions go answered but ultimately need no answer, since they reflect in themselves all that Rosélie knows or will know about this stranger. Much as the cannibal is named even before the moment of colonial contact, the title of Rosélie's painting supplants an image that already exists in her mind; it is a point of departure masquerading as an endpoint, an invention disguised as a discovery. The identities of Rosélie and Fiéla are indeed meshed, their stories mingled, not because of a common plight of social ostracism, but because they share the same source: Rosélie, a true reflection of the cannibal woman, has consumed Fiéla's story as her own.

By repeatedly invoking the language and modalities of cannibalism in her novel, Condé thus recalls the legacies of colonial power hierarchies as they are inscribed in the lives of these women in their late-twentieth-century existences. The challenge posed by Fiéla and Rosélie's relationship, however, is that it also goes beyond this colonial inscription to explore the contingencies and fluctuations of power hierarchies at stake in this globalized post-Apartheid setting. Reading one-dimensionally through the lens of postcolonial theories of cannibalism thus falls short of accounting for the particular modes through which Condé's characters experience, reflect, imagine, and repeat the violence of incorporation. Indeed, Rosélie's painstakingly detailed experiences of racism and marginalization place the postcolonial reader in the awkward position of either aligning an ostracized black woman with the colonial explorer in order to critique her appropriation of Fiéla's story, or redeeming her gesture as a vengeful reversal of colonial power structures, a framework of "writing back" that would attribute the role of the "centre" to the already demonized and silent Fiéla. By multiplying the novel's cannibalizing gestures in unpredictable directions, Condé frustrates the postcolonial reader's expectations of finding a heroic self-liberating cannibal and a unilateral condemnation of the West, refuting that reader's preexisting knowledge of cannibalism with incoherent and unpalatable reflections.

While Rosélie's insistent identification with Fiéla is the sign of her cannibalizing proclivities, then, that identification is also paradoxically what exposes the limits of postcolonial readings of the novel. The doubling of Fiéla and Rosélie, and the inscription of a mutual condition of marginality into their narrative of cannibalism, forms an obstacle to the culturally mapped power structures that inhere in postcolonial studies and exposes the reluctance in such interpretations to censure a subject whose racial and historical identification places her on the side of the oppressed. To see Rosélie simultaneously as the object of colonially informed injustices and as the perpetrator of ethically suspect distortions, in other words, presents a notion of transcultural and contingent power dynamics that exceeds the purview of postcolonialism. In this respect, Rosélie's exaggerated claims of empathy with her subaltern soul mate can be read parodically, as an implicit reference to the conflation of marginalized subjects. Her mingling of her own identity with Fiéla's ("She could be me") suggests a mocking appropriation and distortion of the collapsing of difference effected by critiques of colonialism: read through the binary filter of West and Other, she and Fiéla might as well be the same person. Rosélie's artistic appropriation, then, suggests not a protest against colonial domination in the vein of literary cannibalism, but a demystification of postcolonial fantasies of the "untouchable" marginal subject, of the cannibalistic inclination to replace difference with sameness.

Conclusion

Signs of Translation

GIVEN THE significant overlap between postcolonial studies and Anglo-American critical theory, the fact that many of the assessments of Condé's work that I have discussed in this study are readings of the English translations of her novels adds an important dimension to the critical dialogue she undertakes in her fiction. With a few exceptions, British translator Richard Philcox has been the sole executor of this task, producing skillful and widely appreciated English renditions of Condé's diverse linguistic and geographical inspirations. It is thus, to put it in radical Spivakian terms, Philcox's work as much as it is Condé's that has made its way into postcolonial literature courses, women's studies courses, and Caribbean studies courses across university campuses; into dissertations, journal articles, and anthologies; into bookstores and libraries. Even as Condé is paired with Assia Djebar or Ousmane Sembene as a "Francophone" writer, or gratefully included in an English- and Spanish-dominated Caribbean literature course by virtue of her linguistic difference, translation has been in many ways the primary vehicle of her impressive rise to recognition and her international stature as writer and critic.

The betrayals and infidelities of translation have been abundantly explored by translators, writers, and critics alike. Since the "cultural turn" in translation studies in the 1990s, points of intersection with the field of postcolonial studies have brought particular attention to the metaphorical utility of translation as a way to assess the aftermath of colonial contact: here translation is akin to imperialism, its very origins, as Susan Bassnett and Harish Trivedi assert, located in colonialism, its process of renaming and substitution a textual realization of territorial conquest.[1] Emily Apter foregrounds the question of marketing, where in the Anglophone-driven postcolonial publishing world the process of selection becomes grounds for the distortion or destruction of minority languages. The problem of cultural commodification thus compounds the desire to acknowledge not only the failure of reproduction that inheres in all literary translation but also the betrayal effected by the suppression of minority cultures. Hence, as Lawrence Venuti advocates "visible" translators and "foreignizing" translations that refuse to let the reader forget that the work at hand has been deformed by the violent act of translation, others foreground transformation rather than equivalence, "skewage" rather than duplication, alterity before transparency, in an effort to impede however minimally the distortion of other voices and the tide of monolingual consumerism.[2]

In some ways Philcox makes himself an easy target for the kinds of accusations generated by this critical discussion. In interviews and translator's prefaces, he has repeatedly expressed loyalty to a metropolitan readership, and boldly claims Virginia Woolf and Bruce Chatwin over V. S. Naipaul and Gabriel García Márquez as inspirations for his translations of Condé.[3] On the politically loaded topic of Creole, he is equally unflappable, as evidenced in his preface to *Crossing the Mangrove*:

> What was I going to do with all those Creole expressions? How was I going to render this most Guadeloupean of Maryse Condé's novels into English? How was I going to translate those distortions of the French language that Creole is so fond of making and at the same time poke fun at standard, academic French? I could have researched the English-speaking West Indian equivalents of many Creole expressions, but this would have distanced the reader from the French and Creole-speaking environment of Guadeloupe and transported him or her to Barbados or Jamaica. I could have invented words in English (I did in one or two cases) but I (and even less the author) have no quarrel with the English language on the same level as Creole quibbles with French. (viii)

Leaving aside the question of Condé's quarrel with the English language for the moment, it is interesting to note that Philcox explicitly rejects recourse to geography as a strategy for translational fidelity. While he does acknowledge the friction embodied by Creolized French through his own liberties (or quibbles) with the English language, his strategy is only occasionally the substitution of words from a neighboring Anglophone island for their Guadeloupean Creole "equivalents." Instead, he places a premium on tone and rhythm rather than lexical markers of geographical specificity, underscoring the cultural, linguistic, and geographical distance between and among Caribbean islands rather than the kind of generalized or "submarine" unity envisioned by Brathwaite.[4]

As problematic as the impulse toward transparency in Philcox's work and statements may be in the context of postcolonial translation studies, however, his comments serve to illuminate the regional essentialism that would necessarily undergird the parallelism of Guadeloupean Creole and Jamaican Creole: the suggestion that sets up an equivalence between the two languages implies that the postcolonial Calibanesque reversals of linguistic dominance would somehow approximate each other enough to be interchangeable, thus (paradoxically) preserving the regional particularism of the original. Jamaican is to English as Guadeloupean is to French, the logic would presumably go, and the "effect" for the English-speaking reader of the translation will approximate that of the French-speaking reader of the original. But, as we have seen, one reclaimed difference dissolves another: in the search for a strategy that illuminates the geographically specific colonial history with which language is infused, differences internal to that region fall out of the frame of consideration. In this respect the argument for regional parallelism seems strikingly similar to the simplistic models of translational politics that superimpose colonial binaries at will or, as Emily Apter writes, that "idealize the minority language as an object of ecological preservationism" ("On Translation," 7).

The title of Richard Philcox's English translation of Condé's *La migration des cœurs* offers an informative example of this relationship between linguistic friction and geographical particularism. Philcox's *Windward Heights,* published by Soho Press in 1998, echoes phonetically and lexically the title of Condé's "cannibalized" novel, Brontë's *Wuthering Heights,* while inscribing a Caribbean space: the term "windward" refers, as Philcox himself has noted, to the division of the region into the Windward Islands that bear the first force of the area's northeast trade winds and the more protected Leeward Islands.[5] While on the whole the translator's use of this felicitous resonance has met with critical approbation, Roger Little objects that the tone struck by the new title, if resonant, is inaccurate because "Guadeloupe is one of the Leeward, rather than the Winward [*sic*] islands" (15n2). Against the backdrop of postcolonial translation criticism, Little's correction suggests that, in his overanxious wish to speak to an Anglophone audience, Philcox peremptorily dispensed with geographical accuracy, and further that the translational success of the title *Windward Heights* depends upon the metropolitan British or U.S. reader's readiness to ascribe an equivalence between the word "windward" and an undifferentiated Caribbean, rather than a knowledge of the particular geographical demarcations of the region's colonial history.

The critique put forward by Little does indeed point out an approximation that seems illustrative of the kinds of misreadings and distortions wrought by culturally exterior translations.[6] But the accusation betrays its own approximations. While the "Windward Islands" do conventionally designate the islands in the southern arc of the Lesser Antilles, and thus do not include Guadeloupe, the assumption that the novel's title *should* evoke the island of Guadeloupe in particular seems a bit hasty. Although the better part of *La migration des cœurs*'s events take place in Guadeloupe, the movement or "migration" signaled by the novel's (original) title might attribute equal thematic importance to sites exterior to the island. Along these lines we could read "Windward" as a reference not to Guadeloupe but to its southern neighbor Dominica, the locus of the novel's fourth chapter which takes place in the capital Roseau and whose section entitled "Season of Migration" ["Saison de Migration"] suggests an additional eponymous affiliation.[7] Alternatively, the "Windward" of the English title could be taken to refer, not to the Windward Islands, but to the Windward Passage separating Haiti from Cuba, thereby evoking the Cuban site of the novel's opening chapter, in many ways the signature moment of Condé's thematic displacement of Brontë.

Without dismissing the potential subsumption of geographical precision to phonetic resonance, then, it nevertheless seems important to consider the restriction implied by Little's remark. The fidelity it demands suggests a confinement of the "Heights" of this translated cannibalization to the landscape of Guadeloupe, endorsing an epistemological abbreviation that conflates writer and text with geography, that reads a Guadeloupean writer's text as a work about Guadeloupe. While the call for geographical and cultural accuracy in nonmetropolitan spaces is indispensable, Condé's work reminds us that the metropolitan penchant for cultural synecdoche in the reading of postcolonial texts might be equally as problematic as historical imprecision. Through the framework of Condé's critical incorporations, the critique of Philcox's eponymous gesture can be seen as a reminder of the constraints imposed by hurried claims to postcolonial fidelity.

Indeed, it is a tribute to the originality of Condé's work that the most conspicuous and unavoidable "loss" effected by Philcox's translations is not the suppression of a fragile endangered language, but instead the textual material he leaves untouched: Condé's persistent and unprecedented use of English and Anglo-American references in a Francophone oeuvre. If the fluid British English of Philcox's translations dilutes some of the tensions of Condé's Creolized French, it also erases the "foreignness" of these Anglophone inscriptions in her work, if necessarily at differing degrees depending on the regional, historical, and political inflection of a given allusion. In *The Last of the African Kings*, for example, Philcox's translation of *Les derniers rois mages,* the politics of everyday life on Crocker Island, South Carolina, are rendered through the skeptical eyes of Spéro, a transplanted Guadeloupean still at odds with his American surroundings after twenty years. For him, English is the language of street signs, coffee shops, music, and conversation; but it is also the language of his wife, Debbie, an African American historian whose ideological positions on racial solidarity form a source of marital discord. As the following passage suggests, the apprehension Spéro experiences in the face of his wife's dogmatism is inseparable from its linguistically marked cultural history:

> Ken venait souvent passer les week-ends à Crocker Island. . . . Ses visites, c'était le triomphe et la revanche de Debbie. Sur sa sœur, sur Spéro, sur Anita, sur toute l'existence en vérité. Elle retrouvait foi en elle-même. Elle gavait le garçon des mythes et des clichés dont elle avait gavé Anita et que des individus tels que Farah et Charles Thomas Jr avaient vainement tenté d'oublier. Quant à Spéro, qui faisait profession de s'en moquer, on voyait bien à quoi il ressemblait! *Let my people go. Up you mighty race. We return fighting. We shall overcome. I have a dream. Free at last.* Ken ingurgitait tout cela avec dévotion. (143–44)

> [Ken often came to spend weekends at Crocker Island. . . . His visits were Debbie's triumph and revenge: on her sister, on Spero, on Anita, on her entire existence, in fact. She regained faith in herself. She stuffed the boy with the myths and clichés with which she had stuffed Anita and which people such as Farah and Charles Thomas Jr. had vainly tried to forget. As for Spero, who spent his life making fun of people, you can see how he ended up! *Let my people go. Up you mighty race. We return fighting. We shall overcome. I have a dream. Free at last.* Ken lapped it all up devotedly.] (93)

That the paradigmatic phrases of the civil rights movement are left in the original English in Condé's passage is as much a nod to their global circulation as it is an indication of the political divide between Spéro and Debbie. But, as Condé underlines here, this is a circulation attained through a series of sound bites, a set of "myths and clichés" diluted and repeated for easy consumption. Given the emphasis on the language of ingestion ("gaver," "ingurgiter") in this passage, Spéro's rebellion against Debbie's ideologies can be seen as a refusal to eat, a refusal to consume the sound bites of racial solidarity. It is in this respect that the untranslated state of these phrases is significant: their linguistic difference signals

Spéro's unwillingness to assimilate them—to ingest them—into his narrative. And it is precisely this untranslated use of English that is necessarily absent in English translations of Condé. Although the italicized phrases in Philcox's translation open up an entirely new politics of recognition within their English-speaking audience,[8] the resulting monolingualism of the passage mitigates the role of language in the fractured ideological politics of the African diaspora. While the inscribed encounter between French and English is but one of Condé's many bilingualisms, it is the one that is most fundamentally altered by the English translations of her work.

Condé's "ingestion" of English in her fiction, moreover, covers a wide cultural spectrum and goes far beyond the lexical. In this regard it is useful to return to the consideration of Philcox's eponymous translation of *La migration des cœurs* as a more intricate example of the "Anglicization" of Condé's texts through translation. For Philcox's *Windward Heights,* as we have seen, not only inscribes a Caribbean geography into the novel's title but also marks a "return" to the original material of Condé's cannibalization, signaling Brontë's *Wuthering Heights* in a way that Condé's "Migration of the Hearts" explicitly neglects to do. While the already less accessible title of a British classic was obscured for the French-speaking readership, then, Philcox's rendition translates by unveiling the concealed object of Condé's cannibalization. Philcox's comments on this choice are revealing, moreover, in that they evoke the politics of marketing that have been a recent preoccupation in postcolonial studies: he explains that "something had to speak to the English-speaking reader of that other text, *Wuthering Heights,* which echoes throughout the book" ("Translating," 80). Although this remark concerns translation from one "metropolitan" language to another, it is also strikingly reminiscent of the kinds of paratextual negotiations that are undertaken in the "packaging" of postcolonial or Third World texts for First World consumption, where the importance of "speaking to" the audience is paramount.[9] More often than not, this question of "relevance" is satisfied by the proclaimed universality of the minority text's themes and preoccupations, by qualities that will reassuringly transcend the particular. Philcox's concern for the "relevance" of Condé's novel to the English-speaking reader thus presents an interesting twist on this formula, in that the recognition upon which this perceived relevance will hinge is the cannibalized text of Emily Brontë, a reflection of the English-speaking audience's own literary canon. The "universal," in this case (as in so many cases), is the particular in disguise; the text will "speak" to them because it is already about them.

The "return" to English exhibited by the translations of Condé's work, and the losses engendered by that return, thus serves to underscore the uniquely crafted bilingualism of Condé's Anglophone borrowings. If Condé has, as Emily Apter claims, "exchange[d] a French literary genealogy for a British one" ("Condé's *Créolité*," 437), she has done so on the most intricate of terms, making the condition of that new British genealogy a committed if tendentious coexistence with the old French one. Given that the inscription of British literature into her fiction occurs so often in the mode of rewriting, or "literary cannibalism," Condé also seems to point back to the genealogy of postcolonial studies itself: her duplication of the "Empire Writes Back" model of postcolonial literature recalls one of the crucial self-defining moments in the field's history.[10] Rather than enacting a parallel imitation of this gesture, however, by interrogating the major works of her own French literary education, Condé deliberately crosses into the linguistic and cultural territory of the paradigmatic postcolonial text, incorporating the revisionary move and reflecting it back as a bilingual project.

In this sense Condé's approximation of the "Empire Writes Back" model is perhaps a little *too* close, confusing the binaries of postcolonialism by implying that a Francophone writer might have two "centres" to write back to: British and French. Condé's critical incorporation of postcolonial rewriting, then, offers as usual a slightly distorted reflection; in this case, it is that very distortion that puts the question of language at the forefront, exposing through its bilingual difference the monolingualism of the model. Given the widespread criticism drawn by postcolonial studies' Anglophone roots in the study of "Commonwealth" literature and its continued domination by the English language, Condé's critique makes an important intervention into current reflections on the shape of the discipline. That her critique is raised by a Francophone voice is also germane, since recent works have focused in particular on the gap between postcolonial studies and Francophone studies, whereby the latter field is considered either an analogy or a forgotten subset of the former, and where the politics of translation severely compromise the relationship between the two.[11]

But despite its potential insolence, Condé's gesture is not, I would argue, the simple condemnation of postcolonial studies' persistent monolingualism. For the aim of such recent works as *Francophone Postcolonial Studies, Postcolonial Theory and Francophone Literary Studies,* and *Littératures postcoloniales et francophonie* is primarily to restore a missing dialogue, one that reconsiders the foundational role of Fanon,

Barthes, and Derrida in postcolonial theory, that brings Bhabha and Spivak into the analysis of Francophone literature, and that rejects language as a principle of disciplinary self-definition.[12] In this respect we might see Condé's work, and Philcox's translations, as key contributions to this project, contributions that embody the exchange between English and French and examine the precepts of postcolonial theory through the lens of that linguistic exchange. By performing a bilingual genealogy of postcolonialism, Condé's literary oeuvre seems to affirm the importance of a continuing dialogue between Francophone studies and postcolonial studies, just as its critical incorporations point the way toward conceptual precision and theoretical rigor in postcolonial approaches to literature.

Notes

Introduction

1. For more on this debate, see Taylor.

2. See Arnold.

3. See Hewitt, *Autobiographical Tightropes*, 168.

4. See Condé, "Unheard Voice" and "Des héros et des cannibales." This literary strategy is discussed further in chapter 7.

5. Further biographical background can be found in Mekkawi and Pfaff. Prizes awarded to Condé include the Grand Prix Littéraire de la Femme (1987), the Prix Puterbaugh (1993), the Prix Carbet de la Caraïbe (1997), the Prix Marguerite Yourcenar (1999), and the Hurston/Wright Legacy Award (2005).

6. Ann Scarboro makes this important point in her afterword to the novel's English translation (187).

7. See Barbour and Herndon; Broichhagen, Lachman, and Simek; and Cottenet-Hage and Moudileno. Other works focusing entirely or partially on Condé's fiction are Kemedjio, McKay, Pfaff, and Suk.

8. Scharfman, "Au sujet d'héroïnes péripatétiques."

9. In her important recent essay, Lydie Moudileno observes that Condé's reputation for insolence has become so defining that she now paradoxically faces the expectation that she surprise her readers ("Positioning the 'French' 'Caribbean' 'Woman' Writer," 144).

10. Condé has, however, expressed a due amount of frustration with the relentless attention offered to the intransigent aspect of her work. See for example "Moi, Maryse Condé," 126.

11. See Cooppan and Shohat. On the exclusion of women from postcolonial theory, see for example McClintock.

12. On the collective projections of postcolonial theory, see Seshadri-Crooks. On problems with the term "globalization," see Amireh and Majaj, Trouillot's discussion of globalization as a "fuzzy word" in "The Perspective of the World," and Appadurai.

13. See in particular Mohanty, "Under Western Eyes," and Mohanty, Russo, and Torres. For an in-depth study of the reception of Rigoberta Menchú, see Stoll.

14. In "Eating the Other," bell hooks writes that "within commodity culture, ethnicity becomes spice, seasoning that can liven up a dull dish that is mainstream white culture" (179). See also Huggan, especially 1–33.

15. See in particular Lionnet, "*Logiques métisses*"; Serres; and Walker's helpful analysis of Serres (206–7). Lionnet has also proposed the term "transcolonial" as a way of rethinking cross-regional resonances (see "Transnationalism, Postcolonialism, or Transcolonialism?"). On transnationalism see also Cohen and Dever.

16. Shohat similarly contends that the term "hybridity" is "susceptible to a blurring of perspectives" and "fails to discriminate between the diverse modalities of hybridity" (110). See also Palumbo-Liu's critique of "universal hybridization" (62), Werbner, and Yuval-Davis. This critique does not always overlook, however, numerous efforts to preserve the internal heterogeneity and divergent modes of syncretic identities, or more generally the concerted engagement with the very problem of ahistoricism in recent theoretical discussions. Dirlik, for example, points out various attempts to define historically and structurally distinct hybridities by such theorists as Paul Gilroy, Stuart Hall, and Gayatri Spivak ("Bringing History," 105). See also Rosello, *Practices of Hybridity*, and Robert J. C. Young.

17. See Spivak, *Critique of Postcolonial Reason*, 260.

18. Said, 59.

19. Bart Moore-Gilbert discusses the split between postcolonial theory and literary criticism that marked the 1990s in *Postcolonial Theory* (5–33).

20. See Jameson, "Third-World Literature," and Ahmad.

1. After Essentialism

1. A recent insightful piece by Nick Nesbitt in the *Romanic Review* has done much to repair this critical gap. Nesbitt too argues against an overly neat separation between fiction and nonfiction in Condé's oeuvre: "In my view, the entirety of her work is very precisely the continuation of the methodological investigation we find in [her] early scholarly texts" (398).

2. This 1988 lecture was published in 1994 as "Pan-Africanism, Feminism and Culture."

3. See also Condé's interview with Françoise Pfaff, where she again praises Naipaul's capacity to unsettle his public: "I believe we live in a world that has a victimization complex. People like to comfort one another. It's not their fault if they are what they are. Naipaul simply felt like making a big splash by saying that victims were also guilty. I like this boisterous side of him. Naipaul writes this way in order to disturb good consciences" (109).

4. "Rassurer," *Trésor de la langue française*, 401–3.

5. Condé cites Proust's passage as the following: "Les beaux textes sont toujours écrits dans une sorte de langue étrangère" (cited in "Métissage," 214), although the actual line reads: "Les beaux livres sont écrits dans une sorte de langue étrangère" (297); Great literature is written in a sort of foreign tongue (267).

6. On the link between the dream and artistic creativity in Condé's fiction, see also Moudileno, "Portrait of the Artist."

7. "My title was criticized for being hermetic. Hermetic for whom? Malinke is spoken in almost all of West Africa: Guinea, Mali, the Ivory Coast, Sierra Leone, a little in Senegal" (*Parole des femmes,* 129).

8. The complete title as it appears on the cover of the second edition is *En attendant le bonheur (Heremakhonon),* reversing the sequence between original and revision as if to supply a translation of the French title for Malinke readers.

9. "In theory, this store offered everything people needed, but it had nothing except Chinese toys of poor quality. For me it was a symbol of independence" (Pfaff, 39). In the same interview, Condé adds an unanticipated connection to this proper name: "I found out much later that Hérémakhonon is also the name of a Malian city where Samori is said to have fought" (39).

10. On the precocity of the skeptical viewpoint in *Heremakhonon,* see Apter, "Crossover Texts," 89–91. On the negative critical reaction to this viewpoint, see Ngate; Pfaff, 42 and 46; and Scarboro, 205. Ironically, according to Condé's 1997 interview with Leah Hewitt, some of this criticism presented Véronica herself as a stereotype: "The Africans considered this character to be a stereotype of an Antillean who doesn't understand anything, and doesn't want to understand anything, about Africa" (549).

11. On Véronica's pattern of alienation, see Arlette Smith and Murdoch.

12. "The novel can perhaps be described as staging a timing which is in conflict with a time that belongs to the mental theatre of the protagonist. To read it only in terms of the central character ignores this possibility (Spivak, "Staging of Time," 88).

13. See for example *Heremakhonon,* 17, 51, 87. On Véronica's political detachment, see also Lionnet, *Autobiographical Voices,* 177, and Spivak, "Staging of Time," 87.

14. See for example Lionnet, *Autobiographical Voices,* 179–83, 194; Murdoch, 581–82; and Clark, "Developing Diaspora Literacy," 306. Christopher Miller insists that this hermeticism not be taken for silence or passivity, but for a powerful expression of irony and conflict (174–79).

15. Spivak gives an extensive analysis of this friction in "Staging of Time" (see in particular 86–90).

16. Clark counts "more than one hundred and twenty-five allusions, both explicit and indirect" in Condé's novel ("Developing Diaspora Literacy," 307). On this topic see also Herndon; Hewitt, *Autobiographical Tightropes,* 178–79; and Lionnet, *Autobiographical Voices,* 174.

17. As Spivak asserts, thanks to the multiple layers of historical and geographical meaning inherent in such proper names, "th[e] text is hybridized not merely by the provenance of the heroine" ("Staging of Time," 89).

18. On this function of the proper name, see in particular Clarkson, 41–42, and Ragussis.

19. Clarisse Zimra characterizes this nominal substitution as an interference with Véronica's understanding of her father as well as of the "real live Africans of her daily life" (236).

20. See for example Condé, *En attendant le bonheur,* 11–12.

21. See Spivak, "Staging of Time," 88.

22. On Condé's use of cliché, see also Hewitt, *Autobiographical Tightropes,* 179–80, 185; Christopher Miller, 176–77; and Suk, 92–94.

23. In an insightful reading of Rushdie's *The Ground Beneath Her Feet,* Florence Cabaret proposes that the author uses etymological shifts toward the varied origins of the English language to produce a similarly alienating effect.

24. See for example Berrian, 20; Condé, Interview, "I Have Made Peace with My Island," 124–25; and Mouralis. As Elizabeth Wilson has noted, the narrative structure too seems to underline the lack of spatial freedom that plagues Marie-Hélène ("'Le Voyage et l'espace clos,'" 45, 48–49).

25. "The hero is not . . . an outsider to the same extent as the villain; he is more an 'insider-outsider.' He shares the general moral perspective of the community he serves, but is forced to spend most of his time outside it, in an unpleasant world to which he is professionally adapted, and to behave in a way that is only just tolerable to the community" (Palmer, 25).

2. Fixing Tituba

1. On the marketing and paratext of the French novel and its English translation, see Manzor-Coats. On the U.S. reception of *Tituba,* see Breu and Moss.

2. See for example Barnes; De Souza, "Demystifying Female Marooning"; Peterson, Simon, and Wilson, "Sorcières, sorcières."

3. On the debate concerning Tituba Indian's race, see Hansen, Moss (9–10), Rosenthal, and Tucker.

4. See for example Mudimbe-Boyi; Angela Y. Davis, "Foreword"; and Manzor-Coats. As Mudimbe-Boyi has noted, the epigraph frames the narrative as a translation, a mediation of a text in which the writer/interpreter yields authority to the newly empowered speaker (752).

5. As Mara Dukats proposes, Tituba's unacknowledged agency in the construction of the dominant cultural identity echoes the dynamic between Africanist presence and American identity elaborated by Toni Morrison in *Playing in the Dark* (144–45).

6. Trudier Harris notes further in an analysis of Ann Petry's fictional account of Salem the corrective impulse that motivates Puritan violence: "The world

can only be righted again if some convenient scapegoat is identified for physical punishment, banishment, or death" (107). See also Bernstein's analysis of those condemned as "sorcières," who function as "scapegoats for all that is evil in the various communities" ("Ecrivaine, sorcière, nomade," 123), and Mudimbe-Boyi's observation that the witch was "in actuality, the resounding projection of the fears and obsessions of a community" (755).

7. In his reading of Petry's *Tituba of Salem Village,* Melvin B. Rahming points to the reductive quality of the Puritan worldview, suggesting that the category "witch" is the easiest way in which to conceive of Tituba's alterity: "Witchcraft is the most accessible phenomenon by which her accusers can most easily label her ontological difference from themselves" (36). See also Suk, 125–28.

8. See also Araujo, 222; Anagnostopoulou-Hieschler, 45; Bernstein, "De-mythifying the Witch's Identity"; Simon, 425; and Condé's own comments on the conception of witchcraft in Africa (Scarboro, 206).

9. See in particular Moss, Rosenthal, and Tucker.

10. On the association between Native Americans and evil in Puritan New England, see Breslaw, 65–88, and McWilliams.

11. On the question of race as a meaningful category in critical discourse, see Gates, *"Race," Writing and Difference;* Gilroy; and Appiah. I discuss this debate further in chapter 5.

12. A. James Arnold examines the critical tension that results from *Tituba's* parodic dimension as an inscription of the novel's postmodern quality, claiming that Condé's specific type of parody "reappropriates postmodern techniques and subverts them to specifically West Indian purposes" (714). On this interpretive instability see also Wilson, "Sorcières, sorcières."

13. See Gates, *Signifying Monkey,* especially 103–24.

14. See Christopher Breu's analysis of the novel's denunciation of American racism (279–81). On the anachronisms in Condé's novel, see also Duffey, Moss, and Scarboro.

15. See also Breu, Duffey, Moss, and Simon.

16. "I don't know whether I quite understand or agree with the word *feminism,* because I come from a part of the world, the Caribbean, where we have a sort of different approach to the problem of women" ("Counterpoints," 7).

17. On this textual ambivalence in *Tituba,* see Barbour.

18. On the demonization of Tituba's sexuality, see Breu, 279–80, and Gyssels, 234–35. A. James Arnold argues that Tituba's interest in sex is "the ultimate disturbance of patriarchal order" (715). Condé notes a similar backlash against Véronica's sexuality in *Heremakhonon* ("Order," 133).

19. See Lisa Bernstein's analysis of this reference to the Billie Holiday song "Strange Fruit" ("Ecrivaine, sorcière, nomade," 129).

20. Davis recounts that this conceptual paralysis was such that it at times completely obscured the political message of the song: "In a Los Angeles club

a woman requested that Holiday sing 'Strange Fruit' by saying, 'Why don't you sing that sexy song you're so famous for? You know, the one about the naked bodies swinging in the trees'" (*Blues Legacies*, 195).

3. Imperfect Genealogies

1. On this topic see Lionnet, "*Traversée de la mangrove* de Maryse Condé," and Rosello, "Caribbean Insularization."

2. Françoise Lionnet describes Sancher as "an everyman, the prototype of the island dweller, with uncertain origins, multiple geographical, sentimental, and sexual ties, the nomadism of a rebellious adventurer, the fragility of a dissatisfied intellectual" ("*Traversée de la mangrove* de Maryse Condé," 481).

3. A. James Arnold evokes this inaccessibility by underlining the novel's engagement of an "unspeakable origin of contemporary culture in the French West Indies" (716). See also De Souza's analysis of the identity quest in *Traversée de la mangrove*, particularly of Francis Sancher's fascination with his own hidden past ("Crossing the Mangrove," 368).

4. I borrow the notion of "imperfect repetitions" from Carol Jacobs (379).

5. This skeptical view of interpretive community echoes not only modernist and postmodernist revaluations of allegory but also postcolonial reconsiderations of history and interpretive authority that further undermine the one-to-one correspondence to which the mode aspires. On the revival of allegory in modernism and postmodernism, see Paul Smith. Jameson's embattled essay on Third World literature underlines the epistemologically reparative disposition of allegory ("Third-World Literature").

6. Mireille Rosello characterizes Sancher as "the symbolic point to which everyone converges in their differences" ("Caribbean Insularization," 572).

7. See Lydie Moudileno's analysis of this character as an inscription of the marginalized Antillean writer in *L'Ecrivain antillais*, 144–67.

8. "Columbus's ritual of naming is . . . an extension of allegorical consciousness in that it 'reads' the territory of the 'other' by reference to an anterior set of signs already situated in a cultural thematics, and by this process the 'new' world is made contingent upon the old" (161).

9. As Maureen Quilligan proposes, allegory rests on the "curious, almost physical power of language that operate[s] by a sympathetic magic of names, whereby to name is somehow to know, and to know the name is to control the force" (163).

10. In fact, it is just this distance between the satellite and its truth that is particular to the allegorical mode, and it is precisely what distinguishes allegory from symbol. While the symbol participates in the representation of a "Unity" in the sense that it is of the same nature as what it symbolizes, an allegorical sign fails to close the gap between narrative and reference, between "inside" and "outside". It is this gap that is at the heart of Benjamin's theory of allegory, in which the distance between interpretation and meaning is constituted as a loss. On this topic

see Jameson, *Marxism and Form*, 72–73; J. Hillis Miller, *Topographies*, 144–49; and Paul Smith, 106.

11. Jean-Xavier Ridon describes Sancher as a phantom whose death refuses collective appropriation (220–21).

12. See Patrick Chamoiseau's discussion of the tangled structure of the novel (391) and Leah Hewitt's inscription of this structure in the metaphorical image of the mangrove ("Inventing Antillean Narrative," 85).

13. As Lionnet points out, Condé's novel contests such a project, articulating a "refusal of any form of nostalgia, of any historical, esthetic, exotic, or political prejudice that would attempt to fetichize the past or slavery and to idealize political commitment, nature, or the people" (*"Traversée de la mangrove* de Maryse Condé," 477). See also Stuart Hall, who, in a discussion of Caribbean cinema, refutes the notion of recovering a past "which is waiting to be found," noting that "this is no longer a simple, factual 'past,' since our relation to it is, like the child's relation to the mother, always-already 'after the break'" ("Cultural Identity," 213).

14. In the original text, the French translation of the Creole sentence appears in a footnote, this paratextual gesture bringing further attention to the link between Quentin's question and the problem of translation (229).

15. On the trope of the windowpane as a division between outside and inside, between human and other, see Van Ghent, 161–70.

16. See Françoise Lionnet's analysis of the New World syncretism at work in this scene ("Narrating the Americas," 77–78).

17. Swamy, 68; see also Lionnet's critique of this reading ("Narrating the Americas," 87n5). While Anthuria's potentially incestuous origins certainly resonate with the narcissistic ethos of Brontë's families evoked by Bersani, the child's existence, taken alongside the creation of numerous siblings, aunts, uncles, and cousins envisioned in Condé's narrative, seems also to point to a genealogical world that escapes the careful control of the hermetic Linton-Earnshaws.

18. The diverse perspectives at work in the telling of this tale also disturb the chronological framework of the tale; while Brontë's text, as Dorothy Van Ghent has proposed, mitigates the potentially taboo nature of the story of Catherine and Heathcliff through a consistent temporal and rhetorical distance (159–60), Condé's novel presents instead a constantly shifting temporal frame for this narrative.

19. Swamy's article cogently elaborates the ways in which Condé's novel "make[s] the 'silences' of Brontë's novel 'speak'" (61); see also Lionnet, "Narrating the Americas," 72.

20. On the relationship between Heathcliff's name and his position in the Linton-Earnshaw clan, see Goetz, 366.

21. Bersani argues that patterns of repetition so dominate the narrative that "certain configurations of characters begin to compete for our attention with the individual characters themselves . . . Heathcliff is no longer, so to speak,

entirely within himself; he 'occurs,' in modified versions, elsewhere in the novel" (199–200). Similarly, Giles Mitchell suggests that Heathcliff is locked in a Freudian repetition compulsion (33–34).

22. As Lionnet points out, the incest reading doubles an interior one, in which the "curse" upon Anthuria would refer to the fact that she is "the dark-skinned descendant of two doomed characters" ("Narrating the Americas," 84). On Condé's use of free indirect discourse in this closing line, see also Sanders, 166–67.

23. Carol Jacobs has proposed that a central anxiety in *Wuthering Heights* is the fact that its familial repetitions are imperfect repetitions, that characters only partially resemble the members of this self-enclosed society, and thus that the duplication of names and images functions to obscure or close this potentially threatening gap. Jacobs argues further that the pattern of inheritance follows this same logic of constructed repetition, that the will to usurpation manifests "less a desire for possession than . . . a bizarre desire for imitation" (379).

24. Carine Mardorossian offers an insightful reading of Cathy's shifting racial identifications as a rewriting of both biological and social constructionist approaches to race (36–43).

25. In *Traversée de la mangrove,* for example, one character evokes the oral tradition of her ancestors through such an exchange: "Our ancestors used to say that death is nothing but a bridge between humans, a footbridge that brings them closer together on which they can meet halfway to whisper things they never dared talk about" (161). And as Carol Sanders notes, death also seems to provide a privileged space of proximity and exchange in *La migration des cœurs* (155–57). Emily Apter suggests a paratextual extension of this kind of transcendent communication, reading Condé's dedication of *La migration des cœurs* to Emily Brontë as a resurrection of the British author from the dead ("Condé's *Créolité,*" 442).

4. Breaking the Compact

1. Caruth, *Trauma* and *Unclaimed Experience.*

2. Along with Caruth, see for example Felman and Laub, and LaCapra, *History and Memory, Representing the Holocaust,* and *Writing History.* On psychoanalysis and trauma see Abraham and Torok, and Leys.

3. On the comparability of the Holocaust, a question to which I return at the end of this chapter, see LaCapra, *History and Memory,* 43–72; McBride, 139–42; and Caruth, *Trauma,* 4. For studies in African American criticism and trauma theory, see Bouson, Mandel, McBride, and Morgenstern.

4. The traumatic is also a crucial aspect of Glissant's reading of history, as a delaying effect that projects the assessment of suppressed past events into the Antillean present. As Jeannie Suk argues, this vision of communal trauma generates a conception of contemporary plenitude through "transversality" that is perhaps overly celebratory (70–83).

5. See Morrison, "Unspeakable Things Unspoken."

6. On the link between the maternal and the traumatic in neoslave narratives, see Morgenstern.

7. Licops reads urban space in *Desirada* as a text of "multiple contradictory narratives" (115) that recall Michel de Certeau's concept of "urban polyphony" (117n11).

8. As Scharfman notes, this laugh represents "the black hole of the unknowable, of the impossibility of knowing, that puts into question the entire search for origins" ("Au sujet d'héroïnes péripatétiques," 145). Similarly, Moudileno reads the grandmother's laughter as a crucial moment in the narrative that cruelly undermines both Marie-Noëlle's hopes for paternal identification and the reader's expectations of an archetypical Caribbean grandmother ("Le rire de la grand-mère," 1155).

9. For further discussion of the novel's title, see Bosshard, "Maryse Condé," 151–52, and Abeysinghe, who notes the etymological resonance of the novel's title in the reference to longing and lack in the Latin verb *desiderare* (327).

10. The passage also suggests a link to Homi Bhabha's study of "border lives," especially given his epigraphical evocation of Heidegger's "Building Dwelling Thinking" (*Location of Culture,* 1). Indeed, Condé's vision of immigration patterns in this novel would seem to advance a reconceptualized notion of "dwelling" as an activity that can occur in the absence of fixed sites.

11. On the theme of monstrosity in the novel, see also Moudileno, "Le Rire de la grand-mère," and Bosshard, "Maryse Condé."

12. Alexander terms "cultural trauma" a phenomenon by which "members of collectivities define their solidary relationships in ways that, in principle, allow them to share the sufferings of others" (1).

13. See Leys and Allan Young. Susan J. Brison discusses the double bind presented by the question of credibility in *Aftermath,* pointing out that in order to maintain validity as a victim of trauma one by definition cannot recover from it (70–71).

14. Claude Lanzmann examines the ethical implications of articulating through narrative an event that defies understanding, thus normalizing it as a comprehensible experience.

5. The Margins of Race

1. These include Homi Bhabha, Stuart Hall, Iain Chambers, Paul Gilroy, and, importing the French term *métissage,* Françoise Lionnet. On the colonial inflections of the term *métissage,* see also Vergès, *Monsters and Revolutionaries.* Stuart Hall vigorously protests the caveat against using the term *hybridity* in "When Was the Postcolonial."

2. Christiane Makward identifies Célanire's defiance of chronology as another example of her narratological transgressions in the novel ("Cut-throat or Mocking-bird," 416–17). See also Joan Dayan's eloquent analysis of Célanire's transgressions through gender and ritual knowledge.

3. On the links between the creature's gaze in Shelley's *Frankenstein* and the Freudian model of the Medusa figure, see Salotto, 194–96.

4. See, for example, Ellen Moers's reading of *Frankenstein* as a "birth myth" (92), Fred Botting's analysis of the inscription of the French Revolution in Shelley's text, or Chris Baldick's reading of the "mad scientist" anxiety (141–42).

5. Baldick proposes this reading of the Frankenstein myth through Foucault's etymological definition of the monster as a being or object to be *shown* (*monstrare*) in order to *warn* (*monere*) humanity of the potential consequences of vice or unreasoned behavior (10).

6. On the function of the fantasy in *Frankenstein,* see Jackson.

7. The conception of Shelley's novel as a monstrous narrative, first suggested by the author herself in her introduction to the 1831 edition of the novel with a reference to her "hideous progeny" (25), has been taken up by a number of critics. Fred Botting, for example, has described the novel as "an 'assemblage' of fragments, a disunified text that subverts the possibility and implications of textual and semantic coherence" (27), while Eleanor Salotto proposes that Shelley's text falls into the monstrous inasmuch as it is an autobiographical text, the self-representation of a multiple subject. See also Baldick, 30–33.

8. On this aspect of the fantastic, see Morse.

9. Todorov's definition of the genre has not, of course, escaped criticism (see for example Brooke-Rose, Lem, and Sandor), but his emphasis on the *simultaneity* of conflicting interpretations captures an essential component of Condé's narrative.

10. In his work on myths and the fantastic, Sandor uses the image of the scar to evoke the confusing simultaneity of the genre: "The fantastic suggests a scar that cannot be smoothed out, a scar that cannot heal" (349).

11. Again, Célanire's affirmation recuperates Frankenstein's censored material, since the geographical setting of the doctor's anxiety points to a colonial preoccupation hovering also in the shadows of Shelley's novel: in Frankenstein's imagination, it is in the New World that the creature and his bride would have released their race of devils upon an unsuspecting earth. As Helena Woodard has proposed, this reproduction of the Other is the ultimate colonial fear, "a colonial power's worst nightmare: Caliban's threat to Miranda to people the world with 'little Calibans'" (26).

6. The Coherence of Caricature

1. "The title 'La Belle Créole' is a trap, an *oratio obliqua* that does not name the book's subject" (345).

2. Coursil provides an extensive list of contrasting usages of the word "créole" to demonstrate that "the French expression 'Belle Créole' is a re-imported exoticism, a Creolism (in reverse) for people who are just passing through" (345n1).

3. As Marianne Bosshard notes, "*La Belle Créole,* despite its title's promise of a beautiful love story in exotic colors, created a scandal in Guadeloupe, and

for good reason. Everything in it sinks, including the beautiful sailboat that carries its name" (rev. of *Célanire cou-coupé* and *La belle créole*, 1312).

4. For a discussion of the role of storytelling in the courtroom, see West.

5. Here I am following the argument of Mieke Bal, who examines the relationship between reading and wholeness in "De-disciplining the Eye": "The desire for wholeness informs the compulsion to project unity onto the image or text and thus to ignore incoherent details that threaten to break the unity" (509). In many ways Condé's novel plays out the very tension Bal analyzes, between "realist" readings that preclude any awareness of incoherence and "textualist" readings that acknowledge the construction of wholeness as a process.

6. On the deployment of the synecdochical mechanism of caricature in the construction and perpetuation of racial stereotypes, see Rosello, *Declining the Stereotype*, and Banta. In his analysis of Charles Dickens's *Little Dorrit*, Daniel Novak underlines the false stability engendered by caricature: "Rather than presenting a chaotic world of parts, . . . the author who mobilizes synecdoche enforces the unity of the body by the swaggering certainty of its immanence—the certainty that the part always refers to a stable body" (24). As we shall see below, this reading of synecdoche through the body also illuminates the problematic of reparations as a question of existential freedom in Fanon's work.

7. The derisive reference to Loraine's "debt" to the black men of Port-Mahault who have shared her bed further underscores this critique of artificiality in the case for reparations: "Loraine was only paying a small portion of the considerable debt to the Race, accumulated over centuries of slave trade, slavery, exploitation of all kinds and humiliations of all forms" (219–20). In a second reference, this portion of Loraine's "debt" is specifically characterized as a "réparation" (225).

8. Chris Buck proposes a cogently argued strategy for reconciling Fanon's later argument in defense of reparations for colonialism and a case for slavery reparations through the Sartrian conception of race as seriality.

9. Nicole J. Simek insightfully explores such temporal breaks in Condé's novel through a consideration of the explanatory value of the past for the globalized subject.

10. Founded in 1932 by Martinican Etienne Léro, the journal *Légitime Défense* is considered one of the foremost landmarks of black cultural production associated with the *Négritude* movement.

7. Unfamiliar Cannibals

1. On cannibalism in Thomas Harris's *The Silence of the Lambs*, see Kilgour, "Function of Cannibalism," 248–59; on Columbus and the *canibales*, see note 7 below.

2. On cannibalism and sexual development in Freud, see in particular Kilgour, *From Communion to Cannibalism*, 11–12 and 230–34.

3. Scharfman's "Criss-Crossing the Mangrove" reads this critique of tourism as a revelation of the "dark side of globalization" in Condé's novel, whose mood she cogently describes as "resolutely post 9/11" (201).

4. On tourism and consumerism, see Bartolovich and Lyons. Bartolovich in particular notes the lists of collected or identified objects and commodities that characterize travel narratives as indications of a desire for infinite consumption (231–32).

5. This iniquity is particularly clear in the context of colonial explorations in the New World, where along with fascinated interest in cannibalism emerged the use of such (suspected or invented) behavior as a moral justification for the extermination of native populations. On this topic see in particular Motohashi, who examines the ways in which the "cruel savagery of the 'canibales' was at the centre of the European imagination which tried to justify the violent colonial enterprise" (86), and notes that this impulse also led to the categorization of natives as either "cruel" or "gentle" with cannibalism as the determining factor. As Motohashi points out, also at play in these distinctions was the confusion between "Canibales" and "Caribes." See also Kilgour's foreword to *Eating Their Words*.

6. Bartolovich posits the viewer as consumer of the film, thus establishing this parallel as a potential conflation between consumerism and cannibalism (205).

7. On this linguistic slippage, see also Bartolovich, 207, and Arens, *Man-Eating Myth*, 44.

8. On this topic see also Hulme and Lyons.

9. Arens responds to critics of his argument, including those who associate his position with denials of the Holocaust, in "Rethinking Anthropophagy."

10. Crain proposes further that the rhetorical affiliation between cannibalism and homosexuality is so close that one narrative may in fact substitute for the other, that the homosexual, in the case of Melville, for example, can be read through the cannibal (49). On the connection between cannibalism and homosexuality, see also Freccero; Jooma, 65; and Kilgour, "Function of Cannibalism," 252.

11. This ostensibly premature naming of a creative project recalls the despairing impotence of the figure of the writer in *Traversée de la mangrove*, where Francis Sancher is paralyzed by the fact that he has already found a title for his work before he has begun it. While the trope takes an optimistic turn in *Histoire de la femme cannibale*, the intertextual parallel seems nonetheless to reinforce the exposure of Rosélie's creative enterprise as a false search for knowledge.

Conclusion

1. "It is now recognized that colonialism and translation went hand in hand" (Bassnett and Trivedi, 3).

2. See Venuti; Apter, "On Translation in a Global Market"; and Spivak, "Politics of Translation." Célestin, DalMolin, and Waters propose that the translator's

art is "translucent" rather than transparent (235); in the same issue Mary Ann Caws evokes the misinterpretations of translation as "skewages" (342–43).

3. Philcox, "Preface" (1997) and "Translator's Preface" (1995).

4. "The unity is submarine breathing air, our problem is how to study the fragments whole" (Brathwaite, 1). Condé discusses Philcox's desire to "maximiz[e] clarity and accessibility" in his translations in her interview with Emily Apter. See Apter, "Crossover Texts," 93.

5. Philcox, "Translating Maryse Condé," 280.

6. As it is framed in Little's piece, Philcox's error would be on par, for example, with the detail examined by Gayatri Spivak in her analysis of Philcox's *Heremakhonon*, where the translation of "Fulani and Toucouleur" for the French "Peul and Toucouleur" presents a modification of migratory history that "the metropolitan reader of the translation will undoubtedly pass over" (*Death of a Discipline*, 17).

7. Dominica is appropriately enough on the cusp both geographically and chronologically between the Windward and Leeward islands, having been transferred from the latter to the former colony in 1940.

8. Hewitt discusses the potential controversy sparked by the release of *Les derniers rois mages* in English. See her afterword and "Condé's Critical Seesaw," 648.

9. For an excellent study on this topic, see Watts.

10. See Ashcroft, Griffiths, and Tiffin.

11. Note, for example, Harish Trivedi's claim that "the postcolonial has ears only for English" (272). See also Murdoch and Donadey, and Forsdick and Murphy.

12. See Murdoch and Donadey, Forsdick and Murphy, and Bessière and Moura.

Bibliography

Works by Maryse Condé

Condé, Maryse. *La belle créole*. Paris: Mercure de France, 2001.

———. *Cahier d'un retour au pays natal: Césaire*. Collection profil d'une œuvre 63. Paris: Hatier, 1978.

———. *Célanire cou-coupé*. Paris: Robert Laffont, 2000.

———. "Chercher nos vérités." *Penser la créolité*. Ed. Maryse Condé and Madeleine Cottenet-Hage. Paris: Karthala, 1995. 305–10.

———. *La civilisation du bossale: Réflexions sur la littérature orale de la Guadeloupe et de la Martinique*. Paris: L'Harmattan, 1977.

———. *La colonie du nouveau monde*. Paris: Robert Laffont, 1993.

———. *Crossing the Mangrove*. Trans. Richard Philcox. New York: Doubleday, 1995.

———. *Les derniers rois mages*. Paris: Mercure de France, 1992.

———. "Des héros et des cannibales: Réécriture et transgression dans la littérature des petites Antilles de langue française." *Portulan* (2000): 29–38.

———. *Desirada*. Paris: Robert Laffont, 1997.

———. *Desirada*. Trans. Richard Philcox. New York: Soho, 2000.

———. *En attendant le bonheur (Heremakhonon)*. Paris: Seghers, 1988.

———. "Globalization and Diaspora." *Diogenes* 46.184 (1998): 29–37.

———. *Heremakhonon*. Paris: Editions 10/18, 1976.

———. *Heremakhonon*. Trans. Richard Philcox. Washington: Three Continents P, 1982.

———. *Histoire de la femme cannibale*. Paris: Mercure de France, 2003.

———. *I, Tituba, Black Witch of Salem*. Trans. Richard Philcox. New York: Ballantine, 1992.

———. Interview. "'I Have Made Peace With My Island': An Interview with Maryse Condé." By Vèvè Clark. *Callaloo* 12.1 (1989): 87–133.

———. Interview. "Is 'I' Still Another?" By Leah D. Hewitt. *Sites* 1.2 (1997): 543–49.

————. Interview. "Moi, Maryse Condé, libre d'être moi-même . . ." By Lydie Moudileno. *Women in French Studies* 10 (2002): 121–26.

————. *The Last of the African Kings*. Trans. Richard Philcox. Lincoln: U of Nebraska P, 1997.

————. "Le métissage du texte." *Discours sur le métissage, identités métisses: En quête d'Ariel*. Ed. Sylvie Kandé. Paris: L'Harmattan, 1999. 209–17.

————. *La migration des cœurs*. Paris: Robert Laffont, 1995.

————. *Moi, Tituba sorcière . . . noire de Salem*. Paris: Mercure de France, 1986.

————. "Naipaul et les Antilles: Une histoire d'amour?" *La quinzaine littéraire* 16–31 Oct. 1984: 6–7.

————. "On the Apparent Carnivalization of Literature from the French Caribbean." *Representations of Blackness and the Performance of Identities*. Ed. Jean Muteba Rahier. Westport, CT: Bergin & Garvey, 1999. 91–97.

————. "Order, Disorder, Freedom, and the West Indian Writer." *Yale French Studies* 83.2 (1993): 121–35.

————. "Pan-Africanism, Feminism, and Culture." *Imagining Home: Class, Culture and Nationalism in the African Diaspora*. Ed. Sidney J. Lemelle and Robin D. G. Kelley. London: Verso, 1994. 55–65.

————. *La parole des femmes: Essai sur les romancières des Antilles de langue française*. Paris: L'Harmattan, 1979.

————. *La poésie antillaise*. Paris: Fernand Nathan, 1977.

————. "Pourquoi la négritude? Négritude et révolution." *Négritude africaine et négritude caraïbe*. Paris: Paris VIII, 1973. 150–54.

————. "The Role of the Writer." *World Literature Today* 67.4 (1993): 697–99.

————. *Le roman antillais*. Paris: Fernand Nathan, 1977.

————. *Une saison à Rihata*. Paris: Robert Laffont, 1981.

————. *A Season in Rihata*. Trans. Richard Philcox. London: Heinemann, 1987.

————. *Ségou: Les murailles de terre*. Paris: Robert Laffont, 1984.

————. *Ségou: La terre en miettes*. Paris: Robert Laffont, 1985.

————. *Segu*. Trans. Barbara Bray. New York: Viking, 1987.

————. *The Story of the Cannibal Woman*. Trans. Richard Philcox. New York: Atria, 2007.

————. *Traversée de la mangrove*. Paris: Mercure de France, 1989.

————. "Unheard Voice: Suzanne Césaire and the Construct of a Caribbean Identity." *Winds of Change: The Transforming Voices of Caribbean Women Writers and Scholars*. Ed. Adele S. Newson and Linda Strong-Leek. New York: Peter Lang, 1998. 61–66.

————. *La vie scélérate*. Paris: Seghers, 1987.

————. *Who Slashed Célanire's Throat?* Trans. Richard Philcox. New York: Atria, 2004.

————. *Windward Heights*. Trans. Richard Philcox. New York: Soho, 1998.

Works by Other Authors

Abeysinghe, Nayana P. "Shattered Pasts, Fractured Selves: Trauma and Memory in *Desirada.*" *Romanic Review* 94.3–4 (2003): 319–27.

Abraham, Nicolas, and Maria Torok. *The Shell and the Kernel.* Vol. 1. Trans. Nicholas T. Rand. Chicago: U of Chicago P, 1994.

Ahmad, Aijaz. "Jameson's Rhetoric of Otherness and the 'National Allegory.'" *In Theory: Classes, Nations, Literatures.* London: Verso, 1992. 95–122.

Alexander, Jeffrey C., Ron Eyerman, Bernhard Giesen, et al. *Cultural Trauma and Collective Identity.* Berkeley: U of California P, 2004.

Amireh, Amal, and Lisa Suhair Majaj. Introduction. *Going Global: The Transnational Reception of Third World Women Writers.* New York: Garland, 2000. 1–25.

Anagnostopoulou-Hieschler, Maria. "*Moi, Tituba, sorcière . . . noire de Salem* de Maryse Condé." *Francographies* 8 (1999): 35–48.

Appadurai, Arjun. "Disjuncture and Difference in the Global Economy." *Public Culture* 2.2 (1990): 1–24.

Apter, Emily. "Condé's *Créolité* in Literary History." *Romanic Review* 94.3–4 (2003): 437–50.

———. "Crossover Texts/Creole Tongues: A Conversation with Maryse Condé." *Public Culture* 13.1 (2001): 89–96.

———. "On Translation in a Global Market." *Public Culture* 13.1 (2001): 1–12.

Araujo, Nara. "The Contribution of Women's Writing to the Literature and Intellectual Achievements of the Caribbean: *Moi, Tituba sorcière* and *Amour, colère, folie.*" *Journal of Black Studies* 25.2 (1994): 217–30.

Arens, William. *The Man-Eating Myth: Anthropology and Anthropophagy.* Oxford: Oxford UP, 1979.

———. "Rethinking Anthropophagy." *Cannibalism and the Colonial World.* Ed. Francis Barker, Peter Hulme, and Margaret Iversen. Cambridge: Cambridge UP, 1998. 39–62.

Arnold, A. James. "The Novelist as Critic." *World Literature Today* 67.4 (1993): 711–16.

Ashcroft, Bill, Gareth Griffiths, and Helen Tiffin. *The Empire Writes Back: Theory and Practice in Post-colonial Literatures.* New York: Routledge, 1989.

Bal, Mieke. "De-disciplining the Eye." *Critical Inquiry* 16.2 (1990): 506–31.

Baldick, Chris. *In Frankenstein's Shadow: Myth, Monstrosity, and Nineteenth-Century Writing.* Oxford: Clarendon P, 1987.

Balibar, Etienne. "Is There a 'Neo-Racism'?" *Race, Nation, Class: Ambiguous Identities.* Ed. Etienne Balibar and Immanuel Wallerstein. Trans. Chris Turner. London: Verso, 1991. 17–28.

Banta, Martha. *Barbaric Intercourse: Caricature and the Culture of Conduct, 1841–1936.* Chicago: U of Chicago P, 2003.

Barbour, Sarah E. "Hesitating between Irony and the Desire to be Serious in *Moi, Tituba sorcière . . . noire de Salem*: Maryse Condé and her Readers." *Studies in Twentieth and Twenty-First Century Literature* 28.2 (2004): 329–51.

Barbour, Sarah E., and Gerise Herndon, eds. *Emerging Perspectives on Maryse Condé: A Writer of Her Own*. Trenton, NJ: Africa World P, 2006.

Barnes, Paula C. "Meditations of Her/Story: Maryse Condé's *I, Tituba, Black Witch of Salem* and the Slave Narrative Tradition." *Arms Akimbo: Africana Women in Contemporary Literature*. Ed. Janice Lee Liddell and Yakini Belinda Kemp. Gainesville: UP of Florida, 1999. 193–204.

Barthes, Roland. "Bichon chez les Nègres." *Mythologies*. Paris: Seuil, 1957. 60–63.

———. *S/Z*. Paris: Seuil, 1970.

Bartolovich, Crystal. "Consumerism, or the Logic of Late Cannibalism." *Cannibalism and the Colonial World*. Ed. Francis Barker, Peter Hulme, and Margaret Iversen. Cambridge: Cambridge UP, 1998. 204–37.

Bassnett, Susan, and Harish Trivedi. "Introduction: Of Colonies, Cannibals and Vernaculars." *Post-colonial Translation: Theory and Practice*. Ed. Susan Bassnett and Harish Trivedi. New York: Routledge, 1999. 1–18.

Berman, Jeffrey. *Narcissism and the Novel*. New York: New York UP, 1990.

Bernabé, Jean, Patrick Chamoiseau, and Raphaël Confiant. *Eloge de la créolité/ In Praise of Creoleness*. Paris: Gallimard, 1989.

Bernstein, Lisa. "Demythifying the Witch's Identity as Social Critique in Maryse Condé's *I, Tituba, Black Witch of Salem*." *Social Identities* 3.1 (1997): 77–89.

———. "Ecrivaine, sorcière, nomade: La conscience critique dans *Moi, Tituba, sorcière . . . noire de Salem* de Maryse Condé." *Etudes francophones* 13.1 (1998): 119–34.

Berrian, Brenda F. "Masculine Roles and Triangular Relationships in Maryse Condé's *Une saison à Rihata*." *Bridges: A Senegalese Journal of English Studies* 3 (1991): 5–20.

Bersani, Leo. *A Future for Astyanax: Character and Desire in Literature*. Boston: Little Brown, 1969.

Bessière, Jean, and Jean-Marc Moura, eds. *Littératures postcoloniales et francophonie*. Paris: Champion, 2001.

Bhabha, Homi. *The Location of Culture*. New York: Routledge, 1994.

Bosshard, Marianne. "Maryse Condé: *Désirada* ou l'ironie du sort." Cottenet-Hage and Moudileno, 149–56.

———. Rev. of *Célanire cou-coupé* and *La belle créole*, by Maryse Condé. *French Review* 75.6 (2002): 1311–13.

Botting, Fred. "Reflections of Excess: *Frankenstein*, the French Revolution and Monstrosity." *Reflections of Revolution: Images of Romanticism*. Ed. Alison Yarrington and Kelvin Everest. London: Routledge, 1993. 26–38.

Bouson, J. Brooks. *Quiet As It's Kept: Shame, Trauma, and Race in the Novels of Toni Morrison*. Albany: SUNY P, 1999.

Brathwaite, Edward Kamau. "Caribbean Man in Space and Time." *Savacou* 11/12 (1975): 1–11.

Breslaw, Elaine G. *Tituba, Reluctant Witch of Salem: Devilish Indians and Puritan Fantasies.* New York: New York UP, 1996.

Breu, Christopher. "Practicing Disruptive Economics: The Remapping of the Economic Space of the Americas in Maryse Condé's *Moi, Tituba, sorcière . . . noire de Salem.*" *Re-placing America: Conversations and Contestations.* Ed. Ruth Hsu, Cynthia Franklin, and Suzanne Kosanke. Honolulu: College of Languages, Linguistics, and Literature, 2000. 272–90.

Brison, Susan J. *Aftermath: Violence and the Remaking of a Self.* Princeton, NJ: Princeton UP, 2002.

Broichhagen, Vera, Kathryn Lachman, and Nicole Simek, eds. *Feasting on Words: Maryse Condé, Cannibalism, and the Caribbean Text.* Princeton, NJ: PLAS, 2006.

Brontë, Emily. *Wuthering Heights.* Ed. Linda H. Peterson. New York: Bedford/ St. Martin's, 2003.

Brooke-Rose, Christine. *A Rhetoric of the Unreal: Studies in Narrative and Structure, Especially of the Fantastic.* Cambridge: Cambridge UP, 1981.

Buck, Chris. "Sartre, Fanon, and the Case for Slavery Reparations." *Sartre Studies International* 10.2 (2004): 123–38.

Cabaret, Florence. "Writing as Translation in *The Ground Beneath Her Feet.*" *Commonwealth* 24.2 (2002): 47–57.

Caillois, Roger. *Anthologie du fantastique.* Vol. 1. Paris: Gallimard, 1966.

Carter, Stephen L. "When Victims Happen to Be Black." *Yale Law Journal* 97 (1988): 420–48.

Caruth, Cathy, ed. *Trauma: Explorations in Memory.* Baltimore: Johns Hopkins UP, 1995.

———. *Unclaimed Experience: Trauma, Narrative, and History.* Baltimore: Johns Hopkins UP, 1996.

Cassuto, Leonard. *The Inhuman Race: The Racial Grotesque in American Literature and Culture.* New York: Columbia UP, 1997.

Caws, Mary Ann. "Retranslation and Its Surrealist Delights." *Sites* 5.2 (2001): 341–49.

Célestin, Roger, Eliane DalMolin, and Alyson Waters. "Introduction." *Sites* 5.2 (2001): 235–41.

Chambers, Iain. *Migrancy, Culture, Identity.* London: Routledge, 1994.

Chamoiseau, Patrick. "Reflections on Maryse Condé's *Traversée de la mangrove.*" Trans. Kathleen M. Balutansky. *Callaloo* 14 (1991): 389–95.

Clark, Vèvè A. "Developing Diaspora Literacy: Allusion in Maryse Condé's *Hérémakhonon.*" *Out of the Kumbla: Caribbean Women and Literature.* Ed. Carole Boyce Davies and Elaine Savory Fido. Trenton, NJ: Africa World P, 1990. 303–19.

Clarkson, Carrol. "'By Any Other Name': Kripke, Derrida and an Ethics of Naming." *Journal of Literary Semantics* 32.1 (2003): 35–47.

Cohen, Margaret, and Carolyn Dever. *The Literary Channel: The Inter-National Invention of the Novel.* Princeton, NJ: Princeton UP, 2002.

Cooppan, Vilashini. "W(h)ither Post-colonial Studies? Towards the Transnational Study of Race and Nation." *Postcolonial Theory and Criticism.* Ed. Laura Chrisman and Benita Parry. Oxford: English Association, 2000. 1–35.

Cottenet-Hage, Madeleine, and Lydie Moudileno, eds. *Maryse Condé: Une nomade inconvenante.* Guadeloupe: Ibis Rouge, 2002.

"Counterpoints: Ama Ata Aidoo, Edna Acosta-Belén, Amrita Basu, Maryse Condé, Nell Painter, and Nawal El Saadawi Speak on Feminism, Race, and Transnationalism." *Meridians: Feminism, Race, Transnationalism* 1.1 (2000): 1–28.

Coursil, Jacques. "*La belle créole* de Maryse Condé, un art d'écriture." *Romanic Review* 94.3–4 (2003): 345–59.

Crain, Caleb. "Lovers of Human Flesh: Homosexuality and Cannibalism in Melville's Novels." *American Literature* 66.1 (1994): 25–53.

Dadié, Bernard. *Un nègre à Paris.* Paris: Présence Africaine, 1959.

Davis, Angela Y. *Blues Legacies and Black Feminism: Gertrude "Ma" Rainey, Bessie Smith, and Billie Holiday.* New York: Pantheon, 1998.

———. Foreword. Condé, *I, Tituba, Black Witch of Salem,* ix–xi.

Dayan, Joan. "Condé's Trials of the Spirit." *Romanic Review* 94.3–4 (2003): 429–36.

De Man, Paul. *Allegories of Reading.* New Haven, CT: Yale UP, 1979.

De Souza, Pascale. "Crossing the Mangrove of Order and Prejudice." *Romanic Review* 94.3–4 (2003): 361–76.

———. "Demystifying Female Marooning: Oppositional Strategies and the Writing of Testimonios in the French Caribbean." *International Journal of Francophone Studies* 3.3 (2000): 141–50.

Dirlik, Arif. "Bringing History Back In: Of Diasporas, Hybridities, Places, and Histories." *Beyond Dichotomies: Histories, Identities, Cultures, and the Challenge of Globalization.* Ed. Elisabeth Mudimbe-Boyi. Albany: SUNY P, 2002. 93–127.

Duffey, Carolyn. "Tituba and Hester in the Intertextual Jail Cell: New World Feminisms in Maryse Condé's *Moi, Tituba, sorcière . . . noire de Salem.*" *Women in French Studies* 4 (1996): 100–110.

Dukats, Mara L. "The Hybrid Terrain of Literary Imagination: Maryse Condé's Black Witch of Salem, Nathaniel Hawthorne's Hester Prynne, and Aimé Césaire's Heroic Poetic Voice." *Race-ing Representation: Voice, History, and Sexuality.* Ed. Kostas Myrsiades and Linda Myrsiades. Lanham: Rowman & Littlefield, 1998. 141–54.

Erikson, Kai. "Notes on Trauma and Community." *Trauma: Explorations in Memory.* Ed. Cathy Caruth. Baltimore: Johns Hopkins UP, 1995. 183–99.

Fanon, Frantz. *Black Skin, White Masks.* Trans. Charles Lam Markmann. New York: Grove, 1967.

———. *Peau noire, masques blancs.* Paris: Seuil, 1952.

Felman, Shoshana, and Dori Laub, MD. *Testimony: Crises of Witnessing in Literature, Psychoanalysis and History.* New York: Routledge, 1992.

Fletcher, Angus. *Allegory: The Theory of a Symbolic Mode.* Ithaca, NY: Cornell UP, 1964.

Forsdick, Charles, and David Murphy, eds. *Francophone Postcolonial Studies: A Critical Introduction.* Oxford: Oxford UP, 2003.

Freccero, Carla. "Cannibalism, Homophobia, Women: Montaigne's 'Des cannibales' and 'De l'amitié.'" *Women, "Race," and Writing in the Early Modern Period.* Ed. Margo Hendricks and Patricia Parker. London: Routledge, 1994. 73–83.

Garane, Jeanne. "History, Identity and the Constitution of the Female Subject: Maryse Condé's *Tituba.*" *Moving Beyond Boundaries.* Vol. 2. Ed. Carole Boyce Davies. New York: New York UP, 1995. 153–64.

Garvey, Johanna X. K. "(Up)rooting the Family Tree: Genealogy and Space in Maryse Condé's Fiction." *Emerging Perspectives on Maryse Condé: A Writer of Her Own.* Ed. Sarah E. Barbour and Gerise Herndon. Trenton, NJ: Africa World P, 2006. 159–78.

Gates, Henry Louis, Jr., ed. *"Race," Writing, and Difference.* Chicago: U of Chicago P, 1985.

———. *The Signifying Monkey: A Theory of African-American Literary Criticism.* New York: Oxford UP, 1988.

Gilroy, Paul. *Against Race: Imagining Political Culture beyond the Color Line.* Cambridge, MA: Harvard UP, 2000.

Glissant, Édouard. *Le discours antillais.* Paris: Seuil, 1981.

———. *Poétique de la relation.* Paris: Gallimard, 1990.

Goetz, William R. "Genealogy and Incest in *Wuthering Heights.*" *Studies in the Novel* 14.4 (1982): 359–76.

Gyssels, Kathleen. *Sages sorcières? Révision de la mauvaise mère dans* Beloved *(Toni Morrison),* Praisesong for the Widow *(Paule Marshall), et* Moi, Tituba, sorcière noire de Salem *(Maryse Condé).* Lanham: UP of America, 2001.

Hall, Stuart. "Cultural Identity and Cinematic Representation." *Black British Cultural Studies Reader.* Ed. Houston A. Baker Jr., Manthia Diawara, and Ruth H. Lindeborg. Chicago: U of Chicago P, 1996. 210–22.

———. "When Was the Postcolonial: Thinking About the Limit." *The Postcolonial Question.* Ed. Iain Chambers and Linda Curtis. London: Routledge, 1996. 242–60.

Hall, Stuart, and Paul Du Gay, eds. *Questions of Cultural Identity.* London: Sage, 1996.

Hansen, Chadwick. "The Metamorphosis of Tituba, or Why American Intellectuals Can't Tell an Indian Witch from a Negro." *New England Quarterly* 47.1 (1974): 3–12.

Harper, Ralph. *The World of the Thriller.* Cleveland: Case Western Reserve UP, 1969.

Harris, Trudier. "Before the Stigma of Race: Authority and Witchcraft in Ann Petry's *Tituba of Salem Village*." *Recovered Writers/Recovered Texts: Race, Class, and Gender in Black Women's Literature*. Ed. Dolan Hubbard. Knoxville: U of Tennessee P, 1997. 105–15.

Hartman, Geoffroy. *The Longest Shadow: In the Aftermath of the Holocaust*. Bloomington: Indiana UP, 1996.

Heidegger, Martin. "Building Dwelling Thinking." *Poetry, Language, Thought*. Trans. Albert Hofstadter. New York: Harper, 1971. 145–61.

Herndon, Gerise. "Gender Construction and Neocolonialism." *World Literature Today* 67.4 (1993): 731–36.

Hewitt, Leah D. Afterword. Condé, *The Last of the African Kings*, 211–16.

———. *Autobiographical Tightropes: Simone de Beauvoir, Nathalie Sarraute, Marguerite Duras, Monique Wittig, and Maryse Condé*. Lincoln: U of Nebraska P, 1990.

———. "Condé's Critical Seesaw." *Callaloo* 18.3 (1995): 641–51.

———. "Inventing Antillean Narrative: Maryse Condé and Literary Tradition." *Studies in Twentieth Century Literature* 17 (1993): 79–96.

Hirsch, Marianne. *Family Frames: Photography, Narrative, and Postmemory*. Cambridge, MA: Harvard UP, 1997.

hooks, bell. "Eating the Other: Desire and Resistance." *Feminist Approaches to Theory and Methodology: An Interdisciplinary Reader*. Ed. Sharlene Hess-Biber, Christina Gilmartin, and Robin Lydenberg. Oxford: Oxford UP, 1999. 179–94.

Huggan, Graham. *The Post-colonial Exotic: Marketing the Margins*. New York: Routledge, 2001.

Hulme, Peter. *Colonial Encounters: Europe and the Native Caribbean, 1492–1797*. London: Methuen, 1986.

Jackson, Rosemary. "Narcissism and Beyond: A Psychoanalytic Reading of *Frankenstein* and Fantasies of the Double." *Aspects of Fantasy*. Ed. William Coyle. New York: Greenwood P, 1986. 43–53.

Jacobs, Carol. "*Wuthering Heights*: At the Threshold of Interpretation." *Gendered Agents: Women and Institutional Knowledge*. Ed. Silvestra Mariniello and Paul A. Bové. Durham, NC: Duke UP, 1998. 371–95.

Jameson, Fredric. *Marxism and Form*. Princeton, NJ: Princeton UP, 1971.

———. *The Political Unconscious*. Ithaca, NY: Cornell UP, 1981.

———. "Third-World Literature in the Era of Multinational Capitalism." *Social Text* 15 (1986): 65–88.

Jooma, Minaz. "Robinson Crusoe Inc(orporates): Domestic Economy, Incest, and the Trope of Cannibalism." *Eating Their Words: Cannibalism and the Boundaries of Cultural Identity*. Ed. Kristen Guest. Albany: SUNY P, 2001. 57–78.

Kemedjio, Cilas. *De la négritude à la créolité: Edouard Glissant, Maryse Condé et la malédiction de la théorie*. Hamburg: LIT, 1999.

Kermode, Frank. *The Classic: Literary Images of Permanence and Change*. New York: Viking, 1975.

Kilgour, Maggie. Foreword. *Eating Their Words: Cannibalism and the Boundaries of Cultural Identity*. Ed. Kristen Guest. Albany: SUNY P, 2001. vii–viii.

———. *From Communion to Cannibalism*. Princeton, NJ: Princeton UP, 1990.

———. "The Function of Cannibalism at the Present Time." *Cannibalism and the Colonial World*. Ed. Francis Barker, Peter Hulme, and Margaret Iversen. Cambridge: Cambridge UP, 1998. 238–59.

LaCapra, Dominick. *History and Memory after Auschwitz*. Ithaca, NY: Cornell UP, 1998.

———. *Representing the Holocaust: History, Theory, Trauma*. Ithaca, NY: Cornell UP, 1994.

———. *Writing History, Writing Trauma*. Baltimore: Johns Hopkins UP, 2001.

Lanzmann, Claude. "Hier ist kein warum." *Au sujet de Shoah: Le film de Claude Lanzmann*. Ed. Michel Deguy. Paris: Belin, 1990. 279.

Lem, Stanislaw. *Microworlds: Writings on Science Fiction and Fantasy*. Ed. Franz Rottensteiner. New York: Harcourt, 1984.

Leys, Ruth. *Trauma: A Genealogy*. Chicago: U of Chicago P, 2000.

Licops, Dominique. "Expériences diasporiques et migratoires des villes dans *La vie scélérate* et *Desirada* de Maryse Condé." *Nottingham French Studies* 39.1 (2000): 110–20.

Lionnet, Françoise. *Autobiographical Voices: Race, Gender, Self-Portraiture*. Ithaca, NY: Cornell UP, 1989.

———. "*Logiques métisses*: Cultural Appropriation and Postcolonial Representations." *College Literature* 19 and 20 (1992/1993): 100–120.

———. "Narrating the Americas: Transcolonial *Métissage* and Maryse Condé's *La migration des cœurs*." *Mixing Race, Mixing Culture: Inter-American Literary Dialogues*. Ed. Monika Kaup and Debra J. Rosenthal. Austin: U of Texas P, 2002. 65–87.

———. "Transnationalism, Postcolonialism, or Transcolonialism? Reflections on Los Angeles, Geography, and the Uses of Theory." *Emergences: Journal for the Study of Media and Composite Cultures* 10.1 (2000): 25–35.

———. "*Traversée de la mangrove* de Maryse Condé: Vers un nouvel humanisme antillais?" *French Review* 66 (February 1993): 475–86.

Little, Roger. "Condé, Brontë, Duras, Beyala: Intertextuality or Plagiarism?" *French Studies Bulletin* 72 (1999): 13–15.

Lyons, Paul. "From Man-Eaters to Spam-Eaters: Literary Tourism and the Discourse of Cannibalism from Herman Melville to Paul Theroux." *Arizona Quarterly* 52.2 (1995): 33–62.

Makward, Christiane. "Cut-throat or Mocking-bird: Of Condé's Renewals." *Romanic Review* 94.3–4 (2003): 405–20.

Mandel, Naomi. *Against the Unspeakable: Complicity, the Holocaust, and Slavery in America*. Charlottesville: U of Virginia P, 2006.

Manzor-Coats, Lillian. "Of Witches and Other Things: Maryse Condé's Challenges to Feminist Discourse." *World Literature Today* 67.4 (1993): 737–44.

Mardorossian, Carine M. *Reclaiming Difference: Caribbean Women Rewrite Postcolonialism.* Charlottesville: U of Virginia P, 2005.

McBride, Dwight A. *Impossible Witnesses: Truth, Abolitionism, and Slave Testimony.* New York: New York UP, 2001.

McClintock, Anne. "The Angel of Progress: Pitfalls of the Term 'Post-Colonialism.'" *Social Text* 31/32 (1992): 84–98.

McKay, Melissa L. *Maryse Condé et le théâtre antillais.* New York: Peter Lang, 2002.

McWilliams, John. "Indian John and the Northern Tawnies." *New England Quarterly* 69.4 (1996): 580–604.

Mekkawi, Mohamed. *Maryse Condé: Novelist, Playwright, Critic, Teacher: An Introductory Biobibliography.* Washington, DC: Howard U Libraries, 1990.

Meyer, Susan. *Imperialism at Home: Race and Victorian Women's Fiction.* Ithaca, NY: Cornell UP, 1996.

Miller, Christopher L. "After Negation: Africa in Two Novels by Maryse Condé." *Postcolonial Subjects: Francophone Women Writers.* Ed. Mary Jean Green, Karen Gould, Micheline Rice-Maximin, et al. Minneapolis: U of Minnesota P, 1996. 173–85.

Miller, J. Hillis. *Topographies.* Stanford: Stanford UP, 1995.

Mitchell, Giles. "Incest, Demonism, and Death in *Wuthering Heights*." *Literature and Psychology* 23 (1973): 27–36.

Mitsch, Ruthmarie H. "Maryse Condé's Mangroves." *Research in African Literatures* 28.4 (1997): 54–70.

Moers, Ellen. *Literary Women.* New York: Doubleday, 1976.

Mohanty, Chandra Talpade. "Under Western Eyes: Feminist Scholarship and Colonial Discourses." *Third World Women and the Politics of Feminism.* Ed. Chandra Talpade Mohanty, Ann Russo, and Lourdes Torres. Bloomington: Indiana UP, 1991. 51–80.

Mohanty, Chandra Talpade, Ann Russo, and Lourdes Torres, eds. *Third World Women and the Politics of Feminism.* Bloomington: Indiana UP, 1991.

Moore-Gilbert, Bart. *Postcolonial Theory: Contexts, Practices, Politics.* London: Verso, 1997.

Morgenstern, Naomi. "Mother's Milk and Sister's Blood: Trauma and the Neo-slave Narrative." *Differences: A Journal of Feminist Cultural Studies* 8.2 (1996): 101–26.

Morrison, Toni. "The Site of Memory." *Inventing the Truth: The Art and Craft of Memoir.* Ed. William Zinsser. Boston: Houghton Mifflin, 1987. 101–24.

———. "Unspeakable Things Unspoken: The Afro-American Presence in American Literature." *Within the Circle: An Anthology of African American Literary Criticism from the Harlem Renaissance to the Present.* Ed. Angelyn Mitchell. Durham, NC: Duke UP, 1994. 368–98.

Morse, Donald E. Introduction. *The Fantastic in World Literature and the Arts.* Ed. Donald E. Morse. New York: Greenwood P, 1987. 1–3.

Moss, Jane. "Postmodernizing the Salem Witchcraze: Maryse Condé's *I, Tituba, Black Witch of Salem.*" *Colby Quarterly* 35.1 (1999): 5–17.

Motohashi, Ted. "The Discourse of Cannibalism in Early Modern Travel Writing." *Travel Writing and Empire: Postcolonial Theory in Transit.* London: Zed Books, 1999. 83–99.

Moudileno, Lydie. *L'Ecrivain antillais au miroir de sa littérature.* Paris: Karthala, 1997.

———. "Portrait of the Artist as a Dreamer: Maryse Condé's *Traversée de la mangrove* and *Les derniers rois mages.*" *Callaloo* 18.3 (1995): 626–40.

———. "Positioning the 'French' 'Caribbean' 'Woman' Writer." Broichhagen, Lachman, and Simek, 123–46.

———. "Le rire de la grand-mère: Insolence et sérénité dans *Desirada* de Maryse Condé." *French Review* 76.6 (2003): 1151–60.

Mouralis, Bernard. "*Une saison à Rihata* ou le thriller immobile." *Nouvelles du Sud* 3 (1986): 23–29.

Mudimbe-Boyi, Elisabeth. "Giving a Voice to Tituba: The Death of the Author?" *World Literature Today* 67.4 (1993): 751–56.

Murdoch, Adlai. "Divided Desire: Biculturality and the Representation of Identity in *En attendant le bonheur.*" *Callaloo* 18.3 (1995): 579–92.

Murdoch, Adlai, and Anne Donadey, eds. *Postcolonial Theory and Francophone Literary Studies.* Gainesville: U of Florida P, 2005.

Nesbitt, Nick. "Stepping Outside the Magic Circle: The Critical Thought of Maryse Condé." *Romanic Review* 94.3–4 (2003): 391–404.

Ngate, Jonathan. "Maryse Condé and Africa: The Making of a Recalcitrant Daughter?" *Current Bibliography on African Affairs* 19.1 (1986–87): 5–20.

Nora, Pierre. *Realms of Memory: Rethinking the French Past.* Trans. Lawrence D. Kritzman. New York: Columbia UP, 1998.

Novak, Daniel. "If Re-collecting Were Forgetting: Forged Bodies and Forgotten Labor in *Little Dorrit.*" *Novel: A Forum on Fiction* 31.1 (1997): 21–44.

Nussbaum, Martha. "*Wuthering Heights:* The Romantic Ascent." *Philosophy and Literature* 20.2 (1996): 362–82.

Obeyesekere, Gananath. "'British Cannibals': Contemplation of an Event in the Death and Resurrection of James Cook, Explorer." *Critical Inquiry* 18 (1992): 630–54.

L'Œuvre de Maryse Condé: A propos d'une écrivaine politiquement incorrecte. Paris: L'Harmattan, 1996.

Palmer, Jerry. *Thrillers: Genesis and Structure of a Popular Genre.* New York: St. Martin's, 1979.

Palumbo-Liu, David. "Theory and the Subject of Asian America Studies." *Amerasia Journal* 21.1–2 (1995): 55–65.

Peterson, Carla L. "Le surnaturel dans *Moi, Tituba sorcière . . . noire de Salem* de Maryse Condé et *Beloved* de Toni Morrison." *L'Œuvre de Maryse Condé,* 91–104.

Pfaff, Françoise. *Conversations with Maryse Condé.* Lincoln: U of Nebraska P, 1996.

Philcox, Richard. Preface. Condé, *The Last of the African Kings,* ix–xii.

———. "Translating Maryse Condé: A Personal Itinerary." *Sites* 5.2 (2001): 277–82.

———. Translator's Preface. Condé, *Crossing the Mangrove,* vii–ix.

Proust, Marcel. *Contre Sainte-Beuve.* Paris: Gallimard, 1987.

———. *On Art and Literature.* Trans. Sylvia Townsend Warner. New York: Carroll & Graf, 1984.

Quilligan, Maureen. *The Language of Allegory.* Ithaca, NY: Cornell UP, 1979.

Ragussis, Michael. *Acts of Naming: The Family Plot in Fiction.* New York: Oxford UP, 1986.

Rahming, Melvin B. "Phenomenology, Epistemology, Ontology, and Spirit: The Caribbean Perspective in Ann Petry's *Tituba of Salem Village.*" *South Central Review* 20.2–4 (2003): 24–46.

Reichardt, Jasia. "Artificial Life and the Myth of Frankenstein." *Frankenstein, Creation and Monstrosity.* Ed. Stephen Bann. London: Reaktion, 1994. 136–57.

Ridon, Jean-Xavier. "Maryse Condé et le fantôme d'une communauté inopéra-toire." *Francophonie et identités culturelles.* Ed. Christiane Albert. Paris: Karthala, 1999. 213–26.

Rosello, Mireille. "Caribbean Insularization of Identities in Maryse Condé's Work: From *En attendant le bonheur* to *Les derniers rois mages.*" *Callaloo* 18.3 (1995): 565–78.

———. *Declining the Stereotype.* Hanover, NH: UP of New England, 1998.

———. "Post-cannibalism in Maryse Condé's *Histoire de la femme cannibale.*" Broichhagen, Lachman, and Simek, 35–50.

———, ed. *Practices of Hybridity. Paragraph: A Journal of Modern Critical The-ory* 18.1 (1995).

Rosenthal, Bernard. "Tituba's Story." *New England Quarterly* 71.2 (1998): 190–203.

Rothberg, Michael. "Dead Letter Office: Conspiracy, Trauma, and *Song of Solo-mon*'s Posthumous Communication." *African American Review* 37.4 (2003): 501–16.

Said, Edward W. *Culture and Imperialism.* New York: Knopf, 1993.

Salotto, Eleanor. "*Frankenstein* and Dis(re)membered Identity." *Journal of Nar-rative Technique* 24.3 (1994): 190–211.

Sanders, Carol. "'Une si belle enfant ne pouvait pas être maudite': Polyphony in Maryse Condé's novel *La migration des cœurs.*" *The Francophone Caribbean Today: Literature, Language, Culture.* Ed. Gertrud Aub-Buscher and Beverly Ormerod Noakes. Jamaica: U of the West Indies P, 2003. 151–68.

Sandor, Andras. "Myths and the Fantastic." *New Literary History* 22.2 (1991): 339–58.

Sartre, Jean-Paul. *L'Etre et le néant.* Paris: Gallimard, 1943.

Scarboro, Ann Armstrong. Afterword. Condé, *I, Tituba, Black Witch of Salem,* 187–225.

Schama, Simon. *Landscape and Memory.* New York: Knopf, 1995.

Scharfman, Ronnie. "Au sujet d'héroïnes péripatétiques et peu sympathiques." Cottenet-Hage and Moudileno, 141–48.

———. "Criss-Crossing the Mangrove: The Literary Nomadics of Maryse Condé." Broichhagen, Lachman, and Simek, 199–214.

Serres, Michel. *Le tiers-instruit.* Paris: François Bourin, 1991.

Seshadri-Crooks, Kalpana. "At the Margins of Postcolonial Studies, Part I." Introduction. *The Pre-Occupation of Postcolonial Studies.* Ed. Fawzia Afzal-Khan and Kalpana Seshadri-Crooks. Durham, NC: Duke UP, 2000. 3–23.

Shelley, Mary. *Frankenstein.* Ed. Johanna M. Smith. New York: Bedford/St. Martin's, 2000.

Shih, Shu-mei. "Global Literature and the Technologies of Recognition." *PMLA* 119.1 (2004): 16–30.

Shohat, Ella. "Notes on the 'Post-Colonial.'" *Social Text* 31/32 (1992): 99–113.

Simek, Nicole J. "The Past Is *Passé:* Time and Memory in Maryse Condé's *La Belle Créole.*" *Memory, Empire, and Postcolonialism: Legacies of French Colonialism.* Ed. Alec C. Hargreaves. Lanham, MD: Lexington, 2005. 51–62.

Simon, Bruce. "Hybridity in the Americas: Reading Condé, Mukherjee, and Hawthorne." *Postcolonial Theory and the United States: Race, Ethnicity, and Literature.* Ed. Amritjit Singh and Peter Schmidt. Jackson: UP of Mississippi, 2000. 412–43.

Slemon, Stephen. "Post-Colonial Allegory and the Transformation of History." *Journal of Commonwealth Literature* 23 (1988): 157–68.

Smith, Arlette M. "Maryse Condé's *Hérémakhonon:* A Triangular Structure of Alienation." *International Women's Writing: New Landscapes of Identity.* Ed. Anne E. Brown and Marjanne E. Goozé. Westport, CT: Greenwood P, 1995. 63–69.

Smith, Paul. "The Will to Allegory in Postmodernism." *Dalhousie Review* 62 (1982): 105–22.

Spivak, Gayatri Chakravorty. *A Critique of Postcolonial Reason: Toward a History of the Vanishing Present.* Cambridge, MA: Harvard UP, 1999.

———. *Death of a Discipline.* New York: Columbia UP, 2003.

———. "The Politics of Translation." *Destabilizing Theory: Contemporary Feminist Debates.* Ed. Michèle Barrett and Anne Phillips. Stanford: Stanford UP, 1992. 177–200.

———. "Poststructuralism, Marginality, Postcoloniality and Value." *Literary Theory Today.* Ed. Peter Collier and Helga Geyer-Ryan. Ithaca, NY: Cornell UP, 1990. 219–44.

————. "The Staging of Time in *Heremakhonon*." *Cultural Studies* 17.1 (2003): 85–97.

Stoll, David. *Rigoberta Menchú and the Story of All Poor Guatemalans*. Boulder, CO: Westview, 1999.

Suk, Jeannie. *Postcolonial Paradoxes in French Caribbean Writing: Césaire, Glissant, Condé*. Oxford: Oxford UP, 2001.

Suleri, Sara. *Meatless Days*. Chicago: U of Chicago P, 1989.

————. "Woman Skin Deep: Feminism and the Postcolonial Condition." *Critical Inquiry* 18.4 (1992): 756–69.

Swamy, Vinay. "Traversing the Atlantic: From Brontë's *Wuthering Heights* to Condé's *La migration des cœurs*." *Journal of Caribbean Literatures* 4.2 (2005): 61–74.

Taylor, Lucien. "Créolité Bites." *Transition* 74 (1997): 124–61.

Todorov, Tzvetan. *The Fantastic: A Structural Approach to a Literary Genre*. Trans. Richard Howard. London: Case Western Reserve UP, 1973.

Trésor de la langue française. Paris: Centre National de Recherche Scientifique, 1990.

Trivedi, Harish. "The Postcolonial or the Transcolonial? Location and Language." *Interventions* 1.2 (1999): 269–72.

Trouillot, Michel-Rolph. "The Perspective of the World: Globalization Then and Now." *Beyond Dichotomies: Histories, Identities, Cultures, and the Challenge of Globalization*. Ed. Elisabeth Mudimbe-Boyi. Albany: SUNY P, 2002. 3–20.

Tucker, Veta Smith. "Purloined Identity: The Racial Metamorphosis of Tituba of Salem Village." *Journal of Black Studies* 30.4 (2000): 624–34.

Van Ghent, Dorothy. *The English Novel: Form and Function*. New York: Rinehart, 1953.

Venuti, Lawrence. *The Translator's Invisibility: A History of Translation*. New York: Routledge, 1995.

Vergès, Françoise. "'I am not the slave of slavery': The Politics of Reparation in (French) Postslavery Communities." *Frantz Fanon: Critical Perspectives*. Ed. Anthony C. Alessandrini. London: Routledge, 1999. 258–75.

————. *Monsters and Revolutionaries: Colonial Family Romance and Métissage*. Durham, NC: Duke UP, 1999.

Walker, Keith L. *Countermodernism and Francophone Literary Culture: The Game of the Slipknot*. Durham, NC: Duke UP, 1999.

Watts, Richard. *Packaging Post/Coloniality: The Manufacture of Literary Identity in the Francophone World*. Lanham, MD: Lexington, 2005.

Werbner, Pnina. "Introduction: The Dialectics of Cultural Hybridity." *Debating Cultural Hybridity*. Ed. Pnina Werbner and Tariq Modood. London: Zed Books, 1997. 1–26.

West, Robin. "Narrative, Responsibility and Death: A Comment on the Death Penalty Cases from the 1989 Term." *Maryland Journal of Contemporary Legal Issues* 1.2 (1990): 161–77.

Wilson, Elizabeth. "Sorcières, sorcières: *Moi, Tituba, sorcière . . . noire de Salem,* révision et interrogation." *L'Œuvre de Maryse Condé,* 105–13.

———. "'Le voyage et l'espace clos'—Island and Journey as Metaphor: Aspects of Woman's Experience in the Works of Francophone Caribbean Women Novelists." *Out of the Kumbla: Caribbean Women and Literature.* Ed. Carole Boyce Davies and Elaine Savory Fido. Trenton, NJ: Africa World Press, 1990. 45–57.

Woodard, Helena. "The Two Marys (Prince and Shelley) on the Textual Meeting Ground of Race, Gender, and Genre." *Recovered Writers/Recovered Texts: Race, Class, and Gender in Black Women's Literature.* Ed. Dolan Hubbard. Knoxville: U of Tennessee P, 1997. 15–30.

Young, Allan. *The Harmony of Illusions: Inventing Post-Traumatic Stress Disorder.* Princeton, NJ: Princeton UP, 1995.

Young, Robert J. C. *Colonial Desire: Hybridity in Theory, Culture, and Race.* London: Routledge, 1995.

Yuval-Davis, Nira. "Ethnicity, Gender Relations, and Multiculturalism." *Debating Cultural Hybridity.* Ed. Pnina Werbner and Tariq Modood. London: Zed Books, 1997. 193–208.

Zack, Naomi. "Reparations and the Rectification of Race." *Journal of Ethics* 7.1 (2003): 139–51.

Zimra, Clarisse. "W/Righting His/tory: Versions of Things Past in Contemporary Caribbean Women Writers." *Explorations: Essays in Comparative Literature.* Ed. Makoto Ueda. Lanham, MD: UP of America, 1986. 227–52.

Index

NEW WORLD STUDIES